The Story
of a Forest

I0025462

ALSO BY ROBERT KUHN MCGREGOR

A Wider View of the Universe: Henry Thoreau's
Study of Nature, revised edition (McFarland, 2017)

A Calculus of Color: The Integration
of Baseball's American League (McFarland, 2015)

The Story of a Forest

Growth, Destruction and Renewal in the Upper Delaware Valley

ROBERT KUHN MCGREGOR

McFarland & Company, Inc., Publishers

Jefferson, North Carolina

LIBRARY OF CONGRESS CATALOGUING-IN-PUBLICATION DATA

Names: McGregor, Robert Kuhn, 1952– author.
Title: The story of a forest : growth, destruction and renewal in the upper
    Delaware Valley / Robert Kuhn McGregor.
Description: Jefferson, North Carolina : McFarland & Company, Inc.,
    Publishers, 2018 | Includes bibliographical references and index.
Identifiers: LCCN 2018000267 | ISBN 9781476665917 (softcover : acid
    free paper) ∞
Subjects: LCSH: Forests and forestry—Delaware River Valley (N.Y.-Del.
    and N.J.)—History.
Classification: LCC SD144.D4 M34 2018 | DDC 634.909749—dc23
LC record available at https://lccn.loc.gov/2018000267

BRITISH LIBRARY CATALOGUING DATA ARE AVAILABLE

ISBN (print) 978-1-4766-6591-7
ISBN (ebook) 978-1-4766-3066-3

© 2018 Robert Kuhn McGregor. All rights reserved

*No part of this book may be reproduced or transmitted in any form
or by any means, electronic or mechanical, including photocopying
or recording, or by any information storage and retrieval system,
without permission in writing from the publisher.*

Front cover image © 2018 iStock

Printed in the United States of America

*McFarland & Company, Inc., Publishers
    Box 611, Jefferson, North Carolina 28640
    www.mcfarlandpub.com*

Acknowledgments

The unusual evolution of this unusual history necessitates a bifurcated set of acknowledgments—an initial bow to those lending critical assistance more than three decades ago, and a newer collection of accolades to those lending their thoughts more recently. As noted in the Preface, this study began as research undertaken on behalf of the National Parks Service by the Public Archaeology Facility at SUNY-Binghamton. Facility Director Doctor Albert A. Dekin kindly offered me the opportunity to participate in the project, while Douglas L. Bailey was instrumental in facilitating the field research. Materials gathered over the course of the study became the basis of my doctoral dissertation in history at SUNY-Binghamton, directed with enormous patience by Doctor Sarah Elbert. Additional members of the examining committee included Dr. Walter Huggins, Dr. Richard Dalfiume, and Doctor Dekin, the outside observer.

Returning to this research thirty-five years later necessitated contact with a vastly different assortment of readers. These included Doctor Robert Titus, professor of geology at Hartwick College; Doctor Michael Kudish, emeritus professor of forestry at Paul Smith's College; Doctor Nina Versaggi, professor of archaeology and director of the public archaeology facility, Binghamton University; Ms. Kirstie Buchanen, curator of the Rockwell Museum of Art, Corning, New York; Ms. Blueberry Morningsnow, poet (and daughter); and Ms. Carla Hahn and Ms. Bonnie Sheard of the National Parks Center for the Upper Delaware Scenic and Recreational River. Each read and commented on portions of the manuscript appropriate to their areas of expertise, assisting a veteran historian attempting to reach across too many disciplines.

None of the pages that follow would ever have left my desk without the approval of the one person who has watched and participated from the beginning in the 1980s to the completion. Deborah Kuhn McGregor and I were married on the Upper Delaware in 1982; she has been my companion in historical investigation and in life ever since.

Table of Contents

Preface

On April 22, 1970, the American people first celebrated Earth Day. I was a senior in high school. My girlfriend observed the day in the company of the school biology club, walking the banks of the Chemung River, collecting trash. She came home muddy, scratched, and sore. I spent that afternoon playing golf. Let us say it was not an auspicious beginning to my career as an environmental historian.

Fast forward nine years. Armed with a master's degree in history from a Midwestern school, I was wandering the aprons of the economy, confirming that I was not meant for the wonderful world of retail. Opportunity knocked unexpectedly. The Public Archaeology Facility (PAF), a cultural resource management organization operated under the auspices of the State University of New York at Binghamton, needed a historian to complement a staff composed mainly of archaeology grad students. Appreciating my sardonic attitude, the director, Doctor Albert A. Dekin, gave me a shot. I proved adept at writing brief historical summaries of obscure localities, earning the title of regional research historian.

Two months in, the PAF landed a critical contract. Congress had declared the Upper Delaware, seventy-five miles of river valley separating New York from Pennsylvania, a wild and recreational river, to be administered by the National Park Service. Cultural resources were an immediate concern; the Park Service recruited the PAF to undertake the initial archaeological and historical survey. More than two years of research and writing lay ahead.

As the sole historian on the project, I spent long hours studying obscure tomes, conducting interviews, combing the archives of five counties, three in New York, two in Pennsylvania. A certain degree of insanity permeated the work; probably inevitable when grad students are turned loose. Well I remember doing ninety on one lane dirt roads through narrow hillside passes, riding an ancient pickup truck driven by the archaeological field director. I found out later he was supposed to wear glasses.

The product was a striking success for the Public Archaeology Facility.

The National Park Service published the multi-volume report we produced, including a "Contact and Euro-American (Historical Synthesis) summary," for which I was largely responsible. My first published book, really. On a personal level, the opportunity meant even more. The Upper Delaware project provided a focus for my academic life.

Returning to graduate work at SUNY-Binghamton, I incorporated the cultural resource experience into my studies, abandoning traditional political history for a combination of social and environmental themes. The Upper Delaware richly deserves the wild and scenic designation; though the scenery is nowhere arrestingly spectacular, the valley is a long and invigorating stretch of forest land in the midst of the heavily populated Northeast. But all the forest is young, second and third growth. This I realized examining late-nineteenth-century photographs in the scattered archives. A century ago, the now wooded hillsides were largely bare. I needed to know why. And how. My Ph.D. research came essentially from materials I first noted while undertaking the historical resource survey. Raw census data. Saw mill records. Newspaper recollections. Unbidden, I was entering new historical ground, embracing environmental history as the field was taking shape. What I needed to do required mathematical skills and a working knowledge of forest ecology— foreign ground for the traditional historian.

Quantitative history was all the rage back then. Like most academic disciplines, history suffers through periodic "revolutions" in interpretation and methodology; social science based on numbers was the latest thing when I began dissertation research. Agreeing to serve as my dissertation mentor, Doctor Sarah Elbert said if I wanted to be Darth Vader, that was my business. So I derived formulas, I crunched numbers, I spewed data. What I identified were the mechanics of a heedless deforestation, devastating to the countryside, in the end with an economically fruitless impact. The numbers said so. In the name of understanding a tragic environmental event, I produced a study vaguely resembling an algebra text.

The book in your hands is pretty much a reversal of the typical scholarly endeavor. Most often, the newly minted doctoral recipient, hired to a teaching position and needing to build a vitae, publishes some version of the dissertation as a first book. I was too impatient to move on. After publishing an article or two, I abandoned the thing in favor of different and happier projects in environmental history and popular culture, eventually publishing four books on widely diverse subjects. I never was cut out to be a really hard social scientist. Numbers still intrigue me; they do tell an often persuasive story. But I was done with the dance of the formulae, the arid quest for scientific rigor. Much of my academic career was devoted to humanizing a history the numbers suggest.

I spent twenty-six years at the University of Illinois–Springfield, teaching and researching environmental history. A difficult task in the Prairie State, where the cornfields stretch to infinity, agricultural chemicals are a way of life, and environmental concerns are too often greeted with severe skepticism. The wooded hills of upstate New York became the backdrop of my daydreams. There are lessons in those hills, reminders of an exploitive past begun when nature was reduced to commodity. I soldiered on, bearing in mind always the grim lessons of what had occurred in the Upper Delaware River Valley, not so long ago.

In retirement, I return at last to my first productive research. If anything, this book is an effort to translate my dissertation into something resembling comprehensible English. More than a determination to distance myself from the original research so driven by the math, the chapters reflect a wider view instilled in me through long years of teaching. A forest history embodies much more than the story of settlers and business men chopping down trees. What was the forest they aimed to consume? A true history needs to record how the wilderness came to exist, how the forest altered through time, the forces responsible for the change, the influences that come now to invest a cultural value in the landscape. Geology. Biology. Ecology. Archaeology. More kinds of history than you can count.

The heart of this history is the accounting of a disaster—a "coarse-grained disturbance"—that befell a forest existing for long millennia, and the renewal of that forest in a most modern form. There are some numbers—chapters four and six are drawn somewhat from the ancient dissertation—but they are muted. A few statistics to illustrate an essential process, no more. Too many numbers get in the way of a story that needs to be told in plain words. What you have is something other than an exposition on historical methodology, an exercise in social science, a physical measure of human exploitation. This is a story, a story incorporating multiple experiences, multiple points of view.

This is a story about a forest.

Introduction

The History and Science of Trees

Trees there were. The potential for productive farming was not much, but trees stretched to the horizon in all directions. White pines seventy to eighty feet tall—ships' masts waiting to be harvested. Lots of feathery hemlock—not worth a great deal, but good for house framing. Held a nail well. Hardwoods here and there, valuable if markets became more accessible. The vast forests of the Upper Delaware Valley were a resource to be considered, perhaps the only resource worth pondering.

The eyes studying those trees belonged to relative newcomers to the valley. Europeans had first entered neighboring lands a century and a half earlier, exploring and settling portions of the Hudson Valley, fifty miles and a mountain range away. By the close of the seventeenth century, the Lower Delaware Valley was witnessing the rise of Philadelphia and Trenton, New Jersey. Settlement extended across the Mid-Atlantic region in most directions as New York and Pennsylvania took shapes suitable to European modes of thinking. The Upper Delaware, hemmed in by steep hillsides, largely bereft of flatlands conducive to extensive agriculture, remained unwanted—until desperation arose.

The newcomers were from Connecticut, claimants to lands along the Delaware deriving from a dubious interpretation of their colony's charter. Connecticut itself had run out of room for new settlements; the only answer was to claim lands beyond their established borders. The emigrating colony was small, a handful of families determined to establish independent farms on both banks of the river. They called the settlement Cushetunk, a corruption of a Native American place name. The hopeful emigrants quickly discovered why the Upper Delaware was bypassed in the ongoing rush to colonize the eastern seaboard. Not only was there little land flat enough to plow; the soil was largely thin and sour. Markets were very far away; the river tempestuous in spring, navigable only for small craft the rest of the year. The settlers would survive; they would not prosper. Not with small, relatively unproductive farms, and markets for foodstuffs practically out of reach.

But there were trees. The process took time, and experimentation, and invention, but eventually the forests of the Upper Delaware became a focus of the local economy, a boom that lasted nearly a century—until the trees were virtually gone. What took place over that century was what ecologists would now consider a "coarse-grained disturbance" of the natural system. There was nothing subtle about it. In the eighteenth and nineteenth centuries, when the descendants of European cultures looked out on the forests, they saw neither beauty nor ecology. They stared at natural resources, standing cash ready for the taking. Axes in hand, the settlers of Cushetunk began a relentless reshaping of their environment, a disturbance of nature with long-lasting consequences, pursued for economic considerations, assisted by rapidly developing technology and a revolution in transportation. There was a cultural component to the carnage as well—Europeans saw duty and God's will in the transformation of the landscape, the making of farms and fields in the stead of wildness. The work continued for as long as profits repaid the effort. Then came abandonment.[1]

The pages that follow trace the history of this long and determined environmental disturbance, a history of the Upper Delaware landscape.

A forest history.

Few tasks offer more pitfalls than the prospect of writing the history of an entity that does not exist. As forest historian Thomas M. Bonnicksen insists, "forests only exist in human minds." A strange observation—"forest" is a concept in very common usage; most everyone calls the proper images to mind when the term is offered. A large community of trees seems a safe enough definition. But there is far more to the picture than that; more than one author sees a forest as "a place of enormous complexity," what with the trees, the smaller plants, the interdependent members of the animal kingdom, the bacteria and the fungi responsible for essential chemical exchanges, and the physical environment upon which the vast web of life depends. A forest ecosystem, a far more recent and scientific term, would seem more representative. But difficulties lie in that direction, too. Originally conceived as a physical grouping of objects in nature, an ecosystem has now become a theoretical entity, a paradigm convenient for organizing research, possessing no real existence in the natural world. What is more, referring to a stand of the tall, woody, leafy things as a collection of "trees" is misleading too. The first conifers—gymnosperms (wind pollinators lacking flowers)—appeared some three hundred million years ago, when amphibians roamed the earth unmolested. Broadleaf trees—the angiosperms (plants with flowers)—evolved one hundred sixty million years later, as the dinosaurs flourished (giving rise to the delightful if unprovable hypothesis that the dinosaurs became allergic to the new plant forms and sneezed themselves to extinction). Referring to the conifers and the broadleafs, with their vastly different biology and histories, under the simple collective generic—"trees"—is a misleading unkindness.[2]

And so it goes. A forest is a convenience of the mind, a useful noun for something in nature too complex to define, populated by large, woody plants distantly related to one another, with vastly different biology. Approach with caution.

Much of this consternation results from the need for the precision fundamental to scientific inquiry. Confronted with large communities of tall leafy plants, people from time immemorial saw trees in a forest. Only when science began to inquire more deeply into the nature of forests did matters become complicated enough to maintain that forests do not exist—scientifically speaking. For the past century and a half, the speakers have been ecologists, specialized scientists with their own burdens of hardship to bear. Not only have ecologists encountered difficulty defining a forest; they have suffered profound hardship trying to define themselves.

The word ecology (originally "oecologie" in German) was first suggested by natural philosopher Ernst Haeckel in 1866, derived from a Greek concept, "oikos," referencing a system of household economy. Haeckel, heavily influenced by Charles Darwin's newly published studies on descent with modification, employed the term to describe research examining the relationship between living species and the physical environment, as good a definition as any for the discipline taking shape. Regrettably, historians of the science have tended to limit the field to research undertaken after Haeckel, minimizing the obvious impact of previous efforts. Alexander von Humboldt's worldwide studies of the relationship between topography, latitude, and plant communities provided the necessary foundation for all subsequent ecological science, while Darwin's theory of natural selection was nothing if not a description of the impact of environment on biological change. In the United States, Henry David Thoreau was undertaking forest research during the 1850s that can only be described as ecological analysis; he is almost never mentioned as a pioneer in the field. Thoreau may have been scientific in his methods; he was not a scientist, a distinction that became very important to ecologists as their field of study developed.[3]

Clarifying self-identity was very important. Science generally is a minefield of conflict: just what constitutes "real" science? To the physicists and their fellow travelers, definition is a matter of numbers and formulae—if the subject matter cannot be reduced to mathematical exactness, it is not genuine science. Generations of researchers in the less exact disciplines—earth science, geology, biology, ecology—beg to differ, but the discrepancy is there. Sensitive to their own standing as scientists, ecologists have proven very determined to rid their ranks of all practitioners failing the test of adequate rigor. No Thoreau. Even Humboldt and Darwin, those gentleman researchers of the early era, are viewed dubiously.[4]

The problem for the ecologists of the late nineteenth century was their close affinity with the naturalists, a large group ranging in expertise from rank hobbyists to avid catalogers. Carrying on the work initiated by Linnaeus, naturalists throughout the Western world were busily identifying, collecting, describing, classifying new species, continually adding to the library of the living world. An absorbing task, but to what end? By the 1890s, those who saw themselves as ecologists sought to distance themselves from the naturalists. Too much description, not nearly enough analysis.[5]

Histories generally cite Stephen Forbes, self-taught pioneer scientist from Illinois, as the author of the first true ecology paper, "The Lake as a Microcosm," published in 1887. To understand any single life form, Forbes argued, the researcher must evaluate the life cycle in the larger biological context—food sources, competitors, predators, and the like. He spent a single season studying the biology of six glacial lakes, contriving a hierarchy of "higher and lower" life forms, anthropomorphizing throughout, referring to "barbaric bream" and "worthless carp." He saw each lake as a life system, the whole greater than the sum of the parts, identifying what he saw as "a steady balance of organic nature." He offered no statistics.[6]

Forbes wrote a great many papers in a fifty-year professional career; "The Lake as a Microcosm" is the only one regarded as ecological in outlook. Despite its paucity, Forbes's "ecological" work set a regrettable tone for much that followed. His focus on defining an identifiable, bounded system—a lake—was an attractive model for several researchers, as was his belief that the sum was greater than the parts. More ominous still was the purpose behind his research: Stephen Forbes aimed to control nature for human profit. He was the leading scientist in his state—head of science faculty at the University of Illinois, state entomologist—in a land wholly devoted to agricultural progress. If state funds were to support scientific research, results demanded practical application—beneficial life forms identified and nurtured, the rest eliminated. Forbes spent much of his career discouraging scientific studies promising no economic benefits.[7]

Here was the nub of scientific ecology's identity problem—why undertake this kind of research at all? Frowned upon by the physicists (where was the math?), belittled by traditional academia (what was the point?), early ecologists sought to separate themselves from the naturalists while justifying their own existence in a too utilitarian fashion. The Progressive Era was a utilitarian age—the purpose behind any form of research, from resource conservation to industry to government, was to better apply management techniques. For ecological study, serious misdirection followed.[8]

Two early-twentieth-century ecologists, Henry Chandler Cowles and

Frederic E. Clements, took Stephen Forbes' ideas and expanded them to incredible lengths, creating popular images the science now deeply regrets. Cowles, a professor at the University of Chicago, undertook a detailed study of the patterns of plant growth in Lake Michigan's sand dunes. Unusually, he came at ecological studies from training as a geologist rather than a biologist, a perspective inspiring him to focus on physical landscape rather than climate while discerning patterns in plant behavior. Observing Lake Michigan's shaping of the sand dunes, Cowles noted that different plant communities associated with each stage of a dune's establishment and growth, ranging from groupings of aquatic vegetation as a dune first took shape at the lake's edge, to successively drier-adapted species as the dune stabilized, the soil becoming more organic with plant decay. Eventually the shoreline altered, leaving the dune well-defined as a hillock, high and dry. Cowles described this final plant community, made more or less permanent by the actions of plant roots holding the structure in place, as an example of vegetative climax. Cowles was not the first to advance the concept of plant succession, but his was the first systematic study of a series of stages beginning with pioneer occupation of a newly opened landscape, closing with a climax, resistant to further change. To be fair, Henry Cowles was flexible in discussions of the climax concept; influences could upset the balance. But balance he saw, and permanence, unless something highly unusual occurred. Later ecologists saw his insight far more religiously. Studying the flora of Isle Royale, an island in Lake Superior, H.H. Addams firmly believed that the bog action he witnessed on the island would eventually extend to include all of the Great Lake, succeeding from open water to sphagnum bog to eventual dry land. Climax. Addams exhibited extreme faith in an idea.[9]

Frederic E. Clements took the idea of plant succession further than anyone; much further than the evidence to support his conceptualization. A professor at the University of Nebraska, Clements was most concerned with the grasslands of the Great Plains—their origins, growth, and, most importantly, their future. The fullest embodiment of his vision appeared in 1916 with the publication of *Plant Succession: An Analysis of the Development of Vegetation*, in which Clements examined the developmental history of plant communities, focusing on the grasslands. Fully embracing the concepts of succession and climax advanced by Cowles, Clements argued that plant associations grew in regular, predictable patterns, dependent largely on climate and soil. Reaching climax, these associations would maintain a more or less permanent self-equilibrating balance, a discernable, distinguishable identity. Clements saw the process as a kind of progressive evolution, inevitably trending toward a natural, determined end, a plant association taking on the attributes of a super-organism. This was not a metaphor. Clements saw his grasslands—and by extension, other forms of climax plant associations, including forests—

as real entities, biological products of evolutionary progress. Grasslands were meant to be. Human beings, standing outside, failing to comprehend, could easily interfere with this natural collectivity, bringing disaster. The ecologist's duty was to educate, to encourage wise management, to discourage human abuses.[10]

For Clements, ecological understanding implied responsibility. And power. Armed with a truer understanding of nature's determined progress, the ecologist could successfully predict changes in the landscape, control the direction of evolution—for the greater benefit of humankind. From mere observer of nature's patterns, Clements sought to shape the ecologist's role into one of the most influential in all of science. Guided by the ecologist, private land use and government policy could be molded to guarantee the survival and more effective growth of the plant association/organism he envisioned. What more could an ecologist ask?[11]

Though attractive and in many ways persuasive, Clements' vision was never fully embraced by his fellows. Clements himself was intelligent and flexible enough to acknowledge careful criticisms of his ideas and adjust his theories accordingly. His theories were modified through the years, but he never abandoned his view of the plant association as complex organism. Twenty years after publishing his book, Clements warned that "Under the growing tendency to abandon static concepts, it is comprehensible that the pendulum should swing too far and change be overstressed." Change there clearly was—too much misguided human change, preventing the natural climax from occurring.[12]

The image of natural climax remained influential for decades. Plant communities themselves seemed to lend confirmation—in the east, the stability of long-existing hemlock forests strongly suggested a climax association, encouraging a "simple, deterministic view of nature that would dominate ecology for much of the twentieth century." The practical implications of climax ecology were especially enticing; armed with the concept, forest ecologists could dream of providing the guiding hand, developing better forest management principles to ensure greater lumber production while limiting attendant damage to soils and streams.[13]

The one much-ignored dissent from the prevailing vision of Cowles and Clements came from Henry A. Gleason, a young botanist at the New York Botanical Garden. Gleason very much doubted the inevitability of plant succession, suspecting there was a great deal more chance at work than predictable progress in plant succession. He said so, in a paper entitled "The individualist concept of the plant association," published in 1926. Gleason concluded that "every species of plant is a law unto itself, the distribution of which in space depends upon its individual peculiarities of migration and environmental requirements." Plant associations were the products of coincidence. Start over from the beginning, any given plant community could develop in a substantially different direction. Gleason did not press the point; the 1926 paper proved his one treatment of the problem. For sixty years, it was a view ignored. Climax was the thing.[14]

One of the many problems invited by Clements' conceptualization of the plant association as integrated organism was the tendency to invest that organism with non-material qualities. Just how did these super-organisms know what to do, how to progress properly toward their inevitable station? Was there, perhaps, some kind of spiritual component at work, some means by which the associated plants communicated? Questions such as these are generally considered outside the realm of science (physics especially), but this did not discourage a handful of ecologists from speculating. One more threat to ecology's standing as a science. Addressing the issue, Arthur Tansley, Oxford University, England, sought to tighten definitions in a 1935 essay published in the journal *Ecology*. Maintaining that complete stability was a condition seldom observed in a world where human beings were plainly integral to the natural landscape, Tansley objected to the determinism in Clements' succession, the less than scientific notions the concept inspired. Seeking a concept better suited to describe the real behavior of succeeding plant communities, Tansley introduced the word "ecosystem," defined as a physical system placing a defined biotic community in the context of the inorganic environment necessary to reasonably stable existence. Study of such systems would be limited to physical exchange; no spiritual considerations need apply.[15]

The ecosystem concept has enjoyed a long and flourishing career.

At the heart of Tansley's ecosystem construct was the observation that while "the organisms may claim our primary interest, when we are trying to think fundamentally we cannot separate them from their special environment, with which they form one physical system." One physical system. Tansley denied Clements' contention that a climax community was a holistic organism, but did argue that the ecosystem was an essential entity in nature, occupying a definable position in a hierarchy of systems beginning with the universe itself.[16]

Arthur Tansley's paper was not intended to introduce any new or revolutionary constructs. His goal was, if anything, reductionist, intended to provide a more clearly articulated framework for what he considered proper ecological science. Mitigating the more troublesome aspects of Clements' organicism, discouraging biological metaphors, the ecosystem concept focused ecological studies exclusively on the physical world, emphasizing the need to fully delineate the relationship between biotic communities and their inorganic surroundings. A tall order, and as much as sound science could hope to achieve.[17]

The ecosystem concept did not make much of an initial splash. Tansley's paper was just one among hundreds attempting to explore the misty horizons of ecology, establish a positive direction for a science without much of a standing. The ecosystem framework did not gain stature until after the close of World War II, when scientists were able to properly attend to an elegant study published in 1942. A young doctoral candidate at the University of Minnesota employed the ecosystem concept to perfect a means of measuring the physical exchange between a defined biota and their environment. Raymond Laurel Lindeman identified Cedar Bog Lake, a small glacial lake close to the University campus, as a bounded system, small enough to study comprehensively, large enough to encompass biological complexity. He was following the path established by Stephen Forbes, mirrored by subsequent researchers. Working with his wife, Lindeman employed trawls to sample the lake's life forms over the course of the seasons, documenting the changes occurring with the shifts of weather, available sunlight, and so forth. Building on pyramid models of the food chain advanced by Charles Elton in the 1920s, Lindeman constructed a hierarchy of the chemical relationships occurring in the lake, a food web he designated as a series of "trophic levels." Beginning with energy entering the system directly from the sun, transformed into usable energy forms by photosynthesizing single-celled lake dwellers, Lindeman traced the transfer of energy from level to level, measuring the amounts of energy used and lost with each transfer. The result was a mathematical expression of the web of life, a series of formulae demonstrating precisely the manner in which the lake system physically functioned. Here was science to please a physicist.[18]

In addition to his trophic measures of current biotic activity, Lindeman sought to place the condition of Cedar Bog Lake in a larger scheme of physical succession. The lake was very shallow and choked with plant life; Lindeman recognized this as the product of advanced age. At the tiny system's beginning—a kettle hole left by glacial retreat—the lake was much deeper and largely free of vegetation. Over thousands of years, vegetation decay had slowly but inevitably filled the bottom with organic debris, a fertile bed for still more vegetation. The cycle continued, until Cedar Bog Lake in Lindeman's time approached senescence—soon the debris would fill the lake bed completely; the area would become dry land. What Lindeman's studies captured was a perfect snapshot of a definable stage in the lake's successional progress; his equations established the energy flow through the trophic levels of the system at one point in the long evolution of the system. The chemical exchange between a biotic community and the surrounding environment at a specific stage of succession was a measurable entity.[19]

Lindeman died very young, but his research had a dramatic impact. The ecosystem had become something greater than an expression of focus; it had assumed definition as the flow of energy through a biologic system—a "hard" science. The approach came to define much of the research in the discipline in the post–World War II era, especially following the publication of Eugene Odum's highly influential textbook, *Fundamentals of Ecology*, in 1953. Odum utilized the ecosystem concept as the organizing principle in his text, expressing the idea in terms of thermodynamics. Nature operated as a balance sheet—the energy entering a system must equal the energy leaving plus the energy stored at each level. The ecosystem thereafter became the most central of ecological methodologies, both in theory and application. Ecology remained primarily a biological science, but with established links to physics and chemistry.[20]

Ecosystems theory may have weakened the specter of Clements' holistic organicism, but it did not kill the image altogether. Odum saw natural balance and stability as defining characteristics of an ecosystem. As plant succession occurred in a healthy environment, development would be progressive, leading to increased biomass stabilization and greater diversification of species. Over time would come greater cohesiveness among the plants and animals in the system, which would in turn exercise greater success in regulating the environment. The notions of self-organization and self-regulation remained, promoting the image of the ecosystem as a complex community. Translated into everyday terms, the ecosystem concept did much to sustain the popular vision of Mother Nature's balance.[21]

The decades immediately following World War II proved adventurous for ecological science, for reasons both good and bad. What defined good and not-so-good very much differed, depending on the perception of the given ecologist. In the United States, the postwar years exhibited many signs of unwarranted hubris, in government circles and in much of the general population. Flush with victory, confident in technological progress, America rushed headlong into an era of ill-considered experiments. These were the days of "atoms for peace," when nuclear reactors were supposed to produce electricity "too cheap to meter," when the government envisioned employing nuclear explosions to transform the landscape, create new harbors where nature had failed to provide. Despite the weakness of ecologists' standing in the sciences, the Atomic Energy Commission sought them out to research the consequences for this all-too-new world. Ecology's first important government support derived from AEC funding.

The dreams died hard. Nuclear testing in the Pacific revealed considerably higher levels of fallout than anyone had expected or hoped. Definite plans to explode a nuclear device to rearrange the Alaska coastline were shelved only when the scientists reported that the risk of radiation contamination could be catastrophic. But the nuclear power plants went up at breakneck pace (two thousand were envisioned for the U.S.) even as safety concerns drove costs to unimagined levels and radiation leaks endangered water supplies. When the ecologists continued to report unwanted news, the AEC withdrew support. The National Science Foundation took up the slack—ecology had become important in an entirely different, if not unrelated context.[22]

Employing their developing formulae, their ever-more sophisticated models, the ecologists had discerned a most disturbing fact: human beings were destroying the environment. Along with the rapid spread of nuclear radiation in the atmosphere, there was also the blanket use of chemicals to alter the environment—rid the world of unwanted bugs, unnecessary plants. In 1962, Rachel Carson published *Silent Spring*, notifying the world that the herbicides and pesticides were failing to do the jobs they were designed to perform while creating a toxic environment endangering life itself, including human life. Warnings of sickness throughout the landscape—gross water pollution, unbreathable air—soon followed. After years acting as the government's pet, ecology now assumed the role of "subversive science," warning the world that all this technological hubris was going to end very badly. By 1970, "Earth Day" had emerged, ushering in the "Age of Ecology."[23]

This was hardly a development ecological scientists desired or wanted. After struggling for more than half a century to build a legitimate identity, develop the methodologies of hard science, and exert a real influence on policy, to be abruptly identified with a popular movement sounding too much like the "Age of Aquarius" was not to be welcomed. Despite the obvious and continued desire to provide an applicable science, the last thing the scientists wanted was to become arbiters of moral issues. To the ecologists, the most fundamental problem was the conflation in the public mind of their work with the more humanist writings of authors such as John McPhee or Edwin Way Teale. Here was the naturalist orientation—that "Mother Earth" thing—all over again. Ecologist Tom Fenchel summed up the attitude of many when he advocated simply surrendering the word "ecology" to the environmental movement, while the scientists provided themselves new, more precise labels.[24]

In their determination to demonstrate themselves as something other than naturalists, the ecologists very nearly lost track of nature altogether. The ecosystem approach lent itself very aptly to modeling, just as the computer age was dawning. The problem with the natural world is the enormous number of variables—all those plants, all those animals, all those soil types, all mixed together helter-skelter, ignoring the boundaries the scientists so much wanted to fix. One answer was to reduce the complexity into a much more manageable set of neat categories, jamming a multitude of species into a few analytical lumps, be they trophic levels or whatever. Too often the models became simplified to the point that real nature was forced into abstract classifications made to fit modeling theories, rather than the other way around.

What emerged was an image of nature as machine, determined to respond to conditions in a predictable, mechanical fashion. The fact that the models seldom jibed with what was really happening out there in the forests became an entirely secondary consideration.[25]

The problem of boundaries continued to plague. When Alfred Tansley offered his definition of the ecosystem, he saw the systems as genuine entities in nature—real places a scientist could point out on a map. As the ecosystem model developed, the structures became far more theoretical, considerably less real. Forbes and Lindeman could employ well-defined tiny lakes to develop the pioneer methodologies employed in ecosystem studies; a system such as a forest or grassland proved far more nebulous, more open and connected to neighboring systems in complex fashions. To apply the science to something as elusive as a forest, abstraction was far more workable. Ecosystems lost identity as discoverable entities in nature.[26]

Apart from "for instance" kinds of models, the only answer was to define an ecosystem not by a population of plants or animals, but by physical characteristics—the Lindeman approach writ large. Imprecision would remain a problem, but the analysis could at least pertain to a real place in nature. One of the more successful applications of this approach was the Hubbard Brook Study out of Dartmouth University, initiated by F. Herbert Bormann and Gene E. Likens in the 1960s. Hubbard Brook and its tributaries flow out of the White Mountains of New Hampshire. Bormann and Likens declared the drainage area to be a bounded ecosystem, and proceeded to organize a somewhat different approach to defining ecosystem function, forgoing energy flow diagrams, instead tracing patterns of nutrient cycling among the living species on land and water. Using chemical nutrients as the system's currency, the scientists could link their work to studies in "geochemistry, soil science, hydrology, and atmospheric science."[27]

The study also opened the door to some ugly criticism. With the rise of environmentalism and the age of ecology, relations with foresters and other applied scientists had become far more adversarial—managerial conservation, once an ecological aspiration, was now repellant practice—in the popular mind at least. If the goal was to use more chemicals to grow more trees quickly to cut them faster, then applied science was anathema. When the Hubbard Brook Study noted that nitrogen levels in streams rose when adjacent forest was cut, foresters protested heavily, maintaining Bormann and Likens were inaccurately laying blame for environmental degradation. The science was not only accurate and correct; it was obvious when you stopped to think about the effects of forest removal. The message was abundantly clear. Whether they desired the role or not, ecologists were now the watchdogs, rather than the friends, of environmental management.[28]

Despite the success of the Hubbard Brook Study and several patterned after it, the ecosystems approach became more and more difficult to sustain. As long as the researcher was willing to avoid much consideration of actual species and focus on a single moment in time, the methods produced satisfactory results. But species did not often maintain behavior as the models anticipated, not for more than a few moments. Succession, burdened with a history of overzealous interpretation, remained a fact of biological life. When succession occurred, as it often did, the response saw individual species behave in surprisingly different fashions, move in different directions on a very local basis. Attempting to capture the realities of change, definable units of analysis grew smaller and smaller.

The eventual answer seemed to be an arrangement of ecosystems into a tiered hierarchical pattern. The largest, most inclusive tier was the ecological region, covering a broad area, composed of the more common plants and animals—simple to suggest, difficult to analyze. The region could then be sub-divided into a mosaic, a quilt of smaller systems together making up the whole—forest, bog, lake, stream, meadow. The components of the mosaic could be identified as individual patches—more fully defined communities with specific constituents—a "relatively discrete spatial pattern"—differing from neighboring patches in nutrient consumption or energy flow. Study of patch dynamics, emphasizing change and the interrelationship among the various patches, would illuminate the patterns of change for the larger region. The units grew smaller, but the goal remained: to establish the pattern creating order and stability in a bordered biologic community.[29]

Dissenters hovered on the edge. Ecosystem analyses demonstrated almost no interest in individual plant or animal species; ignored change occurring over long periods of time. John Harper, English plant ecologist, summed up the issue: "What we see as the organized behavior of systems is the result of the fate of individuals."[30] The skeptics concentrated their efforts on what came to be labeled evolutionary ecology, focused on the dynamics of change and their role in influencing development. Employing the perspective of patch dynamics, emphasizing change, the evolutionists argued that ecological patches displayed varied characteristics because of differing local histories of disturbance—species mortality, fires, windstorms, earthquakes, volcanic eruptions, and the like.[31]

History mattered.

Introducing the book *The Ecology of Natural Disturbance and Patch Dynamics*, S.T.A Pickett and P.S. White offered a definition. "A disturbance is any relatively discrete event in time that disrupts ecosystem, community, or population structure, and changes resources, substrate availability, or the physical environment." To assess the impact of a disturbance, ecologists would have to examine the system structure, the resource base, the life history of each affected species, the nature of the competitive hierarchy, the landscape composition and configuration. The shape each patch assumed following disturbance depended very much on conditions prior to the disturbance. A disturbance might be "fine-grained"—a shift in bird or animal population—or, more radically, "coarse-grained"—something disastrous, a hurricane or severe fire. Or determined people with axes.[32]

The subversive science was about to encounter subversion within the ranks. The interpretation of the environment in terms of stability and equilibrium—the balance of nature image so enticing to Clements and subsequent generations of ecologists, was all a chimera, the evolutionists insisted. Equilibrium was rare; disturbance commonplace.

The most telling blow occurred in 1973, when William Drury and Ian Nesbit of the Massachusetts Audubon Society published a direct challenge to the ecosystem concept, founded on extensive research in northern temperate forests. "Succession," appearing in the *Journal of the Arnold Arboretum*, stated baldly that succession does not end in stability, that change is without direction, subject only to contingency and chance. Species responding to individual needs came from different sources to join together temporarily on common ground; there was no determining dynamic. Today's forest will not be tomorrow's forest; predictions of future composition are pointless. Far too many variables. Research into the deeper past bore them out. Margaret Davis of the University of Minnesota demonstrated that the establishment of new forests following glaciation revealed differing and unpredictable patterns as individual tree species followed contingent paths. "The history of the spread of trees northward during the present interglacial leads inevitably to an individualistic view of plant communities." Climate studies showed wide variation in mean temperatures. Even the amount of carbon in the air varied with time. Add the effects of fire, windstorm, disease, pest invasion, and the like, succession would continue endlessly and unpredictably—until the glaciers returned. There was no such thing as vegetation climax. Henry A. Gleason's objections to Clements' succession were sustained.[33]

From this individualistic, evolutionary perspective, patch dynamics assumed more fundamental importance. Eschewing research concentrating on a theoretical balance of nature at a given moment in time, the focus shifted to studies of disturbance—the manner in which individual species responded to varying degrees of disaster, how new communities took shape, only to fall apart once more. The climax was dead, the ecosystem hardly useful. To approach any real understanding of nature, analyzing change was the key. In less than a century, ecological science had described a large circle. Beginning with species and Ernst Haeckel's appreciation of Darwin, ecologists slowly but surely constructed the image of nature as machine, a machine with a succession history leading to a pre-determined outcome. Recognizing the unfortunate and misleading determinism in their models, they slowly backed away, returning at last to histories of individual species, the not-quite random chances that led to the formation of plant communities that seemed stable, but never really were.[34]

One of the great beauties of science is the process of self-examination that guides interpretation—when over-enthusiasm leads to error, the ability to recover remains. With a century of ecological study and interpretation behind us, we understand forests far more fully than our ancestors, understand the necessity of their existence, the impact of tree species on the natural world, the requirements for their survival, the consequences of their destruction.

We also understand that forests are aggregations of individual species, rather than organic entities. If in some ways we also understand forests a little less than our ancestors, this too is a product of ecological science.

Historians are not scientists. Despite considerable insistence to the contrary, we will never establish formulae to explain the directions of human behavior in the past (much less the future). But we are not starry-eyed romantics either, given to painting rosy-eyed depictions of the past in broad, artistic splashes. Facts are fundamental, as are the methodologies governing their use. Historians stand at the intersection between science and art, commanding a view in each direction. We see the ecologist's patch mosaic of a plant community; we see the artist's forest landscape. The historian's task is to assemble a more holistic understanding of a forest's history, embodying the scientist's precise knowledge, the artist's aesthetic appreciation. Unlike the ecologist, we know that forests exist; generation after generation has seen them, appreciated them, hated them, profited from their existence. In America, forests are an integral part of our past, a challenge to overcome, a beauty to sustain, a resource to conserve. To understand a forest from the human perspective, each of these impulses, so often contrary in intention and result, must be understood.[35]

What follows is the history of one particular forest—or, to give the ecologists their due, one mosaic of forests, defined by the drainage system they inhabit. The forest(s) in question range over the lands of the Upper Delaware River Valley, in the states of Pennsylvania and New York. Much of the analytical aspect of this study will emphasize the New York side—the data is more revealing, more complete. If the ecologists teach historians anything fundamental about their business, it is that all boundaries are arbitrary, no definition absolute. As defined in the pages following, the Upper Delaware drainage in New York consists of slightly more than sixteen hundred square miles, divided into twenty-four townships located in five counties. This is a definition more political than ecological. Town boundaries mostly were decided in the nineteenth century with little attention to topography; the lines were drawn capriciously, the products of convenience and administrative decision making. At best, they are an approximation of the lands of the Upper Delaware. Portions of a few of the twenty-four towns bound streams eventually contributing to the nearby Susquehanna drainage. But the data on forest consumption was collected not by watershed, but by these politically defined boundaries: the census takers worked town by town. The historical statistics chronicling nineteenth-century consumption of the forests is unavoidably imprecise; quite a few of the pertinent trees are included in the analysis, a few unavoidably neglected. What the census takers recorded was an approximation of what happened when settlers of European descent came to occupy the Upper Delaware valley, began calculating the economic value of the timber, the agricultural potential of the soils supporting the trees. Axes went to work. The resulting "coarse-grained disturbance" was long and very thorough, an episode emblematic of the Euro-American to the forest landscapes they encountered. Ecologists consider long-term agriculture to be a "very severe" kind of disturbance, eliminating natural seed pools, requiring a long, drawn-out recovery—precisely what happened, is still happening, in the Upper Delaware. Periodic census records were not intended to track the fate of the forests—the idea was more to celebrate the triumph of human endeavor. Analyzing, interpreting the census data carefully, we can reconstruct the trajectory of the disturbance, discover the fate of a forest.[36]

Whether that forest existed or not.

ONE

The Makings of a Forest

There was a beginning.

Trees may have evolved eons in the past—the conifers 300 million years ago, the hardwoods some 140 million years after that—and certainly trees stood in what is now the Upper Delaware Valley for unfathomably long periods of time. But, just fourteen thousand years ago, there were none. The entire region—almost the entire state of New York—slumbered beneath the enormous weight of an ice sheet as much as a half mile thick, overlaying all. Trees were long reduced to organic dust.

The glacier originated in Labrador. Centered in the mountains near what is now Hudson's Bay, the longstanding Laurentide Glacier, grown ponderously immense after ten thousand years of global cooling, began to flow, pushing enormous streams of ice in a variety of southerly directions. Local glaciers formed in advance of the Laurentide sheet, growing steadily in mountain basins, slowly filling valleys with rivers of ice. Laurentide streams eventually crossed the St. Lawrence River Basin, reaching New York by a variety of routes dictated by topography. One such stream, the Hudson-Champlain lobe, deflected in its path by the Helderberg Mountains, entered New York from New England south of the Adirondacks, close to the valley of the Mohawk River. (A separate Mohawk Lobe flowed due west.) The Hudson-Champlain Lobe, grinding southwestward, crushed all in its path, overrunning the Upper Delaware Valley, continuing southwest well into Pennsylvania, encasing plains, valleys, mountains—everything.[1]

The inexorable advance reached a maximum a little less than twenty-six thousand years ago, the front a vast wall of ice straddling a line extended from Cape Cod to Long Island, across New Jersey and Pennsylvania, and on to the west. Much of Long Island originated as a terminal moraine—heaps of sandy residue plowed ahead of the ice sheet, left piled when the advance reached a final halt. The climate was shifting. Rapidly. For millennia, summers had been too short, too cold to melt the snow accumulated in protracted winters. Now summer melting began to outpace winter freezing. At that moment, forces remaking the landscape of the Upper Delaware set to work. The process unfolded over a period lasting at least twenty thousand years, to some small extent continuing to the present day.[2]

A small digression before tracing the region's reshaping in the wake of the ice... The specter of passing time is fundamental to the work of historians, archaeologists, paleobotanists. Proper chronology is the foundation of every interpretation, every analysis. But each profession approaches the concept of passing time from a separate, occasionally conflicting perspective. The differences in understanding and outlook are never more graphically illustrated than in any discussion of prehistoric eras—by definition, foreign territory to the historian. No documentary evidence will ever come to light for events occurring twenty thousand years in the past; archaeologists and paleontologists must work with a far more approximate sense of time.

To begin, the time spans the paleontologist treats are far longer, and less clearly demarked as to beginning or end. For the historian, an era may constitute twenty-five years—"the Gilded Age." Even a concept as vague and ill-defined as "the Middle Ages" lasted perhaps eight centuries. (It is also a useless conceit for any serious historian.) Twenty-five years is nothing to a paleontologist; eight hundred years an eye blink. The paleontologist works in epochs such as the "Hypsithermal," a period of warmer climate that probably began around 9,000 years ago (or perhaps earlier), and persisted for three to four thousand years, depending. A very important period of time for such scientists; disturbingly long and vague in definition to the historian. The dating, based on ice cores mined from glaciers in Greenland and elsewhere, cannot be made more precise.

Further confusing the issue is the matter of carbon dating, a critical tool developed after World War II. Carbon dating is based on the rates of decay of radioactive carbon isotopes, present in all living organisms. After an organism dies, the rate of decay taking place following the end of life provides an approximate measure of the time between the death and the current day ("the Present"). As the methodology came into widespread use in 1950, the convention was, and continues to be, that the time span since death would be expressed in years prior to that date. When researchers recently published a carbon date for the remains of a mastodon found in Orange County, New York, the date provided was 12,350 +/- 65 years BP. Translated, the mastodon came to grief 12,350 years prior to 1950, give or take sixty-five years. This is as exact as the method allows. The historian, bemoaning the considerable inexactitude, will also be sensitive to the fact (?) that another half century has passed.

Carbon dating is fundamentally important to tracing the renewal of forest growth at the close of the last glaciation. The evidence—the only evidence in the Upper Delaware—derives from the coring of peat bogs and kettle ponds found throughout the region. There is a fair degree of random chance in the content of these corings—some trees produce far more pollen than others, and there are tree species that do not much care for wetter soils. So the evidence must be weighed carefully, allowing for erratic happenstance. Scientists have been collecting pollen core data in the region for sixty years, recording the results provided by carbon dating. That the dates are spread over a period of sixty years and more (a long time to historians), has led to unfortunate confusion.

When initially developed, researchers made the quite reasonable assumption that the amount of carbon in the atmosphere remained more or less constant for the past thirty thousand years. The Greenland ice cores demonstrated that assumption to be incorrect; the carbon dioxide density in the atmosphere increased markedly in the period fifteen to ten thousand years ago, throwing off calculations of age by as much as four thousand years. More fluctuations have occurred in the millennia since. The errors create a thorny conundrum, both for paleontologists undertaking primary research on the glacial epoch and for historians endeavoring to make secondary sense of the information. Many of the pollen cores drilled in the Catskill Mountain area were dated employing the original dating scheme; more recent cores utilize the revised system, making comparisons difficult. Add to this the considerable range of time carbon dating in any case provides; dating of particular events can get pretty fuzzy. (White oak may have reached the Upper Delaware twelve or nine thousand years before the present [1950]. Take your pick.)

For the secondary researcher, the issue is compounded by the dates of publication of the various sources available. A few works, written before the carbon anomalies were discovered, obviously rely on the original system. More recent books at least attempt to utilize the reinterpretations of carbon dating results, leaving their dates at variance with the older volumes. And more than a few are simply unclear on the subject, offering dates without any acknowledgment of the issue. The consequence is inherent vagueness, compounded by technical inconsistency. Different sources at times produce variant results. Radiocarbon dates derived from shellfish remains and pollen cores taken from the same site have differed by as much as five hundred years. Dates do not become reasonably precise until 11,000 BP, when dendrochronology, a separate methodology based on tree rings, becomes available. Naturally, dendrochronology is unavailable for the Northeast—the remaining trees are not nearly old enough. Given this degree of imprecision, writing a coherent history of the Upper Delaware's earliest forest history becomes endlessly entertaining.

What follows is a story of the impact of glaciation, the response of vegetation as the ice slowly melted away. The broad pattern is readily discernible;

the chronology—the ordering of events—is largely indisputable. But the dating for any given event should be accepted dubiously, in the company of large
grains of salt. The numbers could be off by a thousand years or more, one
way or the other.

One thing is certain. The transformation from ice to trees was painfully
slow.

The glacial melt wore on for ten thousand years before the Upper
Delaware was clear. Local glaciers in the higher elevations of the Catskills
persisted for another thousand years after that. Once the ice was gone, the
land rebounded, rising swiftly, spilling meltwater southward. The enormous
weight of the glaciers had compressed the earth's crust down into the mantle
as much as eighty feet; release allowed the land to spring back, rapidly at
first, followed by a more gradual rebound. The newly emerging land was still
very cold—a mountain of ice remained melting close by—and very wet. The
compressions in the land were natural basins collecting icy water, runneled
with runoff streams. Rising, rebounding lands dumped the collected water.
The immediate post-glacial world was a vast, empty marshland feeding torrential rivers seeking the sea. The Upper Delaware was one of these. Local
glaciers, followed hard by the Hudson-Champlain Lobe, had scoured the pre-
existing river course, carving a U-shaped valley to funnel the reborn flow of
water. Close by the melting ice sheet, the emerging river took shape as a network of broad, shallow, braided streams. Laden with glacial sediments,
hemmed in by hilly terrain, the swelling river grew into a raging torrent far
wider than today, carrying the meltwater from an ice sheet two miles thick,
a flood prolonged for centuries. Glacial outwash scoured the floodplain clean.
Formation of a glacial lake to the south impeded the flow, slowing the current
enough to allow the deposition of vast amounts of new sand and silt. As the
meltwaters abated and deposition mounted, the river shifted sideways, seeking new channels. After eight thousand years of flooding, sediment deposition, erosion, and hydrologic response, the Delaware settled into its current
bed. By then, the forests surrounding had come to assume recognizable shape
and content.[3]

Though the glaciers slowly melted away, feeding the Delaware, the Hudson, and numerous other rivers, recession was neither linear nor smooth.
Temperatures fluctuated wildly in the period twenty-six thousand to eighteen
thousand years ago. The overall trend was toward a warmer climate—eventually, much warmer—but cold periods brought the ice melt to occasional
halts, and sometimes provided enough ice to feed a temporary re-advance of
the glaciers. Stillstands of some duration occurred at least three times as the
ice melted in the Catskill region. The first of these, known to geologists as
the Wagon Wheel Ice Margin, came just over twenty thousand years ago,
when a temporary glacial advance along a line in the hilly country of eastern

Delaware County deposited a recessional moraine, marking the farthest forward movement. Renewed warming melted this ice after two hundred years, leaving the moraine behind as meltwater spilled westward, apparently shaping what is now the West Branch of the Delaware River.[4]

The second episode was far more striking. The ice advanced once again roughly nineteen thousand years ago, shaping a new recessional moraine in much the same area as the Wagon Wheel Margin. This Grand Gorge Ice Margin melted slowly, leaving behind a very large volume of icy water trapped between the glacier sitting to the north and the moraine, which acted as a dam to create Glacial Lake Grand Gorge, hundreds of feet deep. The end came catastrophically when the dam broke, spilling a violent cascade down Catskill Creek before raging eastward to shape the now serene, V-shaped Pepacton River valley. The lake level dropped four hundred thirty feet in a geologic eye-blink. Overwhelmed by the sudden wall of water and accompanying sediments, the valley was abraded to the bedrock, broadened and flattened by a vast, short-lived glacial torrent. When the lake emptied, the Pepacton River—the East Branch of the Delaware—resumed a more modest character, becoming a small, meandering stream struggling through a bottomland of marsh, surrounded by a valley much too large. Nineteen thousand years later, the East Branch retains its character.[5]

With the termination of the Lake Grand Gorge catastrophe, the Upper Delaware drainage began to assume something at least approximating modern shape. The last local re-advance, called the Middleburgh, coming perhaps 18,800 years ago, reached into the Schoharie Valley to the north. The Delaware was burdened with meltwaters for long centuries more, but glacial ice was a memory. In another nine thousand years, the ice sheet would melt back to Canada. What the glaciers left behind was an utterly barren landscape, ground down to bare rock, a world reshaped by erosion at its most extreme. A blank sheet, in so far as organic life was concerned.[6]

Glaciers are much more than overgrown cubes of ice. The sheet was a dirty colossus, plowing up sand, soil, gravel, large rocks, boulders, smashed trees, decaying bones, and anything else the ice encountered, pushing and lugging the materials great distances. Glaciers carried so much sediment that trees sometimes took root atop the ice. Released with the thaw, these sediments became an abrasive—eroding mountains, sculpting river valleys, broadening lowlands as they washed away. The Upper Delaware and its tributaries flow through a world carved by glacial action, modified by eighteen thousand years of subsequent deposition and hydrology.

Deposition—glacial drift—assumed two essential forms. Heavier materials—pebbles, large rocks, the occasional boulder often heaped in moraines, were generally the product of rapid drainage, sometimes from the face of the ice sheet, sometimes from streams flowing from beneath. Such outwash clogged stream valleys, shaped peculiar hills known as eskers (one stands in Roxbury, Delaware County), and left kettle lakes behind. Till, the finer stuff laid down directly by the ice, consisted mostly of clay, sand, and silt. Strong winds along the glacier blew away storms of fine dust, depositing the material leagues away as loess soil. In the Catskill region, sand was the major component in the deposition, left behind wherever the runoff slowed enough to drop the load. This sand and the accompanying silt played an essential role in shaping the vegetation patterns of the Upper Delaware, becoming the base material for the development of soils.[7]

Many factors fed the transformation from sediment to soil. The raw material would first be broken down, sifted, shifted by the actions of freezing, thawing, the percolation of ground water, leaching. When plants eventually gained a foothold, root action played a further role. Pioneers such as alders, lupine, and ceanothus, bearing nitrogen-fixing bacteria in their root systems, augmented thin soils. Dying, the vegetation, broken down by fungi, bacteria, and various invertebrates, fed organic strains into the mix. Larger animals played their part, leaving their droppings and eventually their bodies to be absorbed into the chemistry. Flatter, poorly drained places such as the upper reaches of the East Branch provided greater opportunities for early plant colonization, as deposition was much finer and heavier, creating some fertile expanses. Aquatic plants took hold.[8]

The fifteen thousand years that have passed since this formation commenced is a very tiny expanse of time, so far as soil development is concerned. While a few bottomlands in the region support soils as much as one hundred feet thick, the average soil depth is just thirty inches—not nearly enough to support many species of trees. The Upper Delaware soil profile is largely comprised of a very thin biological layer overtopping bedrock. There is not much limestone in that geologic layer, meaning the soils are for the most part acidic.[9]

Trees were a long time coming. Even as the glaciers melted back, the immediate vicinity remained inhospitable for long periods. The warming of the earth may have encouraged a "temperate" melt, but the extreme temperature differential between the cold air emanating from the ice and the ambient warmth kicked up violent weather fronts. Winds could blow up to one hundred miles per hour, mounting raging dust storms. Thrashing thunder and lightning tempests were frequent. And of course, the grounds close to the ice were perpetually waterlogged—a challenging landscape for any vegetation to gain much of a foothold. For long periods, about the only plants were of the aquatic variety.[10]

Yet the gradual, episodic melt of the glaciers created opportunity. Plants responded as conditions allowed, accompanied by the smaller forms of animal life critical to shaping their environments. Larger animals followed long after.

When the glacial advance was at maximum some twenty-five thousand years ago, an open landscape of parkland and tundra stretched from what is now the New Jersey Pine Barrens as far south as South Carolina. Nearest the glacier's leading edge lay a band of permafrost—ground frozen solid for much of the year. In high summer, the top layer briefly thawed—just a few inches close to the ice, as much as three to four feet down further away. The unfrozen ground became a vast marsh, populated largely by sphagnum mosses—the muskeg now found in the frozen Arctic. Patchwork remnants of the permafrost, sixty miles wide, persist in New Jersey and Pennsylvania to this day.[11]

South of the permafrost lay an arctic zone populated by sedges, grasses, a few miserable trees, and a variety of wildflowers offering a riot of color in the short months of summer sunshine. Precise definitions of the components of this parkland-tundra are much discussed. This was wooly mammoth country. Paleontologists argue that the zone took on the character of a "mammoth steppe," made up primarily of plant life especially suited to a mammoth's dietary needs. The hairy elephants required a lot of vegetation—as much as four hundred pounds a day to meet the basic nutritional requirements. The beasts—fourteen feet high at the shoulder, weighing ten tons—played a key role in shaping this parkland environment. Quite probably they knocked over most of the trees struggling to establish roots in the arctic zone.[12]

The few trees that did sustain existence in the tundra were of species especially adapted to extreme cold. Huddled in occasional groves, providing some measure of mutual protection against the icy winds, jack pine, red, white and black spruce, and tamarack survived. These were the trees most tolerant of cold weather, especially adapted to the dangers of extreme cold via a mechanism known as extracellular freezing. Cold is the great challenge for most trees—species can endure freezing temperatures only so low before the fluids in their cells freeze, eventually bursting the cell walls and killing the tree. Four of these conifers—jack pines, white and black spruces, tamaracks—evolved a mechanism to allow cellular fluids to ooze out of the membranes into intercellular spaces, where they crystallize without doing harm to the cell structure. The trees can survive in temperatures as low as 112 degrees below zero Fahrenheit. Red spruce, less tolerant of the cold, can suffer severe freeze injury killing up to ninety percent of the tree, yet somehow survive. Between the bitter cold, the ice-laden winds, and the elephants, there were not many of these conifers, but there were a few, the advance pioneers of the invasion to unfold. South of this arctic zone stood a belt of arctic forest, made up largely of white spruce.[13]

When the great melt began, vegetation responded, though not immediately. The lands emerging from the glacial burden were far too harsh for any immediate plant invasion. As the ground slowly healed, the preponderance of the meltwater drained away, vegetation began to colonize. Species by species, plants migrated northward. The earliest invaders, naturally enough, were the parkland-tundra associations, the grasses, sedges, hardy shrubs, and cold-enduring trees from the immediate south. As the ice sheet slowly melted back, halting occasionally, re-advancing when colder climate temporarily returned, the tundra marched cautiously behind, eventually occupying the opened spaces, adapting to the slowly moving line of permafrost, adding organic materials to the soil chemistry, preparing the ground for the more temperate species to follow. The growing season was just three months, but it was enough. Organic materials began to appear in Upper Delaware soils some two thousand years after the ice initially melted away. In the Catskill–Upper Delaware region, the tundra-parkland zone took root and persisted for roughly eight hundred years, beginning at 15,500 years before the present, moving on by 14,000 BP.[14]

This was a unique corner of an arctic world, populated by such cold-adapted large animals as caribou, musk oxen, and possibly a few wooly mammoths following the plants northward. Caribou—the only deer species adapted to cope with extreme cold—dominated the landscape, dining on the lichens so prevalent in the tundra. Then and now, caribou migrated hundreds of miles seasonally, sheltering in woodlands to the south and east during winter, moving to coastal lands in summer to birth young in conditions freer of insects. The musk oxen followed similar strategies, migrating to assure themselves of sufficient food resources. Dire wolves followed the arctic herds. More scavenger than predator, the dire wolf was the largest known canid to ever live, half again as large as the modern gray wolf. With a heavier body, shorter, more powerful legs, robust jaws and teeth, the dire wolf was a fearsome creature hampered by a small and simple brain.[15]

The mammoths raise interesting questions. Very few remains have been identified in New York State, none at all in the Catskills or the Upper Delaware. Quite possibly New York was at the far edge of these elephants' range; most fossil sites are located in the central and western portions of the state. The particular components of the "mammoth steppe" may not have penetrated into the Upper Delaware. Some geologists argue that the lack of mammoth sites indicates a "temperate deglaciation" of the region, in which the composition of the tundra vegetation shifted quickly. But tundra of some sort persisted for eight hundred years. For one thing, yellow-cheeked voles and collared lemmings, small rodents currently resident in the tundra of the arctic north, left fossil remains in the Upper Delaware. Lemmings and voles, but no mammoths. For whatever reason, wooly mammoths left no visible impression in the Upper Valley, or in the Catskills.[16]

The trees accompanying the arctic plants—the jack pines, the spruces, the larches—moved north with the tundra, contributing to the changes in the land necessary for the less hardy species to follow. Forest colonization was limited by two critical factors apart from the extreme cold. The first was ice abrasion—the needles of ice blowing off the glacier or banks of snow in gale-force winds, stripping leaves, shredding bark, twisting tree trunks. Such trees as survived were stunted affairs, little more than scraggly shrubs, hunkered down against the wind, huddled together in clumps for protection. The second factor was the almost barren chemistry of the soil. In the cold, dying vegetation required considerable time to decay—bacteria acted very slowly. Humus was a long time forming. Where the ground dried out quickly, no humus survived at all. In such conditions, the conifers possessed an "evergreen advantage." Bearing needle-like leaves that lasted several years, the trees could begin photosynthesis much earlier than any broadleaf, and could continue to manufacture nourishment in temperatures reaching as low as 13 degrees Fahrenheit. This ability to stretch the limited resources available ensured survival.[17]

As the glacial melt continued, conditions moderated in the Upper Delaware, making the beginnings of a kind of forest possible. The pioneer species crouching in the tundra served as "nurse trees," providing shelter for new species advancing northward. This forest band initially took root commencing roughly fourteen thousand years ago, beginning a process that would last some three thousand years. The cold weather ecosystem—the boreal forest—saw continuous shifting in composition as individual species arrived, competed, and cooperated to gain advantage. The landscape became a patchwork quilt of ecological habitats, offering welcome conditions for one species, poor opportunity for another. Bare soils weak in nutrients alternated with deposits of vegetation litter, shallow duff, rotten wood that offered opportunities for new arrivals. Drainage mattered much, as did elevation, exposure to wind and sun. Fire was one more critical factor. Ignited by lightning strikes, fires consumed growing piles of dead vegetation, imparting essential nutrients to starved soils, clearing the ground to provide seeding opportunities for incoming species. Blazes seem to have come at fairly regular intervals, combusting every century or two as dead brush built up. Jack pine was especially dependent on the flames—the seed cones would open only in extreme heat.[18]

Species bearing windblown seeds were the first to arrive in newly opened zones, outpacing trees bearing winged seeds, fruits, or nuts. Wind pollinators possessed an advantage over insect pollinators; the season for insects was short, but the wind blew constantly. Most of the pioneers were conifers—balsam fir, red pine, and white pine joined the spruces, jack pines, and the tamaracks. Two species of cold-tolerant willow, together with poplar and aspen, added broadleafs to the mix, along with paper birch, which soon became abundant, if short-lived. White or red spruce dominated initially, eventually giving way to a forest made up largely of white pine and birch, two species somewhat tolerant of shade, unlike most of their neighbors.[19]

These initial incarnations of the boreal forest were less than imposing.

The growing season remained short, frosts long and heavy. Taking root in thin soils reluctantly transitioning from tundra, the new trees grew in haphazard conditions. With each thaw, pronounced frost heave upset fragile soil stability, creating a landscape of depressions, bumps and hillocks. Clinging by shallow root systems, the trees leaned every which way imaginable—a "drunken forest."[20]

The conditions were singular, the development contingent on the independent fortunes of individual species arriving at various times and places. Spruce was an especially aggressive colonizer, while birches, for reasons unknown, were unusually rare. Broadly similar to the forests currently found adjoining the tundra in the extreme north, the boreal forest of the Upper Delaware nonetheless bore a character entirely unique—a product of slow-moving migration in response to glacial melting.[21]

This forest, constantly shifting with the addition of newcomers, changes in climate, the recession of the ice sheet, was similarly populated by a colonization of new animals, strikingly different from the previous denizens of the tundra. There were a few grazers to take advantage of open lands—longhorn bison and ground sloths ten feet long, eating roots, stems, seeds, flowers. More important to the forest were the browsers—leaf, cone and twig consumers that played an important role in the ongoing shaping of the landscape. Woodland caribou, elk, moose, woodland bison occupied the woods, along with giant beaver and, most importantly, mastodon.[22]

Mastodons were ancient cousins to the wooly mammoths, evolved some ten million years earlier. They carried longer, more "piglike" bodies on shorter legs, and depended on heavier muscles. By far the most common mastodon relics are teeth—very different from mammoths, efficient grinders to deal with a diet of tough, woody vegetation. Mastodons preferred spruce forests and open woodland, habitats they helped to shape by moving among the trees, knocking down a few, breaking the lower branches of more, opening the understory. A thinly rooted spruce had no chance against a ten-ton elephant. Most often, mastodons moved along lakes and streams, browsing on reachable branches, also consuming large amounts of swamp vegetation. The elephants were a "keystone species," opening up the forest floor, shaping a more parklike habitat. Unlike the mammoths, they seem to have been quite plentiful in southeastern New York. Twenty-two major fossil discoveries have occurred in Orange County alone.[23]

If the thought of elephants in New York is intriguing, the presence of giant beaver should spark the imagination. Think of a beaver two-thirds the size of a black bear, weighing as much as 440 pounds, grown to nine feet long. If their habits had in any manner resembled those of the modern beaver (sixty pounds), giant beaver might have done much to shape the boreal forests of the Upper Delaware. They were the largest rodents known to history, native only to North America, and most common south of the emerging Great Lakes basin. But, despite the imaginative efforts of some wildlife artists, they were nothing like the modern beaver. Their tails were round rather than flat (like giant rats), their legs were very short for their size, and their brains were tiny. Rather than building dams and managing their environment, recent research demonstrates that giant beavers were clumsy, "hippolike" creatures, living in marshlands, burrowing in the soft earth, subsisting on large amounts of aquatic vegetation. Their diminutive cousins would be the ones to influence the shape of the changing forests.[24]

A mix of ancient and modern predators roamed these woods—the familiar big cats and black bears, and the far more intimidating short-faced bear. More predatory than modern bears, the short-faced variety inhabited the damper regions of the forest, chasing down prey on very long legs supporting a relatively short body. As the name suggests, these bears had a short face, though with a wide muzzle. And a small brain.[25]

Beginning in roughly 12,900 BP and lasting some twelve hundred years, a cold snap known as the Younger Dryas overtook the earth, apparently caused by the sudden drainage of the voluminous glacial Lake Agassiz (west of modern Lake Superior) through the Great Lakes Basin, the newly opened St. Lawrence River and into the Atlantic Ocean. The rapid chilling of the North Atlantic shut down the Gulf Stream, ushering in a colder climate. Cold tolerant spruce and fir came to dominate the boreal forests of the Upper Delaware for the duration of the cold. At the end, temperatures moderated abruptly; the earth was tracking toward much warmer weather. The Gulf Stream regenerated. In the space of just half a century, the climate grew warm—truly warm, and drier. By 11,000 BP, birch had become the major component in the region's forests. In another thousand years, white pine, capable of surviving on dry, poorer soils, was well established, able to expand widely in the absence of deciduous trees. The warming climate saw the growth of dense forests throughout much of the northeast.[26]

One factor in the mounting density of the forests may have been the lack of elephants. Judged by the dating of fossil remains, the mastodons were extinct by eleven to ten thousand years ago, along with the wooly mammoths, the dire wolves, the short-faced bears, the ground sloths, and the giant beavers. The quickest way to provoke an argument with a paleontologist is to take a stand as to why this wave of extinctions occurred. Across North America, some seventy species of megafauna—large animals—disappeared during the timeframe, a very large coincidence. Hypotheses regarding cause run from the effects of rapid climate change to the carnage of human hunting to the impact of new diseases. A curious feature of the debate is the often stubborn insistence on monocausality—it had to be one or the other. With an event this large, probably a number of interrelated factors played a role.[27]

The rapid climate change surely created challenges to habitat. Drier weather altered the composition of the parkland-tundra, diminishing the "mammoth steppe" that provided sustenance to the wooly elephants. Dry conditions meant lessened habitat for the ungainly giant beaver. And climate change could have altered the vectors of disease. The argument that epidemics rarely jump from one species to another cuts little ice; such occurrences have been common throughout history.

Humans had indeed reached the Northeast by this point, and are known to have hunted mammoths, although there is no evidence to suggest the aboriginal hunters killed any mastodon. But humans were not the only newcomers. The small-brained dire wolf, probably a lone hunter, would have faced severe challenges from incoming packs of gray wolves, smaller but far better organized, and known to attack lone wolves. Short-faced bears suffered competition from more efficient brown bears, newly arrived from Asia. As giant beaver habitat diminished, the opportunities for modern beavers, another well-organized species, increased. The sleek inherited the earth.[28]

By 10,000 BP, the ice sheet had melted back as far as northern Canada. The tundra belt followed northward in response, the boreal forest zone advancing behind. With the glacier long gone, ambient temperatures in the Upper Delaware grew more temperate. Soils, fed by thousands of years of organic decay, became richer. The boreal forest, the home of conifers and a few hardy broadleaves, now saw the arrival of another range of species, trees that would eventually crowd out the preponderance of the old. Individual examples had been taking root in the boreal zone for some time—red cherry, mountain ash, black ash, white oak, hemlock. Hemlock seeds, windblown northward from the Southern Appalachians at the rate of perhaps 270 yards a year, took root as early as 14,000 BP, were far more at home in the new forest assuming shape. The hemlocks preferred thinner, damper soils—there was a lot of that in a land still recovering from glaciation—but did require seedbeds of organic materials.

More species followed, in greater numbers. At 9,100 years ago, the transition was largely complete. The character of the forest was so changed that the boreal zone could now be discerned to lay northward, displaced by a different, northern hardwood forest. For the next five hundred years, sugar maples and beech would prove the prevailing species. Other trees included yellow birch, red maple, and black cherry, with scatterings of white ash, elm, basswood, and hop hornbeam. A few components of the old boreal zone remained—white pine especially, and paper birch, taking advantage of openings in the canopy. The forests of the Upper Delaware were fundamentally altered—no longer boreal, not yet the woods to come. Gradual but eventually substantial change continued to define the history of the woodland.

How did the newcomers arrive? The succession from park-land tundra to boreal forest was a matter of plant species advancing northward behind the melting glaciers; later tree migrations were more complicated. The boreal forest was a community of cold-tolerant species reproducing by seeds borne with the wind. The newer species required different degrees of assistance. Red cherry, black cherry and mountain ash produced seeds enveloped in fruit; they depended on birds or animals to eat the fruit and defecate the indigestible seed at some distance, a much slower means of migration. White oaks were dependent in much the same manner, bearing acorns that required feet or wings to carry them very far. Still other species produced nutlike seeds, or fluttering winged seeds that expanded the parent tree's range very slowly. Journeys long in time and distance lay behind their arrivals in the Upper Delaware. Every migration story was different.[29]

At the peak of the glaciation, much of North America's climate was inhospitable to most tree species. Forced southward into narrow enclaves known to paleontologists as *refugia*, trees such as white pine, tamarack, balsam fir, and white oak held on. The white pines took refuge in the southern Appalachians; the tamaracks, the firs, and the oaks still farther away in the lower Mississippi Valley. With glaciation at full extent, the depth of the Atlantic Ocean was dropped by four hundred feet, exposing the eastern continental shelf. The Atlantic coastline stood as much sixty-two miles farther east. The southern portions of this extended coastline provided refugia for several plant and animal species; mammoth fossils appear in fisherman's nets off the coast in the present day.[30]

When the glaciers melted back and the climate warmed, trees species began their slow march northward. Birds and animals became the agents of environmental change. Fruit-eating birds deposited undigested seeds in all directions, a few on open ground to the north, increasing the tree's range a few hundred yards. Squirrels collected nuts, caching them in the ground and occasionally failing to return, leaving the seeds to sprout. Blue jays were critically important to the northward migration of the oaks. Jays are especially raucous in autumn, disputing the possession of acorns, a favored food. Carrying the heavy seeds away in their bills, the jays will occasionally drop an acorn in the ground litter, thereby assisting the spread of the oak. Ranging northward on blue jay wings, progress from the lower Mississippi was relatively steady, but the oaks advanced at an average of 380 yards per year—less than a quarter mile. Estimates of arrival in the Upper Delaware region vary considerably, anywhere from ninety-six hundred to seventy-five hundred years BP. Once the blue jays and the squirrels brought them, white oaks established themselves as a major component in the continually developing northern hardwood forest.

Table 1.1: Important Trees Species, Upper Delaware Valley

Family	Species	Arrival, UDR	Seedtype	Seed Distribution	Freeze Survival Temperature	Soil Preference	Shade Tolerance	Refugia
PARKLAND TUNDRA								
pine	jack pine	15.5–14.04K BP	cone	wind	-112F	poor, dry, sandy	intolerant	—
pine	white spruce	15.5–14.04K BP	cone	wind	-112F	thin, cold	intermediate	—
pine	black spruce	15.5–14.04K BP	cone	wind	-112F	thin, cold	intolerant	—
pine	red spruce	15.5–14.04K BP	cone	wind	-45F	rocky, acid	tolerant	—
fir	balsam fir	15.5–14.04K BP	cone	wind	-112F	moist, boggy	tolerant	south
larch	tamarack	15.5–14.04K BP	cone	wind	-112F	swamps, bogs	intolerant	west
BOREAL FOREST								
Willow	poplar	14.04–9.6K BP	catkin	wind	-112F	moist, valleys	intolerant	—
Willow	aspen	14.04–9.6K BP	catkin	wind	-51F	sandy, wet or dry	intolerant	—
pine	white pine	14.04–9.6K BP	cone	wind	-128F	light, dry, deep	intermediate	South Appalachians
birch	paper birch	14.04–9.6K BP	catkin	wind	-112F	moist	intolerant	—
rose	redcherry	14.04–9.6K BP	fruit	birds	-43F	edge habitats	intolerant	—
rose	mountain ash	14.04–9.6K BP	fruit	birds	-40F	cool, moist	intolerant	—
olive	black ash	14.04–9.6K BP	winged	wind	-38F	wet, floodplain	intolerant	—
hemlock	hemlock	14K BP	cone	wind	-76F	thin, cold, wet	tolerant	South Appalachians
birch	yellow birch	14K BP	cone	wind	-47F	rich, moist	intermediate	—
beech	white oak	10.08–7.3K BP	acorn	cache, jays	-40F	hard, stony	intermediate	Lower Mississippi
pine	red pine	9.1K BP	cone	wind	-112F	sandy, dry	intolerant	South Appalachians
NORTHERN HARDWOOD FOREST								
maple	sugar maple	9.1–8.4K BP	winged	wind	-43F	rich loam	tolerant	Lower Mississippi
maple	red maple	9.1–8.4K BP	winged	wind	-40F	rich loam	intermediate	Lower Mississippi
rose	black cherry	9.1–8.4K BP	fruit	birds	-43F	variety	intolerant	—
olive	white ash	9.1–8.4K BP	winged	wind	-10F	well-drained upland	intolerant	—
elm	elm	9.1–8.4K BP	winged	wind	-40F	moist	intolerant	—
linden	basswood	9.1–8.4K BP	nutlike	wind	-112F	moist	tolerant	—
birch	hop hornbeam	9.1–8.4K BP	nutlike	wind	-42F	dry upland	intermediate	—
beech	beech	8.4K BP	nut	cache	-42F	rich loam	tolerant	Lower Mississippi

Sources: Thomas M. Boonickson. *America's Ancient Forests: From the Ice Age to the Age of Discovery* (New York: John Wiley & Sons, 2000); David R. Foster, ed., *Hemlock: A Forest Giant on the Edge* (New Haven: Yale University Press, 2014); Michael Kudish, *The Catskill Forest: A History* (Fleischmans, NY: Purple Mountain Press, 2000); Peter J. Marchand. *Autumn: A Season of Change* (Hanover: University of New England Press, 2000); Peter J. Marchand, *North Woods: An Inside Look at the Nature of Forests in the Northeast* (Boston: Appalachian Mountain Club, 1987); E.C. Pielou, *The World of Northern Evergreens*, 2nd ed. (Ithaca: Comstock Publishing Associates, 2011); Gil Nelson, Christopher J. Earle, and Richard Spellenberg, *Trees of Eastern North America* (Princeton: Princeton University Press, 2014); Stan Tekiela, *Trees of New York: Field Guide* (Cambridge, MN: Adventure Publications, 2006).

The warmer weather continued to beckon important new species. Sugar maple arrived on winged seeds by 9100–8445 BP, settling on rich loams, gradually becoming a major element in the forest population. No sooner did the maples take root than they had to endure a brief, sudden cold snap—the 8.2K Event. More icy waters entering the North Atlantic.[31]

When warmer days soon returned, they arrived with an emphasis; at 9000 BP, the earth had begun to really warm, a dramatic climate shift known as the Hypsithermal. The 8.2K Event was a brief interruption, no more than three or four centuries. Temperatures climbed once more, eventually becoming on average 4 to 5 degrees Fahrenheit hotter than today. The hot weather lasted roughly four thousand years, peaking around 5500 BP. In the central portions of the North American continent drought conditions prevailed, with frequent gales kicking up dust storms persisting for weeks, baking the landscape to near desert. In the Northeast, much the opposite conditions prevailed—rainfall increased, leading to wetter forest floors. Tree populations in the Upper Delaware adjusted slowly to the damp heat. White pines extended their range northward, while beech trees, assisted by caching squirrels, found their way into the region. More new species—chestnuts and various oaks especially—reached into the southern fringes. For close to three thousand years, the valley would be populated by a forest composed primarily of oaks and hemlocks.[32]

Scientists view hemlock as a "foundation species"—not merely a dominant component of the forest in numbers, but a tree instrumental in defining the character of the entire ecosystem. In the Upper Delaware forests of the Hypsithermal, hemlocks made up the preponderance of the vegetation while acting as the underpinning for a long, well-connected food web. Hemlocks are patient trees, able to sustain themselves in deep shade for years on years, growing little if at all. When an opening in the canopy provided sufficient sunlight, the trees seized the opportunity, growing rapidly, shading out competitors. Fully grown, a hemlock's abundant branches, thickly layered with two-ranked flattened needles, effectively absorbed most of the sunlight and rain, an inopportune environment for shade intolerant competitors. The ground beneath became a carpet of fallen needles overlaying thin, acidic soil. The species thriving in such conditions—plants, animals, bacteria, fungi— were not many; hemlocks limit diversity. And they can stand as long as four hundred years. The most long-lived of the region's tree species, hemlocks played an essential role in defining the nature of the forest taking shape in the damp heat of the Hypsithermal. White-tailed deer depended on their presence in winter, yarding up beneath the feathery, protective branches to escape wind and snow. Red squirrels and snowshoe hares ate the foliage; porcupines ate the bark. And fishers ate the porcupines.[33]

The good times lasted until perhaps 5,000 years ago. The warm days of the Hypsithermal drew to a close; the climate turned colder and stayed wet, ushering in an epoch known as the Neoglaciation. The glaciers indeed re-advanced—though not reaching nearly so far as New York. The forests of the Upper Delaware were forced once again to adjust to significant climate change. A few species contracted their range, cooler weather trees took up newly opened spaces.[34]

The shift was complicated by the nearly complete disappearance of the hemlocks, the foundation trees. Beginning just as the climate change took hold, the hemlocks steadily died out over a period of seven centuries, ultimately vanishing throughout almost the entire Northeast. Again the reasons are much debated. With this much coincidence, there is tentative consensus that climatic changes were somehow involved—perhaps a series of droughts along with the radical shift in temperature—but it seems inexplicable that the disaster was so selective, singling out the hemlocks. Changing weather conditions may have allowed some devastating disease or insect to flourish; there is no way of telling.

Whatever the cause, the effects were chilling. Hemlocks died out almost completely in the Upper Delaware; a small refugium may have held on near present-day Margaretville, in Delaware County. With the old foundation dead and disappeared, the character of the woodland changed. The canopy opened, providing new opportunity for a range of species. Birch, oak, elm, sugar maple, white pine, and beech soon took up the available spaces. More sunlight reached the ground, making for warmer days and cooler nights beneath the canopy. Summers were warmer, winters colder; yarding shelter less adequate. Soils dried out at the surface, grew wetter inches down without the hemlock roots to take up moisture.

The effects were not entirely negative. As the forest adjusted, the volume of trees probably doubled. Streams grew warmer without the hemlocks to overhang the banks, creating new habitats for aquatic life. A larger diversity of birds and animals flourished in the more open woods. (Woodpeckers did especially well while the snags of deceased hemlocks still stood.) But ants missed the hemlocks, as did a few bird species (black-throated green warblers, hermit thrushes, Acadian flycatchers), small mammals, and amphibians. The decline lasted more than two thousand years.

By 3300 BP, the conditions felling the hemlocks had mitigated. Windblown seeds once more began taking root on organic seedbeds lining the forest floor; hemlocks took root and grew, patiently waiting on forest openings to reclaim position. Once re-established, the hemlocks steadily assumed their former role, reshaping and defining the forest system, this time in association with the oaks and the white pines. Numerous, patiently competitive, determining, hemlocks would nonetheless fail to approach the numbers standing tall before the crash. Competition was more fierce. The forest world continued to alter.[35]

Forest composition was a constantly shifting dynamic, conditioned by weather, by the actions of various species, by the effects of fire. In the more than four thousand years since the beginnings of the Hypsithermal, tree species came and went—like the preceding boreal woodlands, the northern forests of three thousand years ago have no analog today. The warming climate created conditions conducive to continued change. Pitch pine, a new conifer, entered the region, less cold tolerant, more acclimated to warmer climes. Mainly the newcomers were broadleaf trees bearing nuts. Three new species of oaks entered at least the southern portions of the Upper Delaware, along with walnuts, hickories and, slowest of all, chestnuts—advancing at a snail's pace of 108 yards per year. These trees needed assistance to move northward, agents to carry the heavy seeds. The blue jays did their part, and the squirrels, caching nuts in the ground to be neglected. But probably the most important agent was a relatively new arrival. People may have entered the Delaware Valley as long ago as 14,000 BP. Over nine thousand years, their presence grew enough to begin influencing the direction of change in the region's ecosystems. They were not alone in their efforts. From tiny bacteria to massive brown bears, the agents conditioning the vegetation of the Upper Delaware were many and active in shaping the environment, mostly in small ways that added up to a lot. And the trees themselves were hardly passive, competing for space, for nourishing soil, for water, for sunlight. An ecosystem is a complicated entity, never entirely at rest. The Upper Delaware would continue to change.[36]

Table 1.2: Timeline: Early Forest History of the Upper Delaware

28,200–23,700 BP	Wisconsinian Maximum
	(Terminal Moraine: Cape Cod, Long Island, New Jersey, Pennsylvania)
23,700–18,200 BP	Early Glacial Recession
	(Standstill Margins: 20,020 BP, 18,800 BP, 18,200 BP)
19,400 BP	Earliest Human Presence in Northeast, Western Pennsylvania
19,300–17,800 BP	Deglaciation
15,500–14,000 BP	Parkland-Tundra Takes Root
14,000–12,900 BP	Boreal Forest Established
14,000 BP	Dutchess County Cave Paleo-Indian Site, Orange County
12,900–11,700 BP	Younger Dryas Cold Period
	(rapid climate change at close)
11,600–8,200 BP	Warmer Climate
	(hemlock, beech, oak advance)
10,300 BP	Glaciers Melt Back to Canada
	(3000 additional years to disappear)
9,100 BP	Northern Hardwood Forest Established
8,200 BP	8.2K Event: Brief Cold Period
8,000–5,000 BP	Hypsithermal
	(hot, damp climate, warmest point 6,000 BP)
5,500–4,000 BP	Human Populations Flourish
5,000 BP	Neoglaciation
	(colder climate, continued wet)

5,000–4,300 BP	Hemlock Crash
4,000 BP	Atlantic Ocean Reaches Current Level
	(coastlines assume modern shape)
3,300 BP	Hemlock Recovery: White Pine-Hemlock-Oak Association Established

Fifteen thousand years of forest development is a long time, far longer than historians are accustomed to considering. But that is how long the process required, from the initial seeding of tundra vegetation to the eventual rise of the hemlock–white pine–oak association that would characterize much (though not all) of the region in historic times. Looking back across the long years, the temptation to organize this long paleontological history into a shorthand series of defining eras is very obvious. With the melting away of the great glacier, the shifting Upper Delaware environment can be said to have supported a discernable succession of vegetation bands, beginning with the parkland-tundra, moving on to the boreal forest, growing eventually into a northern hardwood association much modified through the millennia. The descriptive is elegant, simple and handy to use, and entirely misleading. Reading this shorthand, the results appear determined: the weather got warmer, the glaciers melted back to Canada, the trees arrived in waves predictable in their survival characteristics. True in a very limited sense; this is a model that obscures far more than it explains. Dozens of tree species made up the history of the Upper Delaware forests at one time or another, to say nothing of the herbaceous undergrowth, the vast variety of supporting plants adding to the mix. The animal kingdom supplied countless representatives populating these woods, each giving and taking according to nature and need. From majestic white pine to tiny fungi, time and chance happened to each and every species. Each lived according to the dictates of its particular biology, flourished and died with conditions that shifted in unpredictable fashion. Every species has its own history, its own story of local advantage and misfortune, of competitive success and untimely failure. Every history is complicated. Add them together in their thousands; they comprise a past intricate enough to defy all but the most threadbare, nearly empty descriptive analyses. If the forest history of the Upper Delaware defined a simple pattern, the pattern needs vast oversimplification to work at all.

A forest is a community of living and dying, entering and leaving. That is the one characteristic that never alters. Everything is change. Human analysis imposes the patterns. Too often we mistake the map for the territory.

Two

Human Agency
in the Woodlands

If a forest is more than a collection of trees, the definition derives from the inescapable fact that the location, the health, the survival of plant species so often depends on outside agencies. Topography, climate and weather are obvious; the actions of creatures ranging from microbiological fungi to large ungulates are acknowledged ecological agents. But, the role of one particular animal raises troublesome issues, scientific and philosophical. Just how and where do human beings belong in the patterns of forest ecology? Early in the twentieth century, the highly influential models of Frederick Clements held no place for human agency. People stood outside the equation, witness to the workings of collective super organisms striving to achieve vegetation climax. We could help, or more likely we could interfere; we could not participate.

Echoing the reservations of later generations of scientific ecologists, archaeologist Chuck Redman in 1999 expressed grave doubt that environments unaffected by human activity have existed for a very long time. People have manipulated the natural world, evolving any number of survival strategies and philosophical perspectives to mirror their images and their needs. We live in a world considerably of our own making, a process that began long before modern *Homo sapiens* walked this earth. We cannot restore the natural world to any model of perfection predating human existence— we are an integral component of this world. In a word, we are part of nature.

Drawing on long years of archaeological fieldwork in varied corners of the earth, Redman perceived that efforts to shape nature to human desire began well before the invention of agriculture, growing steadily more influential as human populations flourished, technologies diversified, needs increased, and belief systems intensified. Throughout the world, people became an increasingly dominant component of the natural environments they occupied, encouraging and eventually altering more than a few of nature's webs, discouraging and even destroying others. Dependent on nature for survival, human beings did what they could to better their odds. They were strikingly successful.[1]

The Upper Delaware is one more corner of the world molded in part by human endeavor. When Europeans first explored the region early in the seventeenth century, they encountered a forest environment shaped extensively by fellow human beings who had occupied the ground for something over twelve millennia. Longfellow's "primaeval forest," standing pristine, untouched from the creation, never existed. The degree of influence may shift with locale; the Catskill peaks saw relatively little human activity in comparison to, say, the lower Delaware, but nothing remained untouched. Hunting, gathering, exploring, fire all had their effects. Tracing the story of human presence in the valley discloses a history of gradual but unmistakable environmental change.

Table 2.1: Timeline: Human Presence in the Upper Delaware

23,700–17,800 BP: Terminal Glaciation
    Meadowcroft Rock Shelter: 19,400 BP
14,900–12,900 BP: Boreal Forest established
    Dutchess Quarry Cave: 14,020 BP
11,500–8,200 BP: Climate Warms
    Paleo-Indian (fluted point culture): 14,000–10,000 BP
    Late Paleo-Indian: 10,000 BP
    Shawnee Minisink: 10,590 BP =/- 500 years
    Early Archaic: 10,000–8,000 BP
9,100 BP: Northern Hardwood Forest established
8,200 BP: 8.2K cold event
8,000–5,000 BP: Hypsithermal—hot, damp climate
6,000 BP: peak of warming
    Middle Archaic: 8,000–6,000 BP
6,000–4,000 BP: Southern Hardwood Forest established
5,000–4300 BP: Hemlock crash
    Late Archaic: 6,000–4,000 BP
5,000 BP: Neoglaciation
4,000 BP: current coastlines established
    Archaic-Woodland Transition: 4,000 BP–2800 BP
3,300 BP: Hemlock recovery—White Pine-Hemlock-Oak Association established
1,800–1,300 BP: Little Climatic Optimum
    Woodland: 2800 BP–400 BP
        Early Woodland: 2800 BP–2,000 BP
        Middle Woodland: 2,000 BP–1,000 BP
        Late Woodland: 1,000 BP–400 BP

Like every aspect of the Upper Delaware's prehistory, the precise moment when human eyes first saw the valley will never be known for certain. The first evidence of human presence in the American Northeast continue to be topics of debate, partly the consequence of unavoidable scientific imprecision, partly the fault of archaeological dogmatism. Between 1973 and 1977, archaeologists investigated a rock shelter known as Meadowcroft, located in southwestern Pennsylvania. Careful excavations revealed several layers of human occupation ranging over thousands of years, mostly reflecting the reasonably well-understood stages of Native American presence in the Northeast. The layers lying beneath the rest ignited the controversy. Radiocarbon analysis of organic materials found in those bottom layers provided an occupation date 16,000 to 19,400 years ago. There were no forests at all in the Upper Delaware then; the land was probably frozen tundra, still rebounding from the enormous weight of the glaciers. The dating came as an enormous shock, antedating the almost universally accepted beginnings of human presence in interior North America by as much as five thousand years. Archaeological interpretations of the time clearly contended that the first peoples were manufacturers of a unique "fluted" projectile point (unstemmed, bearing a channel or flute on each face) known as Clovis, widely dated to a six hundred year period beginning around 11,200 BP. The Clovis people were thought to be the first into the American interior, Alaskan migrants moving south at the end of glaciation. Anything predating Clovis by three millennia had to be wrong. Experts advanced a variety of explanations for the "error," each scotched by the Meadowcroft excavators. So the matter ended in maddening uncertainty. Forty years later, enough earlier sites have emerged to confirm that folks were in the Americas south of Alaska long before any Clovis migrants; whether some of them occupied Meadowcroft remains controversial. If any Meadowcroft people did venture far enough east to witness the upper Delaware's emergence from the ice, we will never know.[2]

The first peoples to leave definite traces close to the Upper Delaware Valley probably arrived sometime around 14,000 BP. The oldest known site, Dutchess Quarry Cave, lies on private land near Goshen in Orange County, New York, a little south of the Upper Delaware. A few additional sites have come to light close by, illuminating the presence of people who witnessed the nativity of the Upper Delaware's first forests, boreal woodlands comprised largely of cold-resistant conifers—spruces, firs, and a few hemlocks, together with yellow birch.[3]

The world was a vastly different place. The Delaware River had yet to settle into its current bed—torrents of meltwater had shaped and reshaped the valley for two thousand years, leaving thick deposits of sand and gravel, nodules of flint handy for shaping tools and the fluted points. Glacial lakes and ponds stood everywhere, marshy ground predominated the level spaces. The seasons saw seemingly endless migrations of musk ox and caribou. Elephants roamed the sparse but growing woodlands, browsing the trees, knocking down a few. It was a hunter's dream.

Archaeologists once portrayed these first inhabitants—the Paleo-Indians—as big game hunters, doggedly following the large herd animals through harsh weather, working in parties, prepared to fling home those fluted points at the earliest opportunity. These were the hunters supposedly responsible for the extinction of the Ice Age megafauna, certainly one of archaeology's more contentious controversies. Native American myths surviving into recorded history include a couple that very much appear to be ancient memories of mastodons, handed down from generation to generation.[4]

A more nuanced interpretation has now emerged, portraying these men and women as foragers, generalists who took advantage of a considerable array of plant and animal resources, sometimes including—though not depending on—the larger beasts. Apparently people journeyed in small groups, perhaps as small as a single extended family, moving often through large but well-understood territories, at intervals returning to base camps located on higher ground, close to potable water sources. One such camp occupied a terrace slope close by the Musconetcong River in Warren County, New Jersey, below the Delaware Water Gap. Dated to 13,000 BP, the Plenge Site is the largest Paleoindian site in the Northeast, yielding fifteen hundred artifacts, some fashioned from material originating in Maine. Fluted points date to the early, middle, and late Paleolithic, suggesting repeated visits over a four-thousand-year period. Much disturbed by collectors, Plenge offers little information regarding the lifeways of the visitors. Archaeologists interpret the site as a base visited by hunters journeying "from the Delaware River to the mucklands and lake regions of northern New Jersey and into the Walkill Valley and New York State." The Upper Delaware would be a likely route, but again, we will never know.[5]

If a similar base camp ever existed in the Upper Delaware Valley, the evidence has washed away or lies deeply buried under thousands of years of sedimentary deposits. Paleo-Indian sites are few and far between throughout the Northeast, most undoubtedly lost to thousands of years of erosion, deposition, and disturbance. The surviving site closest to the Upper Delaware lies some thirty-three miles to the south of modern day Port Jervis, at Shawnee Minisink, dated to roughly 10,600 BP. Apparently a base camp, the site stood on a terrace overlooking the junction of the Delaware River and Brodhead Creek in Pennsylvania. Caribou remains have come to light, but the occupants more fully depended on deer and elk for sustenance, along with small game including squirrels, rabbits, beaver, geese and ducks; a variety of plants; and fish. There were no mastodon remains.[6]

The hunters did carry their fluted-point spears into the Upper Delaware. An archaeological survey conducted in the 1970s located a few "faint traces" of Paleo-Indian presence, including two of the fluted points. Whether these may be classified as Clovis points depends very much on which archaeologist you ask—with so few surviving artifacts, every discovery becomes a point of controversy. Clovis or not, this fluted point tradition seems to have made its way into the interior of what is now upper New York along the treacherous pathways of the Delaware River. Hunting expeditions, surely. Foragers trekked through a shifting, unstable environment. Even as the Shawnee Minisink encampment took shape, the climate was beginning to warm, a trend to continue for more than three thousand years. Recognizing that deer, their favored prey, flourished best in "edge habitats"—border areas where wood and grassland adjoined—the hunters began to assist nature, employing fire to burn off the understory vegetation, create more open areas. The fires served that purpose, and more besides. Added to the actions of natural fire, these set conflagrations speeded release of nutrients to the soil, cleared away dead brush slow to decay, and provided openings for new tree species to take root. Ten thousand years before Europeans entered the region, Paleo-Indians were manipulating, shaping nature to their needs, in the river valleys especially. From this point forward, the forests would become an ever-increasingly complex weave of lifeforms, with human beings an essential component of the fabric.[7]

Archaeology is a maddening science, precise and unavoidably vague at once. Inevitably, any reconstruction of the Upper Delaware's human prehistory rests heavily on the determinations of archaeological science, explorations and analyses that shape our understanding of peoples living in an otherwise unrecorded past. Such comprehension as we possess must be constructed from the study of material objects—hard material objects. Anything fashioned from organic materials such as wood long ago rotted in the Upper Delaware's acidic soils. The prejudice of the material colors our understanding, a fact to bear in mind.

With so little to go on, there also exists the natural temptation to fill in the blanks with images provided by the creative fancy. What we know from the evidence and what we believe in our hearts is often inextricable. The prehistoric peoples of the Upper Delaware, the Northeast, occupy a prominent space in historical imagination. The image varies with time and place, wavering from one extreme stereotype to another. These people were the aborigines, the Indians, the Native Americans, however you want to label them. With the names come a set of preconceived images, ranging from unrepentant barbarian to innocent dweller of the forest. The images influence our comprehension in unfortunate ways.

Native Americans saw nature differently from the Europeans who came much later—tens of thousands of years of differing cultural trajectory will have that effect—but the harmony with nature we perceive was with a world they did much to create. Leaving aside the debate over the paleolithic extinctions, the fact remains that the prehistoric peoples manipulated nature to secure an environment conducive to their own survival. In the Northeast, this meant more open forest, more edge habitat, more deer. Fire was the primary tool. Foodways brought further changes to the Upper Delaware woodlands. Population growth would exert greater pressures on the environment. Eventually would come agriculture, and the extensive reorganization of the natural world cultivation implies.

Among the folk traditions of the Algonquians who once hunted the lower reaches of the Upper Delaware Valley are stories suggesting that the harmonious relationship with nature was an approach learned the hard way. One folk tale preserved by the Lenapé (Delaware) Indians tells of "When the Animals left Lenapé Land." One day, the animals, especially the larger game species, simply disappeared from the forests. After much searching, an owl discovered the animals were living in an "enclosure of trees" protected by a race of giants. Determined to stage a rescue, the Lenapé attacked, fighting bitterly for days while the animals stood by, indifferent to the outcome. Finally came a truce and parlay, in which the people asked the Elk, spokesman for the animals, why they made no effort to assist in their own escape. The Elk contradicted the assumption—the giants had not forced the animals into the enclosure, did not imprison them. The animals had migrated voluntarily, glad of the giants' protection. Because the people had treated the animals poorly, taking their lives without respect, without gratitude. "You have wasted our flesh; desecrated our forest homes, and our bones; you have dishonored us and yourselves. We can live without you, but you cannot live without us!" Native Americans came to respect their prey only when the animals (in some ecological fashion) demanded as much. The perceived Native American harmony with nature was not instinctive, natural. It was a learned behavior, born of hard lessons lived in the forest. Prehistoric peoples were not ecological saints, no more than they were savages. They were human beings, the same mix of traits good and bad, hopeful, intelligent, determined to survive—the same as every other collection of human beings to grace any corner of the earth, any time in history.[8]

Archaeologists divide the ten thousand years of human occupation following the close of the Paleo-Indian presence into three broad eras: the Archaic, the Woodland, and the Contact Periods. The Archaic and the Woodland are subdivided into Early, Middle, and Late Periods, reflecting behavioral developments and shifts in material culture. Bearing in mind that the dates represent a rough convenience rather than historical exactness, the Periods break down like this:

Table 2.2: Human Presence in the Northeast

14,000–10,000 BP	Paleo-Indian
10,000–8000 BP	Early Archaic
8,000–6,000 BP	Middle Archaic
6,000–4,000 BP	Late Archaic
4,000–2,800 BP	Transitional
2,800–2,000 BP	Early Woodland
2,000–1,000 BP	Middle Woodland (1–1000 CE)
1,000–400 BP	Late Woodland (1000–1600 CE)
400–240 BP	Contact (1600–1760 CE)

Source: William Andrefsky, "History and Archaeology 4.3 Part B: Contact and Euro-American (Historical Synthesis)." Albert A. Dekin, Principal Investigator. *Cultural Resource Survey: Upper Delaware National Scenic and Recreational River, Pennsylvania and New York* (Philadelphia: National Park Service, 1982), pp. 1–3.

The Paleo-Indian Period faded to a close roughly ten thousand years ago. Few surviving sites in New York date that late; for whatever reason, the first people seem to have forsaken their hold on the region centuries earlier. A gap of long years intervened before humans again took up residence in the area, beginning the Archaic (10,000 BP), a period lasting more than seven thousand years.[9]

The shaping of Early Archaic culture seems to have been a response to shifting environmental conditions. Initially, populations were small compared to the earlier Paleo-Indian presence. Like their predecessors, early Archaic groups were foragers, pursuing a variety of plant and animal resources. What was different was the availability of those resources. The boreal forest was largely disappeared outside the higher reaches of the Catskills, retreated far to the north, close to the glacial tundra. In its place stood the Northern Hardwood forest, comprised largely of sugar maple, yellow birch, and beech, in association with conifers, including hemlock. The rise of the hardwood forest enhanced the resource base available to the various game animals, white-tailed deer especially. Populations flourished. Very soon, human populations began to flourish as well. The Northern Hardwood forest offered a far greater carrying capacity than the Boreal environment.[10]

In most ways, the Early Archaic lifeways mirrored the experience of the Paleo-Indians. Large occupation sites were few—people travelled much of the year in small groups, pursuing whatever food resources became available with the changing seasons. Camps were no longer situated on high ground—the river's course had stabilized by now, allowing freedom to choose sites on the floodplains. Elk and deer were more abundant there, as were turkeys and raccoons. Geese and ducks flew the length of the river in spring and fall; the Delaware was (and still is) an essential landmark of the Atlantic Coast flyway.

The archaeological survey undertaken in the 1970s identified four camp sites in the Upper Delaware, two on the Pennsylvania side, two in New York, all located toward the northern end of the river. The sites were consistent with the Early Archaic throughout the Northeast, characterized by "bifurcate base points." Fluted projectile points were ancient history. Groups seem to have kept to themselves and their territories much of the time—trade in hard artifacts was limited.[11]

The hunting may have been good in the emerged Northern Hardwood forest, but nuts—product of more southerly hardwoods—represented an essential component of the diet. Lots of nuts. Chestnuts, acorns, walnuts, hickory nuts. Solid nutrition, readily gathered with the autumn. Availability increased with the passing decades; nut trees in large numbers took root in the southern portions of the Upper Delaware region during the Early and Middle Archaic (10,000–6,000 BP). Gray squirrels did their part, caching nuts far away from the parent tree, occasionally neglected the treasure. Blue jays too, providing wings for heavy acorns. Crows, passenger pigeons, grouse. Ravens, perhaps. But the most important agent in the growth of this new forest was the work of the human beings.[12]

This was true for two reasons. The first was the simple gathering of the nuts, presumably in baskets. Occasionally a collection would spill, a few rolling away, hiding in the leaf litter, provided an opportunity to germinate. Others might be tossed away at camp sites, too burdensome to transport for a group often on the move. Unconsciously, people were planting nuts in new places. More importantly, people were at work clearing the ground, creating open spaces where an oak or a chestnut could grow. The tool was fire, employed by their Paleo-Indian predecessors, ignited often by Archaic foragers. People were actively engaged in the making of a new forest, one that would define the southern portions thereafter. They were not the sole agents—the squirrels and blue jays were there too, and the process was surely aided by the massive die-off of the hemlocks, the "Hemlock Crash" that lasted for seven centuries (until 4,300 BP), leaving considerable open space in the woods. But people were an integral part of the process.

The result was the eventual establishment of a Southern Hardwood forest in the southern twenty miles of the Upper Delaware, a marked shift in vegetation pattern from the northern three-quarters of the valley. The Southern Hardwood forest was dominated by oaks and chestnuts—chestnuts could comprise as much as forty percent of the woodland in the hilly reaches of the valley. Chestnuts did especially well on upper slopes and ridges, preferring open forest. They stood in the company of oaks, red, black and scarlet, along with hickory, walnut, and several associated species. This was a forest largely dependent on fire to maintain open spaces—many of those species were intolerant of shade. Such forests, rich in food resources, were home to a still wider and more concentrated variety of game animals—whitetail deer, black bear, raccoon, beaver, woodchuck, muskrat, gray squirrels, cottontail rabbits.[13] In the northern portions of the valley, hemlocks recovered from their mysterious crash by 3,300 BP, again dominating the cooler, wetter landscape they helped to establish. The hemlocks made up as much as seventy percent of the northern forests, defined as a White Pine–Hemlock-Oak Association. Several thousand years down the line, the differences in forest composition north and south in the Upper Delaware would have an impact on European economic patterns.[14]

TABLE 2.2: Important Trees Species, Upper Delaware Valley

SOUTHERN HARDWOOD FOREST

Family	Species	Arrival, UDR	Seed-type	Seed Distribution	Freeze Survival Temperature	Soil Preference	Shade Tolerance
beech	scarlet oak	6–4K BP	acorn	cache	-20	dry, sandy	intermediate
beech	black oak	6–4K BP	acorn	cache	-15	dry, sandy	intolerant
beech	northern red oak	6–4K BP	acorn	cache	-20	moist, dry	intermediate
beech	chestnut	6–2K BP	nut	cache	-50	hard, stony	intolerant
walnut	hickory	6–4K BP	nut	cache	-20	moist, upland	intermediate
walnut	walnut	6–4K BP	nut	cache	-20	rich, well-drained	intermediate
walnut	shagbark hickory	6–4K BP	nut	cache	-45	rich, moist	intermediate
pine	pitch pine	6–4K BP	cone	windblown	-41	dry, sandy	intolerant

SOURCES: Thomas M. Boonickson, *America's Ancient Forests: From the Ice Age to the Age of Discovery* (New York: John Wiley & Sons, 2000); David R. Foster, ed., Hemlock: *A Forest Giant on the Edge* (New Haven: Yale University Press, 2014); Michael Kudish, *The Catskill Forest: A History* (Fleischmans, NY: Purple Mountain Press, 2000); Peter J. Marchand, *Autumn: A Season of Change* (Hanover: University of New England Press, 2000); Peter J. Marchand, *North Woods: An Inside Look at the Nature of Forests in the Northeast* (Boston: Appalachian Mountain Club, 1987); E.C. Pielou, *The World of Northern Evergreens,* 2nd ed. (Ithaca: Comstock Publishing Associates, 2011); Gil Nelson, Christopher J. Earle, and Richard Spellenberg, *Trees of Eastern North America* (Princeton: Princeton University Press, 2014); Stan Tekiela, *Trees of New York: Field Guide* (Cambridge, MN: Adventure Publications, 2006).

As the Southern Hardwood Forest took shape, the Early Archaic became the Middle and Late Archaic in the eyes of archaeologists. The weather grew very warm and damp—the Hypsithermal had arrived. Not too much changed, really, though people left behind more evidence of working with plant foods. Newly developed stone implements included anvils and grinding stones (for crushing those nuts and acorns), nutting stones, hand axes, and celts (a kind of axe or wood planing tool). Mobile foraging patterns persisted, attuned to the cycle of the seasons. Bands separated into smaller groups to pursue seasonal opportunities, gathered at base camps on occasion. Judging by artifact remains, movement in the Upper Delaware seems to have increased with time, the likely response to the increase of game resources accompanying the growth of the Southern Hardwoods. In Wayne and Pike Counties, Pennsylvania, Late Archaic sites far outnumber those of earlier periods. Diagnostic points littered an eight-and-a-half-mile stretch of the Upper Delaware between Narrowsburg and Cochecton. At least four multicomponent sites have come to light—seasonal hunting camps.[15]

Overall, Northeastern populations were growing, intensifying the demands on the forest environment. The consequence seems to have been a more active definition of territory, with the occupying groups exhibiting more divergent cultural characteristics. Each group was subtly different yet much the same, sharing a more or less common language, similar technologies, comparable life strategies. At this juncture, some 5,200 years ago, these Northeastern populations, classified as the Laurentian, exhibiting "a unity within diversity," might be labeled proto–Algonquian. This was the earliest identifiable expression of an extensive cultural tradition that eventually figured in historical events from the Atlantic Coast to the Upper Great Lakes. A lot of territory, and there subsequently developed several culture groups classified as Algonquian, based on language, cultural practices, artifact production. Linguistic experts maintain that people communicated in the basic Algonquian language at least as far back as 7,000 BP. The divisions of the Algonquians into their several sub-groupings apparently began in the Middle Archaic. By the Late Archaic, two overarching traditions had emerged.[16]

At first glance, the differences between the two traditions seem artificial and minor. Each employed the familiar mobile strategy, radiating outward from well-positioned base camps to utilize resources shifting with the seasons. Each tradition operated in small bands, maintaining defined territories with relatively low population densities. Both employed minor variations of the standard Late Archaic projectile point. The differences lay primarily in the resources available to each culture group. Spreading eastward from the Great Lakes, the inland tradition, known to archaeologists as the Lake Forest, were positioned to enjoy access a considerable array of resources, moving from one to the next employing the vast network of rivers and streams. Dietary habits shifted markedly through the seasons; they were adaptive and flexible people, spending much of the year in small encampments in the forests, gathering at prominent water spots when the weather grew warm.

From New York's Finger Lake region southward, the Coastal Tradition—occasionally identified as the "Mast Forest Tradition"—occupied lands closer to the Atlantic Coast, including considerable territory extending out onto the now submerged continental shelf. (Sea levels would not reach their current level until 4,000 BP.) Resources were not quite so plentiful in these regions. People hunted a lot of deer, and became well-versed in fishing, both freshwater and saltwater varieties. As the "Mast Forest" label suggests, they consumed a great many nuts. Competition among the Coastal bands apparently grew more pointed—remains exhibit signs of violence, suggesting territorial disputes.[17]

By the close of the Archaic at 4,000 BP, there were two quite similar traditions: small but steadily growing populations; a few hints of territorial hostility, with important implications for the future. Lake Forest territories shifted to Coastal territories close to the headwaters of the Delaware River—archaeologists recognize "separate archaeological complexes for the Susquehanna and Delaware drainages." Collectors have found elements of each in the Upper Delaware—Laurentian points carried from the Hudson Valley, Lackawaxen points from the south. The Valley had become a land between the two traditions, a potentially unstable situation.[18]

The world was changing, shifting in fundamental ways. By 5,000 BP, the weather had turned cold. The Hypsithermal had ended, ushering in a period of damp chill persisting off and on for a thousand years. The glaciers readvanced, though not very far. Tree species shifted ground. But the oceans continued to rise, washing up against modern coastlines by 4,000 BP, depriving the Coastal peoples of considerable territory. In the lower portions of the Upper Delaware, the Southern Hardwood forest was now fully established, culminating a development reaching two thousand years into the past.[19]

People were changing too. Archaeologists see the 1,200-year period beginning at 4,000 BP as a time of transition, a slow adjustment to new challenges, new ideas that brought an eventual adaptation in Archaic lifeways pointing to the Woodland Period. The material marker demarking the transition is a bowl. A very heavy stone bowl.

Archaeologists suspect that the Archaic Period saw wooden vessels used for boiling—red hot stones dropped into wood bowls to heat the water they contained, a clumsy and highly unsatisfactory approach. At the transition, stone bowls begin to appear in artifact inventories, bowls carved from steatite or soapstone, very shallow and awkward to transport. It was a better way to cook nuts, and a diagnostic marker that archaeologists appreciate. The idea seems to have originated south of the Upper Delaware, slowly travelling northward, a wellspring for more inventive ideas to come.

People lived more sedentary lives. Campsites were often located along major rivers; the occupants stayed there for longer portions of the year. (Those bowls were heavy to move.) Fish became a more important component of the diet. Judging by the heavy concentration and considerable diversity of projectile points, the Upper Delaware seems to have been a meeting place of different cultures, a locus of trade and social exchange. Centuries passed. Human behaviors resembled characteristics of the vanishing Archaic less and less, the coming Woodland more and more.[20]

The Woodland, beginning around 2,800 BP, is reckoned to encapsulate the Northeastern human experience over a period exceeding three thousand years. When the Europeans began to explore North America in the sixteenth century of the Current Era (CE), they encountered a bewildering variety of

Woodland peoples, many of them engaged in deadly competition. Differences in the two traditions reach back into the Archaic; conditions in the Woodland Period invited conflict.

The essential characteristic of the Early Woodland Period (2800–2000 BP) was the development of clay pottery. Seeking to create a lighter, handier stone bowl, artisans began experimenting with clay, initially shaping clay vessels in the same shallow shape, actually blending bits of steatite into the clay to lend substance before firing. A better stone bowl. But it did not take long to realize that clay was a far more malleable medium for shaping than a block of steatite or soapstone, and far more readily available. A variety of clay vessels in assorted shapes and sizes began to appear. Competing cultures adapted different characteristic styles, unconsciously providing archaeologists a superb diagnostic tool for distinguishing between groups.[21]

Like the preceding steatite bowls, the primary use of clay pots was to cook nuts to extract the oil. Nuts remained an essential item in the diet—walnuts, butternuts, hickory nuts, acorns—boiled down to provide crucial proteins, fats, and carbohydrates. Various wood implements must have been important as well, judging by the large numbers of adzes, celts, and scrapers uncovered at Early Woodland sites. People stored gathered food in large underground pits, reflecting the more settled lifestyle, though seasonal movement continued.[22]

Early Woodland presence in the Upper Delaware seems to have been minimal, reflecting conditions throughout the Northeast. Camps were small, populations apparently sparse. Archaeological survey identified just ten examples of material evidence, one of them a burial at a rock shelter near Callicoon. A very few projectile points have come to light, leading analysts to conclude the region was lightly travelled. Yet the few points are revealing. Most are examples from what is classified as the Meadowood Phase, common to central and western New York. But a few are Adena points, significant enough to attract archaeological attention. The Adena were people of the Midwest, migrating in small numbers from what is now the Ohio country, carrying ideas for mortuary symbolism. Trekking into the Chesapeake region, representatives then filtered northward, following the valleys of the Delaware and the Hudson, trading as they went. What resulted was a collection of small Northeastern Early Woodland sites littered with a few artifacts originated in the Midwest, as far away as Lake Superior. Early Woodland peoples may have been few in number and conservative in outlook, but they took an interest in arresting concepts.[23]

The seasons cycled, time moved inexorably on. Measured by the modern conventions, the Early Woodland became the Middle Woodland as the Current Era began. Like all archaeological divisions, the dating is a bit arbitrary, yet essential, recognizing a series of critical developments among Northeastern peoples. True, much went on as before; in summer, people organized their lives around camps largely devoted to fishing. Autumn saw them break down into smaller groups to hunt. Ceramic innovation continued, new styles signifying differing local traditions. Evidence of a Point Peninsula culture appears in the Upper Delaware, including a rock shelter site at Ten Mile River, representative of influences from as far away as Southern Ontario. Fishing was indeed the primary activity. The archaeological survey undertaken in the 1970s identified Middle Woodland sites at sixteen locations, all bearing artifacts similar to finds on the Middle Delaware and the Upper Susquehanna Rivers. The variety was striking—"workshops, burial mounds, cemeteries, temporary camps, seasonal camps, larger semi-permanent camps." The Upper Delaware saw considerably greater use than in the Early Woodland, though lifeways remained much the same.[24]

The continuity masks two essential developments, each with a bearing on life in the region. One was the gradual adoption of agriculture. The second was the emergence of two competing cultural identities resonating into the historic period: the Algonquians and the Iroquoians.

Once upon a time, a really good way to start a fight at an archaeological convention was to make some pontificating remark about the origins of agriculture in North America. The evidence is slippery; the intellectual investment in one theory or another large. Agriculture is a marker, a dividing line crucial enough to be characterized as a "revolution" in human history. The Neolithic Revolution. In earlier, more chauvinist days, anthropologists tried very hard to establish the superiority of one people over others by postulating just which culture "invented" agriculture. Once invented, the idea supposedly travelled slowly across the world, communicated by cultural diffusion. That prejudice is thankfully gone; careful, less narrow-minded studies grant that agriculture was independently invented at least three separate times—in the Middle East, in Southeast Asia, and in America. That too is a misleading conclusion.

The problem is with the verb "invented." The word conveys an entirely false impression, as if someone awoke one spring day with a bright idea, went out and planted a field. All else followed. Theoretically, crop agriculture in the Americas began to take shape with the cultivation of maize in Mexico. More truthfully, intensive plant management emerged dozens, if not hundreds, of times in the Americas. Each of these essentially unrecorded events was a response to growing pressures on the gathered food supply, and each was governed by local circumstance. Populations were growing larger, band territories smaller in consequence. Feeding more people required greater production from a more limited resource base. The Agricultural Revolution was a long, slow process of trial and error, repeated many times in many places.

The gathering of plant foods was a necessary activity in any culture; always there were available a variety of edible seeds, herbs, stalks, fruits, berries, nuts and such, available for collection. The variety was endless—Algonquians recommended chewing the sap of white spruce trees as a laxative; the Iroquois chewed pitch pine sap.[25] The mere act of gathering wild plants profoundly influenced local ecosystems. The advance of the Southern Hardwood Forest into the lower portions of the Upper Delaware was largely a consequence of human dependence on nut foods. Women, harvesting nuts, tubers, herbs, berries, and fruits, exercised a process of artificial selection, choosing the choice fruits of some species while ignoring others. Spillage and leftovers, spread about the grounds near encampments, sometimes took root, becoming selected plantings of preferred floras.

The idea of planting crops—making plants do what people wanted them to do—grew out of such gathering experiences. The more heavily people utilized a basic food source, the more readily it betrayed the effects. Squash, an early Northeastern cultigen, provides a sufficient example. When human populations were small, the pressure on seedbearing squash gourds was very light. People gathered the gourds as a food resource during the yearly round, but the plants remained in a typically wild condition, growing willy-nilly wherever gourds might thrive. As more people began to depend more heavily on the gourds as a food source—as occurred when storage pits came into general use—more gourds were picked over, and more completely. Plants growing in marginal areas were unable to withstand the higher demand, and began to die off. Plants in favorable locations flourished, as seeds dropped in the intensified harvest sprang from the fertile earth. Before long, gathering women learned that plants responded to human management.

The critical moment came when the gatherers stopped gathering the best seeds for consumption. In a culture devoted exclusively to exploitation of wild resources, the obvious tendency was take the best, leave the poorer. As intensified seed management became the norm, ingesting the best available seeds had a dilatory effect on the following year's crop. When the gatherers took the next step in the logical sequence—saving the best seeds until the following spring, sowing them in the most favorable locations—determined plant management was underway.[26]

The emphasis on maize production has created an unfortunate interpretive bias in the comprehension of agriculture's history. The tendency has been to date the beginnings of agricultural endeavor in any group to the first evidences of maize consumption. Maize cultivation *was* a consequence of cultural diffusion. Maize is wholly a product of human manipulation, the result of domestication experiments begun in Mexico some 4,700 years ago. Carefully selecting and encouraging seeds of a native annual called teosinte, Mexican Indians eventually developed a plant dependent on human intervention for survival and propagation—people must manually remove the seeds from their tightly bound cobs and sow them in the earth for the plant to reproduce. Maize migrated north from Mexico only because people carried seed kernels from place to place. Movement was slow, as the plant had to acclimate itself to differing temperature and rainfall regimes in the different latitudes of the Americas. Maize demonstrated a remarkable adaptability, eventually establishing itself (with human help) in any place providing sufficient water and 140 consecutive frost-free days each year. Every Northeastern culture recalls a legend of how maize came to the people—in a variety of ways benign or violent, but always from the outside. The plant reached the Northeast by the seventh century CE. (Recall the Adena peoples journeying eastward late in the Early Woodland, carrying trade goods. And seeds as well?)[27]

Initially, maize was not regarded as an important food source—more as an entertainment, the source of popcorn and a mildly alcoholic beverage. As time passed and populations grew, maize became more essential (though never more than half the dietary intake), a reliable source of calories. And cavities—maize produces a lot of sugars. By 600 to 700 CE, a variety of maize known as Eastern 8-row had become common throughout the Southern Great Lakes region. A genetic descendant, Northern Flint corn, was cultivated by both Iroquoians and Algonquians as the historic period began.[28]

The problem with the insistence on maize as a marker is that the event completely discounts any earlier experimentation with more local plants, including seeds we do not much think of as edible these days. There is good evidence that people in Maine were cultivating gourds as far back as 5,695 BP, the Late Archaic. A great many more experiments may be lost to time.[29]

The date generally cited for the first efforts at agriculture in New York is sometime around 1,000 CE. Suspiciously late. Maize agriculture probably began at that late date; some forms of horticulture may have emerged much earlier. Whenever, the move to cultivation was gradual, more a new wrinkle in the yearly cycle than a revolution in lifestyle. Bands continued to move from place to place with the seasons, pursuing shifting food resources. The evolving cycle might begin in spring with cultivation and sowing, close perhaps to a reliable fishing stream. A summer journey could take the band to some more advantageous resource inland. A return to the fields in autumn would bring harvest and celebration, succeeded by a trek to favorable winter hunting grounds. The following spring would bring renewal. Very gradually, as populations continued to grow larger and territories smaller, dependence on cultivated crops increased. Fields expanded; more time was devoted to sustained agriculture.[30]

The slow but steady development of full-fledged agriculture impacted the forests in limited areas. Native American populations were never that large (perhaps fifty people per square mile by 1500 CE); there was no need to clear large expanses of woodland. But clearing there was. Developing new fields, women along the Delaware generally preferred the floodplains, where soils proved deeper and more fertile than the thin, sour earth characteristic of the uplands. Another attractive choice was the abundant bottomlands left by long-dried glacial lakes and ponds, where organic sediments had collected over long millennia. Men undertook the clearing, women the cultivating, planting, and harvesting. Fields tended to be relatively large, and more or less permanent. Once established, women often employed some form of crop rotation, leaving a few plots fallow and planting the rest, rather than continually opening new ground. Planting strategies enhanced fertility—rather than monocrop agriculture, women often wove plantings of beans and gourds together with maize, the former plants supplying nutrients the corn absorbed from the soil. The overall impact on the environment was small—an abandoned field, given over to goldenrods, asters, meadowsweet, blackberries, and raspberries, would be reclaimed by the forest within decades.[31]

Agriculture there was on the Upper Delaware; archaeological evidence demonstrates the fact; travelers' accounts from the eighteenth century lend support. But probably not much. The valley was narrow and steep, lands propitious for agriculture less than abundant. More to the point, the region was frontier country, a borderland between two similar yet competing cultural groups. To the south lay the population core of an Algonquian group, later known to themselves as the Lenapé, to history as the Delawares; territories to the north came to be inhabited by Iroquoian peoples—eventually known as the Mohawks, the Oneidas, the Onondagas. The lands between were lightly occupied, a kind of border country.[32]

Iroquoian and Algonquian groups shared much in common. Both were Eastern Woodland cultures, adapted to the lifeways of the forest, attuned to the seasonal cycles that brought them the nutritional riches of fishing, hunting, plant gathering, and eventually agriculture. Quite similar myths and legends figure heavily in the traditions of each, revealing their common origin. Each was organized as a matriarchal society. Their languages express common roots. Yet the two were fundamentally different, products of a separation deep in the past, generating the continued evolution of markedly different, at times antagonistic cultures.[33]

The differences were quite plain to Europeans, so strikingly plain that early theorists posited that the Iroquois were intruders, migrants from the Southeast. Their origins remain a mystery, but scholars generally agree that Iroquoian groups originated to the north, probably southwestern Ontario, as long ago as the Late Archaic, five to six thousand years in the past. There is not much to go on, but linguistic scholars have determined that Iroquoian languages emerged from dialects common throughout the Eastern Woodlands. Algonquian and Iroquois arose from a common ancestry.[34]

Among the folk tales preserved by the Lenapé is the story of "How the Pipe Came to the Lenapé." The myth recalls a time in the distant past when there was just one people. A dispute over a sacred medicine, the tooth of a monster bear, led to irreparable divisions. To keep the peace, "it was finally decided to separate into independent groups.... In time, many new tribes came into being, speaking new and different tongues and living in different ways."[35]

Whatever may have happened, the development of Iroquoian societies drove a firm wedge among the Algonquian groups. The eastern tribes, including the Abenakis, the Cree, the MicMac, and the Lenapé became separated from Upper Great Lakes tribes such as the Sauk, the Fox, and the Ojibway. By the Middle Woodland, the differences between the two culture groups were marked enough to allow archaeologists to clearly distinguish between them.[36]

The Iroquoian groups emerged from a culture known to archaeologists as Point Peninsula, dating to the Archaic-Woodland transition, heavily influenced in its later stages by the mound-building cultures of the Midwest. By 800 CE—well into the Middle Woodland Period—the Owasco culture had taken shape, centered in the Mohawk River Valley and the Finger Lakes Region. Architecture (along with the inevitable ceramic differences) was a defining characteristic; prototypical longhouses began to appear. Another two centuries saw the adoption of maize agriculture (with attendant tooth decay). By the early years of the Late Woodland (1000–1600 CE), people were spending much of the year in large, fortified villages. There were troubles. For one thing, the bow and arrow, a most effective attack weapon, had arrived.[37]

Their villages housed hundreds and eventually as many as two thousand people, protected from attack by stout wooden palisades. Just which attackers they feared is difficult to say—neighboring Iroquois or Algonquians? But life had become far more sedentary, constructed around the demands of crop agriculture for much of the year. Grain storage was an important consideration. Hunting expeditions continued in the winter months, though the hunters had to travel farther afield. Large villages consumed larger and larger bundles of firewood—one more burden placed on the forests.[38]

To the south and east, similar developments were taking place among the Algonquian groups. Apparently there was not a great deal of exchange between the forerunners of the Iroquoians and the Algonquians; each arrived independently at essentially similar lifestyles. Variations of Owasco ceramics characterized each culture; with the passage of time, differences in ceramic design marked their separation. Trade was minimal; for the most part the two peoples maintained their distances—Iroquois to the north, occupying territories reaching to the Susquehanna; Lenapé south, on the lower portions of the Delaware River drainage. Between them the Upper Delaware flowed, seventy-five miles of mostly unoccupied country.[39]

Not completely unoccupied. The archaeological survey undertaken in the 1970s found a rich assortment of material artifacts traceable to the Late Woodland, most heavily along the floodplains and at nearby rock shelters. Owasco ceramics were well represented, along with later Iroquois materials, especially in the upper reaches of the valley, close to the sources of the river. The findings confirm reminiscences recorded in nineteenth-century county histories. In the *History of Delaware County*, W.W. Munsell included pioneer memories of two fortified Native American sites on the banks of the Delaware near the mouth of Mill Brook, one on the east bank, one on the west. Projectile points lay about in abundance. Munsell's volume further contended that a Tuscarora village stood near Margaretville on the East Branch of the Delaware in early historic times, while the Oneidas sold land to white settlers as far as Delhi, on the West Branch, known in the eighteenth century as the "Mohawk Branch." The northern reaches of the Upper Delaware lay within the periphery of Iroquois territory.[40]

Seventy-five miles southward, faint evidence of Lenapé presence has come to light in the vicinity of Port Jervis, where the Delaware bends sharply southwest and the Upper Valley (by definition) terminates. Algonquian artifacts have emerged as far north as the mouth of the Lackawaxen River, some twenty miles. The division between Iroquoian and Algonquian materials— and the relatively sparse discoveries of each—points to the unique character of the valley. Unlike the middle and lower Delaware, the Hudson River to the east, and the Mohawk to the north, the Upper Delaware Valley was a lightly utilized region, with minimal sedentary settlement. A small village or two in the upper portions of the valley, a few cultivated fields near modern Hancock—that was pretty much it. David Murray, in his *Centennial History of Delaware County, New York*, contended that the Native Americans visited the East Branch of the Delaware, along with the headwaters of the West Branch, on "annual hunting expeditions." That sounds about right. The valley was inhospitable to more permanent settlement—narrow, rugged, prone to flooding, a little dangerous. Archaeologists have identified very few Early or Middle Woodland sites in Wayne County, Pennsylvania—the northern portion of the Upper Delaware. This was a frontier separating two peoples, lightly travelled to minimize potential conflict.[41]

And that left the condition of the Upper Delaware forests a little different from surrounding regions. Such interstices between differing cultures were ecologically significant. The more heavily populated core regions of home territories exacted considerable pressure on the local environment. Ongoing hunting made game relatively scarce, extensive areas were cleared for agriculture, the demand for wood fuel was considerable. Out on the periphery, something approaching the conditions of a "no man's land" prevailed. Seasonal hunting parties, rarely visiting precisely the same haunts in successive years, taxed the resource base minimally. A little firewood, a tiny field or two; sustained human presence was nearly nonexistent. The one impact was fire, set periodically to renew the forest, create more edge habitat, remove the deadwood. Shape a better hunting ground. The forests of the Upper Delaware were in part managed by human beings, but the actual consumption of forest resources was small, compared to neighboring valleys.[42]

The result: the forests flourished. Animal populations—game animals especially—thrived. Tree species grew large; the pace of succession was slow. Disturbance, apart from the periodic fires, was slight, limited largely to the effects of wind and weather. Functioning as a buffer, the Upper Delaware was a land of ecological richness, a region where the forests could burgeon, individual species proliferate, supplying continued renewal to neighboring regions that supported more intensified human use.

Among the Lenapé, a legend survives of a masked being, Misinkhâlikán, with a face half red, half black. The masked being was the guardian of the forest, moving between the material world and the realm of the spirits, protecting the trees and the animals, ensuring the continued survival of the game. His demands were few, among them the making of a mask mirroring his face, to be worn at ceremonies honoring his presence. Occasionally he was seen in the forest, riding on a buck, herding deer. Misinkhâlikán would have been very much at home in the Upper Delaware.[43]

At least until the 1750s, when a very different cultural regime assumed possession. European pioneers, as ever seeking new lands to farm, encountered an Upper Delaware Valley virtually pristine, or so it appeared. Nut trees abounded in the southern reaches of the valley and grew locally in the northern reaches. Large spaces of open woodland created by fire provided abundant habitat for white-tailed deer and smaller game. The results of human efforts over long millennia. The Europeans were assuming control of a forest world shaped by the efforts of Native American predecessors.

THREE

A Division into Commodities

Recognizing the impact of human agency in a forest's ecology should in no way obscure our perception of parallel influences wrought by other species. Without those mycorrhizal fungi doing their work, feeding the tree roots, encouraging growth, offering protection against disease, there would not be much of a forest at all.[1] From the microbiological to the enormous, a multitude of plants and animals shape the forest economy. One of the more obvious—and historically important—is the beaver. Nature's engineer.

Relatively large as rodents go—though not nearly so large as their extinct Pleistocene cousins, the giant beavers that once enlivened the region—the modern beaver weighs in at forty to fifty pounds, running about four feet long, including the seventeen-inch tail. Their familiar aquatic habits necessitate an especially lustrous, watertight fur coat, composed of two kinds of hair. More obvious are the long, coarse guard hairs, 2 to 2.4 inches long. More important is the one-inch thick soft woolen underfur next to the skin, repelling the water. The qualities of that fur coat would bring ecological change to the Upper Delaware, along with most of the North American continent.[2]

Stating the obvious, beavers build dams. The skill is hardwired in their brains. The sound of running water is an important trigger—encountering such, the beaver's instinctive response is to stem the flow by blocking the waterway, and build a lodge in the pond that forms. A beaver colony consists of the members of a single family—two breeding adults, two to four kits born each year, and two to four yearlings who will depart, usually early in their second year when a new set of siblings appear. Leaving the lodge, they will seek a mate and an unoccupied stretch of stream in need of a dam. Mortality is high; sojourning adolescents are often victims of bad weather, poor diet, and the sharp teeth of wolves, coyotes, bears, and mink. But enough are successful to fully populate any extensive river network; density averages nearly

56

two colonies for every mile of stream, as many as sixty beaver per square mile.[3]

Apart from running water, the critical ingredient to a beaver colony is the presence of trees. Beavers have their preferences. Highest on the list are aspens and willows, shade intolerant softwoods that often take root in the moist soil of stream banks, especially after fire has left a clearing. (Native American's fires probably created attractive habitat for beavers.) Lacking their preferred woods, a colony will devour beech, ash, maple, hornbeam, cherry, birch, hemlock, and, in late winter, pine—the essential components of the Northern Hardwood Forest. Beavers accept spruce and fir only when desperation calls.[4]

Drained by myriad small streams, thick with Northern Hardwood species, sprinkled with clearings made by Indian fires, the Upper Delaware was ideal beaver country. Locating a favorable site, a beaver pair would begin construction work on a dam in late summer, felling poles perhaps seven feet long, propping the sticks against the bank, angled upstream. Heavy stones held the sticks in place; coarse grasses got wedged into the gaps between. Stream flow impeded, water backed up behind the dam, establishing a pond where the lodge would soon take shape. Dam maintenance could continue for several years. New poles floated across the pond were jammed into the original structure while thick layers of mud were added, the whole construction evolving into a compact, remarkably tight embankment.

Years of occupation would leave a mark. Venturing from the central lodge, the beaver family foraged in all directions, clearcutting the forest up to five hundred feet away. Well-worn paths often grew deep enough to fill with water from the pond—canals extending well into the surrounding forest, where a beaver could fell a young tree in fifty minutes. A favorable site might last a good ten years before the reachable food resources gave out; venturing too far from the safety of the pond was dangerous.[5]

The ecological impact of this engineering was considerable. As a dam initially took shape, rising water killed the trees standing at the stream's banks, opening the forest canopy. Stream hydrology altered; the dam slowed and regulated the water's flow, reducing runoff erosion and flooding, extending water availability through the seasons, moderating water temperature. Impounded water raised the surrounding table, benefiting a variety of animals and plants. Thick layers of organic matter collected in newly formed swamps and meadows. Trout took refuge in the pond when water was low. Turtles made homes. Geese and ducks floated on the surface and built nests in marshy areas the dam created. Redwing blackbirds established harems. Grebes, kingfishers and herons found meals. Otters, minks, raccoons. Black bears wallowed in the margins. White-tailed deer drank from the pond. Woodpeckers, chickadees, bluebirds, and tree swallows flew overhead, finding advantage in a woodland reshaped. The beaver lodge itself became a haven for mice, voles, muskrats, moths. Abandoned, the dam eventually disintegrated, leaving a unique corner of the forest, a long-lived "beaver meadow" providing fodder and a yard for deer in winter. Engineering their dams, promoting their own safety and well-being, beavers did much to create and sustain biodiversity in the forest.[6]

The rodents played an integral role in a large and varied system. White-tailed deer were a keystone species, selectively browsing the trees, slowing growth, influencing the numbers and kinds of trees comprising the mature forest. Unchecked, the deer population could multiply exponentially, resulting in denuded woodlands and large die-offs. Predators kept the numbers down—wolves hunting in packs, cougars leaping from boulders and trees, black bears preying on fawns, scavenging carcasses. On a smaller scale, the lagomorphs—rabbits and snowshoe hares—affected plant life too, consuming bark, girdling young trees, thinning the forest. Red foxes thinned the rabbits. Whatever the species, whatever the strategy, the goal was the same: survival, reproduction, growth. Thousands of years of shifting conditions, shifting fortunes had resulted in a dynamic woodland equilibrium—fragile, temporary, easily shifting, but vast enough to secure a definable system. A forest, populated with innumerable plant and animal species large and small, each seeking success on its own terms, had created an elusive, undefinable, ever-shifting, larger whole.[7]

The Upper Delaware was a forest system the first peoples had learned to respect. As historian Anthony F.C. Wallace noted, "Toward the brute creation the Delawares preserved a respectful mien; animals valued for their flesh and skins, like the bear, were not treated with casual brutality but were killed with ceremony and in some cases addressed by the hunter as noble enemies." But this was a learned behavior, subject to potential change as conditions and opportunity shifted.[8]

Sometimes the shifts seemed to shake the earth.

Henry Hudson was the first European to encounter Delaware Bay. An Englishman working for the Dutch, Hudson in 1609 sailed his ship, the *Half Moon*, past Cape May to briefly explore the waters beyond. Balking at the heavy shoals, he spent just six hours in the bay, enough to conclude that a considerable river emptied in, before turning northward to discover and explore the river bearing his name. Sailing the Hudson northward as far as the future location of Albany, New York, he established contact with the Mohawk Indians, guardians of the Iroquois' eastern door. Hudson's crew exchanged knives and hatchets for beaver and otter skins, the beginnings of a trade that would profoundly alter the fabric of life throughout the American Northeast. Even the remote forests of the Upper Delaware would feel the ripples of yet more change.[9]

Henry Hudson was an advance agent, one of several representing the dramatic transformation taking place on the far side of the Atlantic Ocean. For more than a thousand years after the fall of the Roman Empire, Western Europe had survived as a conservative, moribund economy, subject to petty political upheaval, shifting allegiances, and precious little innovation. Culturally united by devotion to the Roman Christian church (not without its own upheavals), leaders of the various geopolitical entities (do not think of them as nations) dreamed of Roman reunification and future glory. Only when the possibility of an empire renewed became genuinely tangible early in the sixteenth century did Europeans realize how unacceptable such an event would be. Geographic self-interest, always present, became paramount; Europe's political entities entered into economic, cultural, and military competition that became global in scale. Emerging nation-states sought economic independence and power over their neighbors, placing the rising tide of capitalist trade above any desire for common cultural identity. The Christian monolith was one obvious victim; various European states adopted differing forms of Protestantism mainly to shake off economic and political limitations.[10]

The quest for new economic possibility, new means of enrichment, new ways to out-compete greedy neighbors led several countries to explore the possibility of new opportunities in distant lands. When the Vikings discovered North America in the eleventh century there was no impact on Europe, no economic desire to be filled. Half a millennium later, the discovery of new lands meant new economic opportunity. Henry Hudson found Delaware Bay while seeking new resources for the Dutch, just as Champlain was doing for the French, exploring the St. Lawrence Valley in 1603, just as the English were trying very haphazardly to accomplish at Jamestown beginning in 1607.

Leaving aside the glamour and adventure of the thing, the objective was everywhere the same: to procure "mercantible commodities." Stuff you can buy and sell at profit.[11]

Unlike the First Peoples, who perceived a shared spiritual life in nature, the newcomers saw nature as so much spiritually lifeless commodity. Human beings were separate from the natural world, superior; nature existed to provide human needs, nothing more. Even the newly developing interest in the scientific study of nature re-enforced the concept. Sir Francis Bacon, the first to articulate the postulates of the scientific method (*Novum Organum*, 1620), emphasized that the purpose behind the research was to better utilize and dominate the natural world. Carrying that thinking to conclusion, René Descartes argued that as animals were spiritually without life, they felt no pain in a meaningful sense. That justified experimentation on animals.[12]

Catching his glimpse of Delaware Bay, sailing up the Hudson River, Henry Hudson measured what he saw with very different eyes from the people who had occupied the region for millennia. He was the agent of an outreaching force that would very quickly alter the natural equation in the American Northeast—in the Upper Delaware and everywhere else.

Hudson's voyage provided justification for Holland, newly emerged from centuries of Spanish rule, to claim control over lands extending from Delaware Bay northward to include much of what is now New York, Pennsylvania, New Jersey, and portions of New England. The English, basing their claims on the voyages of explorers such as John Smith, disputed large portions of this territory, creating confusion that lasted through the American Revolution. Simply put, the boundaries were vague (early maps were not terribly accurate), the stakes high. That the boundaries were not clearly defined is not surprising; Europeans did not officially recognize the national boundaries separating their own countries until 1648.

The Dutch, recognizing the trade advantages offered by the geography of the Hudson River and the obvious port at Manhattan Island, concentrated their efforts on that axis into the interior. The Dutch West India Company founded New Amsterdam at Manhattan by 1624; Beverwijck (Albany) as early as 1631. Stretched thin, the company made little effort to develop claims in the Delaware Valley, doing little more than establishing a single frontier trading post to tap into the rapidly expanding fur trade. One more interloper, the Swedes, horned in, establishing New Sweden on the Lower Delaware (populated mainly by Finns) in 1633. Eleven years later, New Sweden was sending two ships to Europe laden with 6,127 packs of beaver skins.[13]

The Finns and the Dutch transacted business with the Lenapé, descendants of the Algonkian sub-group that had occupied the Delaware Valley for thousands of years. Perhaps 8,000 Lenapé lived along the river in 1600. The Europeans tried very hard to define and treat them as a nation, similar to the nation-states taking shape in Europe. The mistake created endless confusion then and ever since. The Lenapé people shared common cultural bonds, adhering to a system defined by three totems: Wolf, Turkey, and Turtle. Europeans thought the divisions dictated by geographic location, but totem membership cut across geographic and economic divisions among the Lenapé. Totems were a social bonding mechanism, a defined source of common identities among an often scattered people. Any member of a totem could call upon any other member for aid and shelter, no matter the location or circumstance. Inherited, totem lineage was reckoned through the female line, one more convention mystifying the newcomers.[14]

Tribal unity, political and economic, depended very much on the situation and the time of year. The Lenapé were more sedentary, more dependent on agriculture than their ancestors, but they still journeyed with the seasons, breaking away from central villages to pursue hunting and fishing opportunities. Warfare (repeatedly triggered by interactions with the incoming Europeans) might bring more people together for common defense, but large degrees of localism and separation remained the rule. Villages were seldom fortified, even as violence escalated.

Political decisions were guided—not commanded—by sachems (nine in the early 1600s) who garnered varying degrees of authority and loyalty based mainly on personal prestige. There was no overarching leadership structure, no person or persons who spoke for all. No king, no central government. The sachems negotiated alliances among the varying bands of Lenapé as were deemed necessary; these were temporary, created to meet the exigencies of an immediate situation. The totems provided such permanent common identity as people shared.[15]

The newcomers called the Lenapé the "River Peoples," subsequently the "Delawares" when the river itself was provided a European name. Living so close to the Atlantic Coast, easily accessible to the incoming Europeans, the Delawares were among the first of the native peoples to be diminished and displaced by the sudden appearance of the ships from across the sea. Among the folktales preserved by the Lenapé is the story of the "White Men and the Bullock's Hide," which supposedly renders a memory of the initial arrival of the whites, their chicanery in obtaining lands for settlement. The story concluded with the expressed fear "that they would soon want all of our country." How right they were.[16]

The first deadly aspect of European contact struck the Lenapé with merciless speed. Long separated from the germ pools of Eurasia and Africa, Native Americans possessed no immunities to a variety of diseases too common on the far side of the world. Sudden exposure fostered what epidemiologists define as "virgin soil epidemics"—diseases such as smallpox spread through the native communities unchecked, ravaging helpless populations. Entire villages died out; by the late 1650s, Europeans were reporting ninety percent mortality in the Lower Delaware region. Coupled with the culture shock rising from the proximity to the incomers, Lenapé society in the lower valley collapsed. Survivors mostly retreated northward, reorganizing in a region that came to be known as the Minisink, where the Wolf totem predominated.[17]

As a territory, the Minisink defies precise definition, varying in expanse, in tacit boundaries, depending. The southern frontier seems to have rested at the Delaware Water Gap, where the river cut through the Appalachian Mountains. The Minisink extended northward thirty-seven miles across the Lehigh Hills as far as the Neversink River (the southernmost point on the Upper Delaware, Port Jervis now), or maybe Lackawaxen Creek (another twenty-three miles upstream), or perhaps even Callicoon Creek (twenty-four miles further). The Catskill Mountains bounded the territory to the east, separating the Minisink occupants from other Algonkian groups. The western frontier was nebulous, depending very much on what the Iroquois thought.

Establishing new villages in the Minisink, the surviving Lenapé were remote enough from the centers of European colonization to rebuild their fortunes in a somewhat familiar fashion. By the eighteenth century, these bands had become known to the Europeans as the Minsees, or perhaps Munsees—dwellers of the Minisink. They felt no love for the Europeans, regarding them as "heathens." Heathens or not, the Europeans were inescapably close, pushing at the boundaries, offering much, taking much. For the Munsees, for all the Woodland tribes, the fundamentals of life had changed irreversibly.[18]

The horror of strange disease had some impact, and the stress of endemic warfare—against Europeans, against other Indians—played a role in the alteration, but the change in Native American lifestyle was more basic still. The trade that began so innocuously between Indian peoples and European explorers quickly grew into necessity. The Algonkian (and Iroquoian) groups that had lived comfortably for centuries on centuries employing lithic tools, flint projectile points, and clay pots discovered that the Europeans were offering much handier alternatives. Iron hatchets. Steel knives. Shooting muskets. Above all, copper and iron kettles. How much easier to cook a meal in a metal pot, where a person could boil water directly. Slowly but steadily, the Indians abandoned their own manufactures to purchase what the Europeans offered: "rifles, powder, lead, repair parts, flints, traps, knives, iron hoes, steel axes, copper kettles, files, awls, nails, wire, wampum, paint, blankets and blanket cloth, shoes…" the list goes on. The medium of exchange: deer skins and, above all else, beaver skins. (Beaver in Europe were rare, nearly extirpated, and beaver hats were all the rage—no well-dressed man could be seen without.) As one northern Algonkian so famously characterized the deal, "The beaver makes everything perfectly well, it makes us kettles, swords, knives, bread; in short it makes everything…."[19]

Before the trade with Europeans began, the Native Americans had treated the beaver as one more aspect of nature, occasionally hunting the animals for food, for medicine, for warm clothing; taking care not to overhunt. Respect afforded the natural world. Much speculation has been invested in the reasons behind the dramatic change after 1600, but the most probable answer is desire for the convenience found in the new. Metal cookware especially. Note that the first item the Algonkian speaker mentioned was "kettles."[20]

With the advent of the fur trade, the occasional beaver hunt became more of a fulltime preoccupation, especially in winter when the inner fur was most lustrous. One of two methods served the purpose. The hunters might break down the dam, spearing the beaver as they sought to escape the draining pond, or they might cut holes in the frozen pond to attack the lodge directly. Each was exceedingly effective. By 1670, essentially the entire beaver population of what is now New York State was gone. Wars among Indians grew in consequence. In 1642, the Iroquois Confederacy attacked the Hurons living on the northern shores of Lake Erie, seeking control of the Canadian fur trade. The Iroquois would continue to extend their reach northward and westward for more than a century, building an economic and political chain intended to maintain the supply of European necessities. The Lenapé, weakened by disease and too-close proximity to the Swedes and Dutch, entered into uneasy alliance with the Iroquois as subsidiary adjuncts to the Confederacy, an agreement that would end in bitter humiliation. The much-diminished Lenapé traded what they could, relying largely on deer skins as the beaver supply ran out. In the forests, ponds and marshes disappeared, erosion grew, the water table dropped, the forests grew more dense. The water engineers had disappeared.[21]

Just when the first Europeans may have set foot in the Upper Delaware is not much more certain than the arrival of the first peoples, maybe twelve thousand years before. One source points to 1614; another to some time between 1632 and 1640. The impact of the fur trade is visible in the archaeological record; a variety of European trade goods turned up in surveys. The Swedes may have attempted to establish a post near Big Island in 1638 or 1639; if so, the settlement came to nothing. Much of the confusion seems to stem from the varying definitions of the Minisink Territory—how far northward was the extent? Which Europeans ventured how far?[22]

No matter, realistically speaking. The Upper Delaware may have been remote in comparison to the Connecticut, Hudson, and Lower Delaware valleys, but in the end, the Lenapé grandfathers were absolutely correct; the Europeans wanted to have it all. Killing or evicting your trading partners seldom makes good business sense, but as the beaver skin supply ran low and tribal resistance weakened, the one last desirable commodity the natives retained was the land. Europeans were more than willing to bargain.

Land transactions between Native Americans and Europeans were unavoidably tainted by each party's misunderstanding of the other's cultural practices. For their part, the Indians possessed no concept of land ownership—the idea that a parcel could be delineated, bounded, and sold, becoming private property alienated to all others. The Lenapé understood the idea of naturally bounded territory; they had maintained a frontier understanding with the Iroquois for centuries. The familiar practice was a matter of determining who got to hunt where without causing conflict; the land itself remained free, like the game, the water, the air. When the Lenapé, the Iroquois, and dozens of other tribes began selling to Europeans, they at first assumed they were selling the use of the land, not the land itself. The Native Americans reserved hunting and fishing rights in early land transactions, encountering stunning surprises when the Europeans built fences on the lands they purchased and accused the Indians of trespass.

For their part, the Europeans sought to purchase land by negotiating with individuals they often erroneously perceived as chiefs—men with authority to deal. This presumed an authority that was often lacking; sachems led by persuasion rather than command. Often, Europeans mistook war chiefs for political decision-makers, making attractive offers to people possessing no power to bargain, only to see the transaction repudiated by the true sachems. Temptations were large. European trade goods were supremely valued; alcohol flowed freely. Locating tribal representatives bearing nothing but a patina of authority, Europeans could entice signatures to a land deed and defy subsequent protests from the true decision-makers. Land acquisition was often little more than formalized racket. Transactions in the Upper Delaware make a very good example.[23]

The Upper Delaware, a scarcely navigable stream flowing between intimidatingly high hills, with little potential farmland and not much else in the way of resources, was hardly the most desirable of potential land purchases. Nonetheless, portions of the seventy-five miles of valley were subject to claims disputed by four different colonies, mainly purchased through three highly dubious land grabs. The transfer of the Upper Delaware from tenuously held Native territory to colonial ownership was a tangled affair.

The controversies were rooted in the presence of the Dutch. South of New Netherlands lay Virginia, with vague land claims extending as far west as the Mississippi River, as far north as anyone's guess. To the Northeast lay the New England colonies, four in number by 1660. The boundaries between Dutch and English were much disputed; the Dutch claimed eastward as far as the Connecticut River, as far south as Delaware Bay. New England maintained the boundary was at the Hudson River, while Virginia was always seeking lands northward. The presence of New Sweden was an annoyance the Dutch overcame, conquering the colony in 1655. The Dutch were an annoyance the English overcame soon after, the Navy entering at Manhattan in 1664, forcing surrender.[24]

The problems were just beginning. A new king sat on the English throne, Charles II, the beneficiary of good fortune when supporters brought about the restoration of the monarchy in 1660, ending eleven years of Parliamentary Protectorate. Heavily in debt, the restored king nonetheless felt obligated to reward his key allies. The answer was land in America; easy enough to give away, seeing the king owned the territory in name only. His brother James, Duke of York, was awarded New Netherlands on the condition he conquer the colony from the Dutch. Easy pickings—much of the New Netherlands population felt little loyalty to their Dutch overlords. New Netherlands became New York, a proprietary colony (a colony owned and operated by a private individual—to be managed and governed as the proprietor sees fit, so long as the governance does not contradict English law). Charles reserved parts of the newly conquered territory for other purposes—what is now New Jersey he awarded to two proprietors who divided the land into East and West Jersey. In 1682, Charles bestowed a further generous parcel of the Dutch territory to the son of yet another supporter, William Penn, so he could establish a haven for the persecuted Society of Friends—the Quakers. The Pennsylvania grant apparently abrogated (without saying specifically) a clause in the charter granted to the colony of Connecticut back in 1662, setting the boundaries of that colony between 41 and 42 degrees north latitude, extending from the Atlantic Ocean to the Pacific. In all, Charles II established the groundwork for three new proprietary colonies out of the lands taken from the Dutch, while seemingly revoking the western claims of a fourth. Got all that? It only gets worse.

New York became a Royal colony (managed and government directly by the king in Parliament) when the Duke of York succeeded to the throne on the death of his brother in 1685, becoming James II. An attempt to reorganize the New England colonies and New York into a single entity called the Dominion of New England fell apart when the Glorious Revolution deposed James; New York survived as a separate Royal Colony under William and Mary.[25]

The new owners faced an old problem—just where did the boundaries of New York lie? Seeking to firm up the colony's claims to extensive holdings, New York's Royal Governors bestowed unbelievably lavish land patents on a few wealthy and powerful colonial residents, figuring that private ownership under New York's aegis would be an indisputable argument in any boundary dispute. The last decade of the seventeenth century saw two small patents awarded at the southern end of the Upper Delaware—a tiny grant to settler William Tietsort, 1,200 acres to merchant Thomas Swartout and partners. Small potatoes. The remainder of the eastern half of the Upper Delaware Valley was swallowed in a single breathtaking gulp, known to history as the Hardenbergh Patent.[26]

Johannes Hardenbergh, born in Albany, was the High Sheriff of Ulster County, located upriver on the west bank of the Hudson. In 1708, Hardenbergh wangled an obscure Esopus Indian into granting him a deed for lands between the Hudson and Delaware Rivers (including the Catskill Mountains) amounting to roughly one and a half million acres, for which he paid the princely sum of sixty pounds. Hardenbergh joined with six partners to petition New York's Governor Edward Hyde, Lord Cornbury, an interesting individual. (There is a quite famous painting of Cornbury walking along the walls of the fort at the foot of Manhattan Island. In drag.) Cornbury was not above land fraud, and the deal certainly furthered his mandated policy of strengthening New York's boundaries through patents to individuals. Despite the extremely dubious authority of one Esopus Indian to even offer such a windfall (there was really no such entity as the Esopus Indians for one thing), Cornbury confirmed the patent. Queen Anne, looking to strengthen the borders of a Royal colony, added her blessing. The Royal government had given away an immense property, parts of which no one was certain belonged to New York at all.[27]

The problem was New Jersey. The Proprietary ownership of East and West Jersey had not done well. Queen Anne reclaimed the land in 1702, reuniting the halves to create the Royal colony of New Jersey. Despite separate government administrations, Anne placed New York and New Jersey under the direction of a single Royal Governor. Dispute and general unhappiness ensued. This lasted until 1738, when New Jersey saw the appointment of a Royal Governor of their own, and complete separation from New York. Establishing a precise boundary between the two colonies now became imperative.

A joint commission comprised of New York and New Jersey surveyors in 1719 had concluded that the northern boundary should be set at Station Rock, at a bend in the Upper Delaware, basing their opinion on a generous interpretation of "the bounds formerly set for the Minisink." A majority of the commission must have hailed from New Jersey; Station Rock lies some fifty miles north of the current boundary. New York's Assembly promptly repudiated the agreement, ushering in several decades of comic opera as officials of the two colonies arrested one another, assessed conflicting taxes, indulged in mild violence. The current border—at the Neversink River—was finally negotiated in 1772. King George III confirmed that boundary a year later, but no one was paying him much attention by then. The Continental Congress (that ineffective body) finally resolved the issue, along with the rest of the myriad colonial boundary disputes, in 1782.[28]

The ongoing controversy dampened enthusiasm for colonial settlement of the region. The prospect of being charged property taxes by two governments was not an attractive one. Efforts to even organize the lands for potential sale moved at snail's speed. By the time owners of the Hardenbergh Patent got around to negotiating a deed for their one and a half million acres from the Munsee Indians, the eight original patentees were dead. The Munsees, who had largely departed the Minisink, confirmed the deed in 1746; the land was surveyed, divided into lots three years later. Sales were tepid.[29]

While New York and New Jersey did what they could to discourage settlement of the Upper Delaware's east bank, still more advanced forms of chicanery were brought to bear in the west. By the charter Charles II bestowed in 1682, the western half of the valley belonged to Pennsylvania, provided the Indians could be persuaded to sell. William Penn, the first proprietor, was most careful with this condition, holding firm to the Quaker belief in the brotherhood of all human beings. Penn negotiated openly and fairly with the various Indian nations occupying the lands bounded by his proprietary grant, enforcing an orderly settlement outward from his capital at Philadelphia, each land transaction carefully worded that each side might fully understand the limits of the purchase. Penn's precise real estate diplomacy brought his colony decades of peace. His descendants were not so scrupulous.[30]

By the 1730s, with William Penn safely dead, Pennsylvania's leadership were casting greedy eyes on the Minisink, the region north of the Delaware Water Gap that included some vaguely defined portion of the Upper Delaware. For decades, the Minisink had proven a stable, relatively unscathed refuge for the Munsees—the surviving refugees of the Lenapé. Digging into long-forgotten records, Pennsylvania officials uncovered "evidence" of a grant from the Lenapé signed over to William Penn in 1686. Unusually, there was no documentation supporting the mention of the grant. Soon after, a map—deceptively labeled—appeared mysteriously out of nowhere. The Munsees remembered nothing of any such deal. Confronted with the produced evidence, their much puzzled sachems in 1737 signed a deed confirming the legitimacy of a "walking purchase." The lands to be conveyed to Pennsylvania would begin from the northernmost point of previous purchases, extending northwestward over the LeHigh Hills "as far as a man can go in one day and a half." What the Munsees envisioned was a normal day's saunter, with breaks for meals, rest, a good night's sleep. What Pennsylvania officials provided were three very fast men, walking a prepared path through the woods for a total of eighteen hours, provisions carried by horses walking behind. More of a run than a walk, the hike covered nearly sixty miles. From there, a line drawn to the Delaware was to bound the purchase. Officials disingenuously drew this line at a right angle, biting off thousands of additional acres, leaving Pennsylvania in possession of 1,200 square miles of new territory, including the Delaware Valley as far as the Lackawaxen River. Victims of breathtaking fraud, the Munsees had been hoodwinked out of their Minisink homeland.[31]

There was nowhere for the Munsees to turn. Their supposed allies, the Iroquois Confederacy, demeaningly confirmed the legitimacy of the transaction at a council held in 1742. The Confederacy condescended to give the Munsees permission to occupy lands at Wyoming (now Wilkes-Barre, Pennsylvania), an inviting spot on the Susquehanna the Iroquois wanted protected. By 1760, just two Munsee families remained in the Upper Delaware. Understandably mistrustful and bitter, most of the surviving Lenapé migrated westward to the Ohio country. Repercussions would be violent—several Lenapé warriors fought with the French in the Seven Years' War (1754–63), terrorizing Pennsylvania's largely unprotected frontiers.[32]

The long, tenuous Native American occupation of the Upper Delaware was ended. Pennsylvania's officials quickly negotiated a purchase with the

Iroquois to take possession of the remaining lands on the west side of the Upper Delaware; the Hardenbergh patentees surveyed their property on the east bank, prepared the vast acreage for sale. Pennsylvania and New York (or maybe New Jersey) had laid the groundwork for colonial settlement of the valley, opened the door. European settlers would claim the region at last, almost a century and a half after Henry Hudson's voyage.[33] The settlers arrived from Connecticut. They claimed the lands they occupied as part of their Connecticut home.

The colony of Connecticut came into existence in 1636, when a determined band of Puritans migrated, separating themselves from Massachusetts—Puritanism in the Bay Colony was not pure enough. Granted a separate charter in 1662, Connecticut from the beginning fostered a determined independence of thought and deed. When James II, preparing to dissolve the colony, demanded the return of their charter in 1686, Connecticut officials were unable to find it. With James safely deposed three years later, the charter came to light, hidden in a tree. Connecticut's population continued to expand, firmly wedded to the New England township system, a land distribution strategy governed by the legislature. Prospective new communities, mostly comprised of high-minded young Puritans, the sons and daughters of previous generations, petitioned for the establishment of a new town, carved from the colony's unoccupied holdings. Allotted lands would be divided into family properties among the community, creating new towns modeled after the old. Maintaining economically independent farms, remaining true to the concept of interwoven religious communities. Connecticut prospered, at least by its own expectations.[34]

The system worked well but for one problem: Connecticut's holdings were far from infinite. A day would come when there would be no more Connecticut to divide into new towns. By the 1740s, Connecticut was a colony tormented by hard choices—young people could no longer hope to live in independent communities. There would be no more new towns; the land was gone. Underscoring this social and economic crisis, religious controversy divided the colonists—"Old Lights" holding strong to the original Puritan vision, "New Lights" seeking reform. The religious divide seems to have influenced the bold economic solution Connecticut attempted. A "New Light" faction in the legislature successfully campaigned for the creation of new towns—in lands belonging to Pennsylvania.

The justification for this maneuver derived from the original Connecticut charter, establishing a colony extending as far as the Pacific Ocean. Not that the "New Lights" were preparing to move that far westward. Their eyes were on the Wyoming Valley of the Susquehanna, the large fertile valley within the Royally acknowledged boundaries of Pennsylvania, claimed as part of the Iroquois domain, occupied by the remnants of a few Munsee bands recently evicted from the Minisink.[35]

The Connecticut Assembly passed legislation organizing the Susquehanna Company in July 1753. By autumn, a committee had journeyed to Wyoming to survey and purchase the land from the Iroquois. A thousand men would arrive with the spring, they promised. Pennsylvania, reacting to this "wicked revival of the Connecticut claims," urged the few bands of Munsees, still smarting from the walking purchase fraud, to remain at Wyoming as a buffer against the Yankee intrusion.[36]

The Susquehanna Company hired John Henry Lydius, a shady merchant even by Albany standards, to negotiate a deed with the Iroquois. At the Albany Congress held in 1754, Lydius managed to find eighteen Iroquois he claimed to be "chiefs," paying them two thousand dollars for their signatures. The Confederacy's sachems repudiated the deal in council, stating that the signers possessed no authority to sell the land to anybody. The Susquehanna Company, armed with a deed they felt legal enough, were prepared to proceed. Settlers began emigrating from Connecticut.[37]

Very bad timing. Tensions arising from English westward expansion and French intentions in the Ohio country brought renewed violence to the frontier, igniting the Seven Years' War. The Yankees wisely retreated to New England as the Lenapé generally threw in with the French and the Iroquois wavered. English overconfidence brought a series of disastrous early defeats, but slowly the tide turned. By 1760, the French were forced out of the Ohio country; the Iroquois held with the English. Elements of the Lenapé, reluctantly pacified, remained at Wyoming. Connecticut determined to try again.[38]

Wyoming remained the prize, but the Connecticut people exercised some caution, organizing a second colonization scheme, the Delaware Company, to establish a base for the extension of their claims. The year 1760 saw a community of twenty men take up residence on the Upper Delaware, near Station Rock, accompanied by a few women and children. Another twenty returned home "for want of provisions." The settlement, called Cushetunk (supposedly derived from an Algonkian word meaning "rock cliff washed by water"), was located on the Pennsylvania side of the river, thirty-seven miles below the junction of the East and West Branches forming the Delaware. The Connecticut men set about the business with New England efficiency, constructing some thirty dwelling houses, three log houses, a grist mill, a saw mill, and a blockhouse for protection. They laid out the bounds for three towns fronting the river, each ten miles long, eight miles wide, divided into eighty lots of 200 acres each. One lot was set aside for a meeting house. Whether a preacher ever showed is not recorded, although, judging by behavior, finer religious feeling was not much of a priority among the pioneers.[39]

The odd part of this operation was that these settlers (or trespassers, depending on who you asked) preferred the east bank of the river—the New York side. No matter how tortured the interpretation of the Connecticut charter, there was no legal justification for claiming territory in a Royal colony conquered from the Dutch by the Duke of York. But the Delaware Company prepared their ground carefully, purchasing three separate deeds from obscure Munsees in the process of vacating the region anyway. Gravitating to lands south of Station rock, the Connecticut people planted themselves firmly on properties still disputed between New Jersey and New York. When the New Jersey tax collectors came, the pioneers said they paid their taxes to New York; when the New York officials dropped by, they claimed to pay New Jersey. Meanwhile, the Chief Justice of the Province of Pennsylvania issued orders of arrest for the nominal leaders of the Cushetunk settlement, chiefly brothers Daniel and Timothy Skinner, for intruding on Indian property. As if Pennsylvania nurtured any scruples regarding that practice.[40]

The Cushetunk people forecast an additional four thousand Yankees to arrive the next spring, but no migration approaching those numbers ever occurred. Wyoming remained the real prize; the settlers cut a road between the Delaware and Susquehanna Rivers in 1762 to facilitate the larger goal. In April of the following year, Teedyscung, nominal leader of the Lenapé still at Wyoming, became the victim of grisly arsonist murder. Two weeks later, large numbers of Yankee settlers began to appear on the Susquehanna, perhaps two hundred by autumn, sustained by grain grown along the Delaware at Cushetunk.

More bad timing. The blatant murder was one more incident nurturing a widespread and growing disenchantment among the Native American tribes on the frontier. The French were gone, ceding North America to the English to end the Seven Years' War. British officials immediately adopted new policies toward the Indians, demanding new land cessions while ending the long tradition of gift giving at councils. From the Upper Great Lakes to Pennsylvania, the frontier went up in flames once more in 1763, the violence misleadingly known as the Pontiac Conspiracy. Teedyuscung's son avenged his father, massacring ten settlers at Wyoming. The remainder fled. Cushetunk came under attack as well; the town barely survived. Once the terror subsided, perhaps sixteen families hung on, the initial and core settlement of the Upper Delaware Valley.[41]

Realistically, the Cushetunk occupants were engaged in a practice that would become familiar as the EuroAmerican population expanded westward. Finding weakly held lands in obscure locations, the pioneers established homesteads, cleared a few acres, planted crops, raised enough cash to pay for the land they squatted once the bill came unavoidably due. The Connecticut people eventually settled their debts with the New York patentees, paid for land warrants on the Pennsylvania side. The plan to extend Connecticut's borders to the Susquehanna and beyond was a hopeless dream, fed by the colony's idealistic desperation.[42]

Upstream from Cushetunk, a small settlement took shape along the West Branch as frontier hostilities flickered out. The East Branch saw the beginnings of a town at Margaretville, founded by settlers emigrating forty-five miles across the mountains from Esopus, on the Hudson. Descendants of New Netherland dominated the little town, teaching Dutch in their school, managing farms along a twenty mile stretch of river. At best a population of thirty souls. Along with Cushetunk, these tiny settlements were pretty much it. Sparse effort, with little to show.[43]

In 1769, a New Jersey merchant and land speculator named Richard Smith traveled the length of the Upper Delaware, part of a "Tour of Four Great Rivers" to judge investment prospects. Smith found the Upper Delaware the least appealing. Employing an Iroquois as his guide, Smith journeyed overland from the Susquehanna in early June, striking the West Branch of the Delaware near Cookooze, a village site where two Indian families remained amidst fields of maize. Canoeing downstream, he found the landscape hilly and full of stones, identifying stands of beech, hemlock, sugar maple, and chestnut, along with a few oaks and hickories. Smith was struck by the fact "the Indians either thro Accident or Design have burnt large Spaces in the Woods," echoing the observations of Peter Kalm and other naturalists exploring the Northeast. One hundred fifty years after initial contact with the Europeans, the remaining Native Americans were still doing what they could to manage the forests.[44]

From Cookooze to Cushetunk, thirty-seven miles downstream, Smith encountered no settlements at all, Native American or European. Passing the "sixteen or seventeen farms" comprising the ragtag Yankee settlement, he saw just one or two more settlers the twenty-two miles of river to Lackawaxen Creek, and "no place fit for another." To Smith's eye, the lands were "miserable"—barren, rocky, hilly, "of little worth." Further south was worse still, stony cliffs overhanging the river. Such timber as he could see was short, scrubby. A dismal outlook, all in all. Measured through eyes that computed nature as commodity, the Upper Delaware was sadly wanting.

What little might be wrested from the forests would be almost impossible to ship to any worthwhile market. Navigating the river was "impracticable at low water"—no boat larger than a bateau could negotiate the frequent rifts, rapids and falls. Cushetunk's farmers sent grain to New Jersey and Pennsylvania markets in small, flat vessels called "Durham Boats" (designed originally to carry mineral ore). Each boat carried five hundred to six hundred bushels, and then only at high water, limiting the shipping season to maybe three weeks out of the year. Not much profit in that. Farmers tried sledding grain down the frozen river in winter—one more measure of desperation. Richard Smith came home to Trenton, New Jersey, unimpressed.[45]

The Revolutionary War suspended all efforts to grow a paying economy.

The valley sheltered nothing of strategic consequence, but provided a convenient avenue leading to wealthier settlements in Pennsylvania. With raiding parties of Iroquois and Tory militia making frequent forays down the river, the residents of Cushetunk and the other tiny communities wisely fled to more populated havens. A few of the Cushetunk folk exhibited loyalist sympathies themselves, removing to Canada at war's end. Seventeen families returned to the Upper Delaware in 1783—thirty-two adults, ninety-six children re-establishing their town, Cochecton now, firmly a part of New York.[46]

Peace encouraged migration into the region. With the boundaries of New York, Pennsylvania, and New Jersey settled at last, the Upper Delaware became marginally inviting, so long as dreams of untold wealth were left behind. By 1792, seven villages had taken shape; by 1800, twenty-two, all very small. In total, there were four taverns, a single store, and six sawmills the length of the valley. The State of Pennsylvania did what it could to encourage economic growth, voting in 1792 to provide funds to improve navigation, largely by removing boulders and like impediments from the river. Road construction, often following ancient Indian paths, connected the valley to larger populations outside, though the effort did not much enliven the local economy. More resources were drawn away than flowed into the region.[47]

The Cushetunk settlement did leave one legacy crucial to the future of the valley. One of the original Connecticut pioneers, Daniel Skinner, had traveled much in his search for personal independence. One occupation was a turn at a Philadelphia shipyard, where he noted the enormous white pines imported from upriver for use as ship's masts. The pines were hugely valuable—a single tree was large enough to constitute a mainmast. In Britain, shipbuilders had long ago been forced to bind three smaller trees together to shape such a mast, a weaker, far less satisfactory arrangement. Later seeking to make ends meet at Cushetunk, Skinner eyed the tall pines lining the river—pure gold, provided he could deliver them to Philadelphia. In 1764, he cut a few, setting them to float down the river, following in a canoe. With the rifts and rapids, the task was hopeless. He lost them all.

Returning home, Skinner experimented, cutting six white pines, pinning them together with strips of wood to shape a raft. Hiring a "tall Dutchman" to assist, he navigated the rapids with his makeshift, shallow draught craft, delivered the pines to Philadelphia, and walked home (a three-day journey) with money in his pocket.

Here was an idea worth copying. Very soon, Daniel Skinner's neighbors had christened him "Lord High Admiral" of the river, saluting him with a bottle of wine before embarking on their own rafting adventure down the Delaware. The key to such economic future as there was had crystallized. The vast forests fronting the river were money, awaiting a market.[48]

FOUR

A Coarse-Grained
Disturbance Begins

The "American Saga" is a myth deeply engrained in the culture, a body
of truth and half-truth imprinted in the old textbooks, invoked by tradition-
alists and antiquarians, celebrated in literature. The Saga encapsulates a simple and logical tale of American development, a story of progress achieved
in recognizable stages. First came the explorers, discovering and describing
what the lands had to offer, followed quickly by the trappers, fleshing out the
picture, identifying the proper routes to the interior. (Never mind the millions
of people already living there—they did not count.) Soon came the lumbermen, those hearty souls who hewed down the forests standing in the path,
turned the trees to useful products. Clearing opened the land to the farmers,
men performing God's own work, bringing forth the true fruits of the earth.
(Women do not figure heavily in this myth either.) Agriculture brought surplus, giving rise to the market economy, feeding the growth of the cities, bea-
cons of advancing civilization. Quite the story, laden with acts of becoming
heroism, honest toil, determined effort. All misleading, in fashions too many
to count.[1]

Anyone perusing nineteenth-century county histories—proud retellings
of local settlement, local growth—will instantly recognize the elements of
the saga. So much is simply assumed in the telling—that fundamental belief
in Christian progress especially. County histories, often produced by national
companies for local markets on a subscription basis, were composed to a pattern—the pattern described above: the early explorers, a few words acknowledging Native American presence, the inevitable struggle, the grim efforts of
the pioneers, culminating finally in pictures of civilized peace and prosperity.
For the Upper Delaware region, the myth of settlement was especially
emphatic on one particular point: the deforestation of the valley was the work
of lumbermen.

David Murray's *Centennial History of Delaware County, New York* illustrates

the case perfectly. Murray edited the volume, a collection of township histories written separately by local authors. In virtually every case, those authors
spoke of a distant past (maybe a century), a time before settlers arrived and
the land was largely occupied by sawmill operators. The mills were gone by
the 1890s, giving way to dairy farmers, paragons of industry and virtue. Each
writer presented the days of the lumbermen as a brief but dark age, benighted
and backwards. Civilization came slowly to Delaware County. The narrative
purpose in these accounts was more than a simple retelling of the past. In
the late nineteenth century, the authors were looking out across a landscape
nearly devoid of trees. Virtual deforestation had left behind a telling image
of scarred, wounded hillsides. It was good to know where to place the blame.[2]

The process so eloquently described by antiquarians was more than
erroneous myth; the story was constructed on a series of false assumptions
that completely obscure the beginnings of deforestation. The truth is much
more simple: the lumberman and the farmer were the same person. In the
pioneering days, this was a person with a very large problem. There were
trees—a Godawful lot of trees, and they had to go. If the farmers had waited
on a separate set of sawmill operators to clear the land, very little serious
agricultural activity would have begun before 1850. Purely from the stand-
point of technological capability and available manpower, lumbering was far
too slow clearing the forests. Before the late 1840s, very little of the forest
ended up at the sawmill. Yet, by 1845—less than a century following the initial
attempts to settle the Upper Delaware Valley—at least a quarter of the forest
had already disappeared.

The aggregate story is told—for the New York half of the valley, at least—
in the cold, cold figures provided by the State Census. The State, apparently
determined to measure the pace of their own staggering economic growth,
began a serious effort to collect data on manufactures large and small as early
as 1821—a task the Federal Census would not take up in a serious way before
1850. The State's initial effort recorded a small number of very telling pieces
of information, collected from each existing township in each county. Census
marshals counted noses of course, providing the population characteristics
of each township. But they also counted the number of sawmills operating
in their jurisdictions, the number of asheries, and, most importantly, the
acres of "improved land." Keeping track of the improved acreage proved an
essential statistic through the years; the instructions for the Census of 1855
provided an exacting definition.

Schedule II. Agriculture and Domestic Manufacture
  23. Acres Improved: land under cultivation or improved, including pasture,
  meadow, arable land and in short everything that has been reclaimed from a state of
  nature, deducting highways, lakes and ponds of water, when the latter exceed ten
  acres in area, but not otherwise.[3]

That term neatly sums up a large body of feeling towards the woods—getting shed of all those trees was improving the land, making the soil truly productive. Most suggestive is the idea that the farmers were "reclaiming" the lands from the state of nature, as if the natural conditions were an intrusion into the intended order of things. (A descent from the Garden of Eden perhaps, as imagined by census marshals.)

The forest confronting the pioneers was a mosaic of hardwoods and evergreens standing in a mix of communities dependent on local conditions—a series of ecological patches. Trees of all ages struggled together for limited space in an often harsh environment. Along the steeper slopes so prevalent in the Upper Delaware, pines and hemlocks were generally more tenacious than their hardwood competitors. Hillsides offered a largely coniferous aspect.

Lack of written records makes more than an approximation of the forest composition impossible. White pines, relative newcomers taking root in the occasional gaps in the canopy, were the most striking and valuable to a settler's eye, but they were relatively few—seven to fourteen per acre perhaps. Twenty percent? Hemlocks dominated the canopy, making up anywhere from fifty to seventy-five percent of the forest stand. The remainder were hardwoods—sugar maples, beech, basswood, oaks, yellow birch. Journeying southward down the valley, the hardwoods became more plentiful, scrub oaks and chestnuts more numerous. On the Pennsylvania side, forests in the southern portions were labeled the "Open Woods"—small groves of "chestnut, oak, hemlock, and pine," islands of trees in a landscape dominated by shrub.[4]

Whatever the species, to the Upper Delaware pioneer, they stood in the path of progress. The figures for improved acreage provide a rough measure of how much forest fell to the axe in the first half of the nineteenth century. In 1821, the New York State census tallied 110,000 "improved" acres out of nearly 1.1 million—just over ten percent of the forest cover. Twenty-four years later, improved land stood at practically 272,000 acres, virtually one-fourth of the forest. In a little less than a quarter of a century, the population on the New York side of the Upper Delaware chopped down at least fifteen percent of the forest, taking pride in the accomplishment. The pace was steady but slow, compared to what was coming.[5]

How much was the work of the lumberman? Or, put another way, how many trees did the sawmills consume? The State Census lists 199 mills operating in 1821, 333 by 1845. A lot of mills sawing away up and down the valley; every stream seemed to power one at least. Technologically speaking, in 1821, each mill was different, yet all were remarkably alike in their capabilities. Technological change would come with time.

The early years of the nineteenth century in the United States are sometimes labeled "the Age of Wood." The raw material was exceedingly plentiful and cheap to utilize, particularly in frontier areas distant from iron foundries and machine shops. Despite the proximity to the Eastern Seaboard, the Upper Delaware in 1821 was not far removed from frontier conditions—low population, no major urban centers close by, poor connection to larger markets, an almost exclusively agricultural economy just emerging. Wood was the material of choice, for everything from houses, barns, and fences down to the gearing for a saw or grist mill. About the only metal bit in an 1820s sawmill was the saw. Waterwheel, gearing, housing, everything else was most often wrought from wood. The machinery was of necessity hand-hewn, making each mill a little different, speaking much to the innovative skill of the local millwright.[6]

Every mill was powered by water. The basic configuration was everywhere the same—a millpond, shaped by damming a small stream or diverting water from a larger source, the milldam jerry-built from local materials to hold back the pond, a sluice with a gate to feed a steady stream powerful enough to turn a wheel. There were a few options when it came to the wheel. All were large, designed to capture as much energy as possible from the flow of falling water. The water could strike the wheel at a variety of points: an "overshot" wheel poised the millrace to feed the wheel just past the highest point—around one o'clock. "Undershot" wheels fed the power to the paddles ahead of the high point—anywhere from six to ten o'clock. Much depended on the local terrain, the knowledge and preferences of the wheelwright.[7]

Most early mills in the Upper Delaware were powered by an undershot wheel sometimes known as a "flutter," for the sound produced when operating. Flutters were simple to construct where water was plentiful and the fall from the milldam six feet or greater. Both qualities were easy to locate in the well-drained and hilly region. A flutter wheel could produce roughly one hundred strokes of the saw per minute.

The overriding characteristic of these early mills was the need for a large supply of water to drive the wheel. Given the primitive, ad hoc quality of the milldams, sufficient water could be had for just a small portion of the year. Generally, this would be in the spring, when meltwaters collected behind the dam, or perhaps after a period of unusually heavy rain. If there was too much rain, fall from the dam would overshoot the millrace, drowning the wheel, leaving the works inoperable. All told, a flutter wheel could function for two and a half to three months out of a typical year.[8]

The flutters, driven by the fall of water, rotated an axle connected to a markedly complicated set of gears located beneath the floor of the mill. The gears imparted a simple up and down motion to a single straightline saw (no circular saws). Workers fed individual trees to the saw, watching their fingers attentively, making as many passes as necessary to produce a pile of boards and enough sawdust to clog smaller streams. No carriage to guide the log, no clamps to hold the timber in place. Just a great deal of patient maneuvering accomplished by human muscle with a minimum of mechanical help. Employing this haphazard technology, a typical mill might produce 108,000 board feet of lumber in a year. That sounds like a lot, but really is not much at all, not in comparison to the number of trees falling. On average, a sawmill of the period might consume two and two-thirds acres of forest in a year. A useful if not overly productive sideline, operated mainly in the spring, before crops could be sown.[9]

Two and two-thirds acres. To repeat, the Census identified one hundred ninety-nine sawmills operated in the Upper Delaware in 1821; the number rose to three hundred thirty-three by 1845. A little simple math with a calculator delivers a most revealing answer: those sawmills were grinding up, on average, 844 acres of trees each year; a bit more than twenty thousand acres all told over a twenty-four year interval. During that period, farmers "improved" a total of more than 160,000 acres. If those sawmills were consuming nothing but trees removed in the "improving," they still accounted for just 12.5 percent of the cleared acreage. About one tree out of every eight removed by a farmer ended up as boards at a local sawmill. Where went the other seven?[10]

That was the aggregate picture. A quarter of the Upper Delaware's forest cover disappeared by 1845, despite a low population, poor transportation, challenging terrain. And just a tiny fraction of the trees gone to sawmills. Larger forces were at work.

Consider the Upper Delaware farmer. Farming was overwhelmingly the occupation for the region's families; nearly eighty percent as late as 1850. The valley's population grew slowly but steadily, augmented by a continued influx of pioneers from New England, source of the region's first EuroAmerican occupants back in the 1760s. The New Englanders brought knowledge and expectation; they were thoroughly skilled in the demands of the agricultural life in less than ideal conditions: sour hilly land, short growing seasons, finicky weather.[11]

Land was readily available for a long time. Depending on location, a prospective settler might purchase from one of the Hardenburgh Patent heirs, or, if he desired land in the slightly more hospitable areas along the Pepacton (East) Branch of the Delaware, he might have to rent. A holdover from the near-manorial practices of the Colonial Era, proprietors continued to rent land to pioneers, retaining a few manorial privileges, a practice continued in Delaware County until the Anti-Rent Wars of the 1840s.[12]

Owning or renting, the newcomer faced precisely the same challenge that confronted Daniel Skinner all those years before; the land he secured was fully populated with trees. To graze cattle, plant crops, grow an orchard, build a house, a barn, and a few outbuildings, the first step was to do away with the forest. Unless he had older sons, he would be undertaking the task on his own. With the population so tiny, surplus labor was essentially non-existent. Neighbors might pitch in for an unusually demanding task, but that was rare. Every farm family faced their own challenges.

With marketable farm production a dream of the future, deriving any kind of cash from the all-too-present forest would be a welcome bonus, but an incidental consideration. There was no farm until the land was "improved." Estimates differ from source to source, but it seems safe to say that a determined farmer could clear somewhere between five and ten acres over the course of a year. To make a one-hundred-acre farm a fully productive concern, the family was looking at ten years at least, probably more.[13]

Drawing on their New England experiences, these pioneers probably took an axe, began chopping down the trees straight off. There was an alternative option, employed elsewhere in New York, perhaps occasionally in the Upper Delaware. Anxious to get crops started, a farmer might girdle the trees, cutting a one-inch gap in the bark circling each trunk. This interrupted the flow of sugar-transporting phloem to the upper reaches of the tree, reducing the flow of sap by half. The tree slowly starved to death. When new leaves failed to appear, sunlight could penetrate to the ground, creating at least patches of ground somewhat receptive to planting. Once dead, the trees could be pulled down with the help of oxen, heaped in a pile, and burned. Back-breaking work still, but easier than cutting live trees, so the claims went.[14]

For New Englanders, direct chopping was the preferred method. Vigorous toil opened a few acres, establishing an initial field littered with stumps that made plowing an interesting challenge. The stumps might remain five years or more, allowed to rot, soften enough for oxen to remove. Each year would find a few more acres cleared, and so the cycle would continue until the property reflected the pastoral image God and farmer desired, a network of tilled fields, green pastures, perhaps an orchard, always a surviving woodlot of a few acres. Fuel for household fires.[15]

The question was, what to do with the felled timber? Clearcutting did leave a few moneymaking options, dependent on the time required, the skill demanded, the transportation available. The first and most obvious choice was to use some of the wood to construct a barn, a house, maybe a shed or two. Hand hewn planking was a typical component of early Upper Delaware domestic structures, a critical step toward creating a home. A lot of absorbing work, but not a task consuming many of the felled trees. Building a barn might put a quarter acre of trees to good use; a small frame house required less. Sheds and outbuildings might take a bit more of the woods, but the total domestic construction could not absorb much more than a tithe of what the farmer was cutting down in a single year. And that only once or twice.[16]

There was the necessity of heating the house. New Englanders were quite lavish in their consumption of firewood; there was, after all, plenty and to spare. Every room would have a fireplace; most would remain lit throughout the day. Estimates suggest northeastern homes, facing unrelenting cold winters, burned as much as twenty cords of wood each year. Picture a stack of logs four feet high, four feet wide, eight feet long. Multiply that image by twenty. It's a large stack of wood. Yet, translated, that large stack was the product of three-quarters of an acre of felled forest. Prodigal to the extreme in maintaining household fires, farm families still could not hope to utilize as much as a fifth of the trees they were cutting down each year. Selling the cordwood to outsiders was beyond the range of the practical; with no urban market within reach, a farmer would lose money transporting a wagon of cordwood to anyone willing to buy. A traveler through the Upper Delaware region early in the nineteenth century remarked on the number of signs he encountered with variations on the theme "Cordwood for sale—you haul." There were not many buyers. According to the Federal Census for 1840, the entire population of Delaware County managed to sell just four acres of cordwood to outside markets; Sullivan County three. Cordwood was a pioneer farm luxury, accounting for very little of the timber removed.[17]

Rafting some of trees was an attractive possibility, provided the farm lay close to an accessible stream. Daniel Skinner demonstrated that. In his time, rafts were comparatively small, perhaps twelve thousand feet of uncut lumber floated to market. With the passing years, experiment and innovation enabled raftsmen to more than double the size of their unwieldy craft, eventually delivering thirty thousand board feet to Trenton, New Jersey, or to Philadelphia.

Farmers generally constructed log rafts to a standard pattern. Over the winter, they chopped down and delimbed logs of equal length—seventy to eighty feet—and dragged them to the stream shore. There they lined up the logs to a width of twenty to twenty-five feet along a gently inclined bank. Heavy rope was a rare and expensive commodity, so farmers stapled the logs together, employing lash poles called halliards, with augur holes bored at each end. Ash staples secured the halliards to the logs. To complete the construction, raftsmen mounted wooden oarlocks front and rear, the stern oar doubling as a tiller. The raft was ready to sail with the spring freshet.

White pine was the lumber of choice in the early rafts; these tall, straight, elegant logs fetched the best price. In the southern portions of Wayne County, Pennsylvania, along Wallenpaupack Creek, a treacherous waterfall discouraged rafting until farmers discovered the market value of pine. The profit was incentive enough to disassemble rafts at the head of the falls, reconstruct them below. But not much of the forest was pine, and soon the farmers throughout the valley were shifting to the far more plentiful hemlock—sturdy, sound for construction, certainly not elegant. The raftsmen would have preferred to ship the more marketable oaks and maples, but hardwoods did not float well enough to make workable rafts. Sometimes hemlock rafts carried hardwood boards on their decks, or a little quarried stone. The extra cash was important. There were property taxes to pay, necessities such as sewing needles to purchase.

Tradition has established several rafting points along the Upper Delaware and its tributaries by the early nineteenth century. A point on the West Branch not far above Hancock became known as Deposit for the rafts assembled there. Late winter was a busy time, as farmers assembled hundreds of rafts and made ready to push off when melting snows swelled the river to navigable depth. Rafting season proved a boon to taverns and innkeepers along the route, many of whom depended on the yearly event for survival. For the farmers become raftsmen, the ready cash from the enterprise was important, but so was the adventure—the annual rafting journey was the one escape from the work of the farm. Farmers from the interior of Delaware County might be gone as long as two weeks, sailing downstream, returning home on foot.

A considerable folklore grew up around the rafting journey—tales of tragic accidents, unlikely wedding trips, the odd transport of the occasional farm animal. Rafting was important, a break from the prosaic routine of a grinding, toilsome existence. What it was not was an effective means of utilizing all the trees the pioneer farmer was clearing away each year to create that ideal farm. A raft twenty-five feet wide might comprise two to three dozen eighty foot logs—not much of a dent in the backlog of trees fallen to earth.[18]

Just how many rafts floated downstream requires a shameful amount of guesswork. Officials operating a dam at the mouth of Lackawaxen Creek kept count beginning in 1828 (because several came to a sad end at that point, provoking lawsuits), but the records do not survive for any year before 1872, when a newspaper began publishing the figures. Far too late to mean much. Based on the number of farms, the best estimate comes to maybe eight hundred to eight hundred and fifty log rafts sailing downriver in 1845. A strikingly large number (probably too high), but a tiny amount of lumber in the context of the rapidly disappearing forest. Seven percent of the yearly consumption at most. Rafting may have created a vibrant folk history, and the adventure undeniably put a little hard cash in farmers' pockets, but the practice did not much contribute to the principles of resource management.[19]

What about the sawmills? Each mill was at least consuming something on the order of two and two-thirds acres of trees each year, perhaps half of what a pioneer might be cutting down. By 1845, there were roughly six thousand farms in the Upper Delaware region, maintaining an average of forty-five improved acres. And 399 sawmills. Not nearly enough to absorb the volume of timber the farms laid waste. The fact was, a sawmill, in service for only a few weeks out of the year (and at much the same time as the rafts were running), was an adjunct to a larger farming operation, an option pursued by a few wealthier settlers. Lumbering was an extra, a part time occupation supplementing a cash flow dependent primarily on the production of the adjoining farm. The Population Schedules of the Federal Census tell the tale. When they began listing occupations (only male heads of households were deemed to have them), every sawmill owner to be found gave his occupation as "farmer." The farm was the thing; the sawmill just one more aspect of the business, like the butter the farmer's wife churned.[20]

That lumbering in the early days was a low-key affair is hardly a shocking revelation. Geography dictated limited production—a more efficient industry could only pile up tons of board lumber that could not be marketed. Local consumption was very small; one or two sawmills was enough to provide the local needs of any township in such an isolated, rural market. Probably ninety-five percent of the lumber Upper Delaware sawmills cut was shipped to the distant cities. For a long time, that meant the river.

Mill production for Philadelphia and Trenton must have begun quite early. No township was limited to a single sawmill very long after initial settlement; local consumption was nowhere near enough to absorb what was sawed. As mill operators depended upon the river to move their surplus, a new kind of raft developed, composed almost entirely of rough cut planking.

The first step in the construction of a sawed-lumber raft was to build a crib. Raftsmen laid an essentially square frame of "grub plank" sixteen to eighteen feet wide, seventeen to twenty-two feet long. They nailed on planks enough to cover the frame, shaping a solid crib. Raftsmen would construct up to five of these cribs, wedging them together with lockets of scantling to make the underlayer of a "colt" raft. Over the top of the underlayer came four or five additional layers of sawed lumber laid in alternating directions, followed by three more layers arranged in a shingle pattern. Nine layers in all.

Embarking from smaller tributary streams at the spring thaw, the raftsmen floated the colts downstream to points on the Delaware where they could be wedged together to become true rafts. As many as four colts—twenty cribs—could be locketed together to form a single plank raft. They did not float awfully well, and steered sluggishly if at all, but they did float. And they fetched much better prices downriver than any log raft. For the lumber industry, the future was bright, though limited. Lumber—even hemlock—was very much in demand at rapidly expanding urban centers; a ready market existed. The constraints loomed at the supply end of the equation, where minimalist technology produced just so many boards, and a shallow, treacherous river effectively barred more delivery. But the trees were there for the asking; the task was to find more efficient means of processing the raw material, and delivering the stuff to market. In 1845, sawmills, operating as adjuncts to the more enterprising farms, were delivering to distant markets about twelve percent of the trees farmers were chopping down.[21]

Lumbering was not the only industry with potential in an isolated valley well-lined with trees, hemlock especially. In 1805, Sir Humphrey Davy, an English chemist, discovered that tannin—the essential ingredient in the manufacture of tanned leather—could be got by soaking crushed hemlock bark in water. An important discovery—previously, oaks had been the sole source. Merchants regarded hemlock-processed leather an inferior product, too ruddy, too reddish. But it was cheap, and hemlock was plentiful enough. Hemlock tanneries could produce shoe sole leather if nothing else.[22]

Hides were more readily transportable than hemlocks; tanneries sprang up close to the forests. Small tanning operations appeared in the Upper Delaware as early as the 1780s, somewhat larger factories by the 1820s. Much depended on the supply of bark. At times, the tanners obtained their bark from the sawmills, but more often they simply stripped trees in the woods, taking the bark, leaving the trees standing to die.

At the most basic, tanning functioned as a cottage industry, another adjunct to a larger farm operation. (Occasionally, a sawmill and a tannery could be found on the same property, operated by the same owner, who still identified himself to the census marshal as a farmer.) Like the sawmill, the tannery was a part-time occupation. The size of the establishment was dictated by the capacity of the bark mill, where the hemlock bark was ground to produce the tannin. This was the one part of the process to require motive power; hide cleansers and soaking vats would be numerous and large if there was much production, but these were inert. At the lowest levels, a farmer could tan a few hides—perhaps from his own and neighbors' cattle, along with a few deer hides—employing a single small vat and bark ground by hand. The next step up was a bark mill powered by a horse walking a circular track. Production was minute. A larger-scale tannery—one meant to produce for markets larger than the immediate locale—required the harnessing of a stream to turn a bark mill powered by a wheel. Most of the tanneries operating between 1826 and 1847 utilized water power in one way or another. As such, they were limited in the same manner as the sawmills—a few weeks of operation when sufficient water flowed to power the bark mill. Bark milling was a seasonal chore. The rest of the operation—the long soaking of the hides for curing (the tannin prevented the skin rotting)—could be left standing through the long months when the mills could not turn. The small sheds sheltering the hide treatment works—the tanning vats, the grinding stones—did little to beautify the neighborhood while raising a stench to heaven. Dumped into streams, exhausted tanning fluids proved toxic, killing fish.[23]

Tanneries were so insignificant in the early economy that the State of New York did not even try to count them until 1835. They found thirty-six in operation in the Upper Delaware, mostly in Delaware County, where a growing dairy industry provided a source of hides. Ten years later, the number had grown to just forty, all relatively small operations. Over in Pennsylvania, just ten tanneries were at work in 1840, four in Pike County, six in Wayne. All were small, local affairs. The problems besetting the lumber industry applied to the tanneries: limited production time coupled to inadequate connection to distant markets. There was just so much leather the local neighborhood could use.

To what extent did the tanneries absorb the raw material produced by the ongoing deforestation of the region—the "improvement" of the land? The calculation is tricky—tanners utilized just the bark, some unknown portion of which came from sawmills. Much of the rest came perhaps from farmers clearing their lands, though some bark was taken from stands deep in the woods, particularly on steeper hillsides where settlement had not reached. So knowing the total number of trees the tanneries stripped provides a number misleadingly high when computing the improved acreage gone to the bark mills. But it is the only figure available, and that the product of some mathematical legerdemain. Simply put, the thirty-six functioning tanneries ground something like forty-five cords of bark each in 1835; ten years later, forty tanneries required around seventy-nine cords apiece. Sources agree that a tannery obtained eighteen cords of hemlock bark per acre of woodland. Jabbing at the calculator, we arrive at maybe 1,418 acres of hemlocks debarked on the New York side in the ten years up to 1845. That's a lot of dead hemlocks, but a mere drop in the bucket in the overall clearing of the forest. Not to belabor the point unduly, the tanners could not have absorbed more than 7.5 percent of all the trees felled up to 1845. And they were only taking the bark from those.[24]

Taken together, the rafting, the sawmills, and the tanneries at most used one tree out of every four Upper Delaware residents were chopping down. What happened to the remainder?

The answer is very simple and straightforward: as farmers "improved" their land, they unceremoniously burned three trees out of every four. The use of fire to clear the forests was a time-honored practice among New Englanders, the predominant settlers. Both Quinlan's *History of Sullivan County* and the Munsell *History of Delaware County* make mention of settlers burning woodlands, though neither appreciated the extent. The process was straightforward and simple, intended to take up the least time and labor possible. Oxen hauled the felled trees into a large clearing, or preferably a pit if one could be found or dug. On a calm day the farmer ignited the pile, which might burn a good while. He had to be attentive; a sudden wind might blow enough sparks to light a fire, endangering the neighborhood.[25]

In some instances, there was an economic incentive to the firing. The ashes left from hardwood stands could be collected and leached with water in large kettles. (One more homely shed on the property.) Potash, the substance resulting, could be sold to a commercial ashery or used at home to make soft soap and tallow candles. Manufacture was not especially attractive; the work was more labor-intensive than might appear, and a considerable collection of hardwood ash produced a minuscule amount of product. The industry was important enough for the New York State Census to count the number of commercial establishments (again, adjuncts to larger farm operations): thirteen in the Upper Delaware in 1821, peaking at thirty-one in 1825, diminishing to twenty-one by 1845. Marshals found the majority of these asheries in areas where sawmills were few. Two factors were probably at work. Areas lacking navigable streams might turn to potash as an alternative to rafting or sawmilling, while regions where hardwoods dominated the landscape would have little choice—the hardwoods would not float. How poor the alternative was is best illustrated by the relative dollar value of sawed lumber to potash. In 1835, Upper Delaware sawmills produced over 277 thousand dollars' worth of planking; the total production of the asheries came to $9,800, a ratio of twenty-eight to one.[26]

Domestic construction, cordwood, rafting, sawmilling, tanning, potash manufacture—the pioneer farmer had a considerable number of options when it came to utilizing the trees standing on his property. No farmer tried them all; the majority had not the wherewithal to take advantage of any save an annual raft or a little potash. A wealthier, more established resident might run a sawmill or a tannery (very rarely both), or perhaps a larger potashery, but still he saw himself essentially as a farmer, a man of the soil. Whatever combination of enterprises he chose to operate on his property to increase the value, encourage the cash flow; his primary focus was on the productivity of the land. With that determination, his biggest obstacle was the standing forest. Reduced to a manageable woodlot (often poorly managed), tamed woods had their place. But most of the trees had to go, more than a quarter million acres by 1845.

Unsurprisingly, the wildlife dependent on the forest diminished as well. Deer, hunted for meat and leather, "roamed in great numbers down to a recent period," David Murray observed in his *Centennial History of Delaware County, 1797–1897*. They were completely gone by the 1890s. Farmers saw woodchucks as an enemy, leaving their bothersome trails through the meadows, along with the three species of squirrels (red, gray, chipmunk), fond of ripened grain. Local squirrel hunts were common, with prizes to the hunter killing the most. Wolves, those sheep eaters, disappeared by 1800 at the latest, a five-dollar bounty on their heads. Panthers too, the big cats that attacked deer, sheep, cows, and occasionally people—Sullivan County paid the last bounty of fifteen dollars in 1806. A few black bears managed to survive the onslaught, despite their habit of attacking hogs loosed in the woods to feed on nuts.

Streams and rivers suffered, too. Shad, once abundant, disappeared completely, along with black bass. Brook trout were greatly diminished. Deforestation was the culprit—as overhanging trees (hemlocks especially) disappeared, streams lay open to a more unrelenting sunlight, heating the water to points several species could not tolerate. Waters laced with tannin did not help.

Lumbering impacted songbirds in contradictory fashions. Several species, including the blue jay, the chickadee, the red-eyed vireo, and the hermit thrush, were indifferent to the cutting, adapting to the changes in the forest. A few, warblers especially, found their opportunities improved as selective removal of mature trees opened the forest canopy. But others suffered from lost habitat, diminishing in numbers, including ovenbirds, wood thrushes, winter wrens, and yellow-bellied sapsuckers. Clearcutting—"improving" the land—left them all searching for new homes.[27]

Any bird of prey stood high on the list of enemies. Hawks (red tailed "chicken hawks" especially), eagles, owls (despite the fact they hunted grain-attacking mice far more than chickens), and crows were ready targets. Some complained of that marauding denizen of the orchard, the robin. Game birds—geese and ducks from the rivers, turkeys from the woods—largely disappeared. Wild turkeys died out for two reasons—their dependence on the mast they used to forage from the vanishing leaf litter, and their favored appearance at the dinner table.

Most emblematic was the fate of the passenger pigeon, once so plentiful that migrating flocks a half mile wide would appear each spring, taking two or three hours to pass. Shooters fired indiscriminately into the flocks, occasionally for dinner, most often for the hell of it. By the 1840s, numbers were noticeably diminished, by the 1870s, they were gone. The very last passenger pigeon died in a zoo in 1914. To establish a proper rural life, the first step was to rid the neighborhood of the least hint of the wild. Elimination of the larger species was obvious; what was happening to the web of smaller creatures and plants was never considered, much less guessed at. To steal a phrase, the valley needed to be made safe for corn and wheat.[28]

The essential goal may have been everywhere much the same as people transformed the Upper Delaware from wilderness to farm communities, but the story does vary a bit from one location in the valley to another. Even in a relatively small, narrowly defined geographic entity, regional variation played a critical role in the patterns of growth. The Upper Delaware can be parsed into at least six sub-regions, defined largely by their economic potentials as seen by the eyes of the time. Gaining a sense of the valley's various sub-regions will assist understanding of the changes taking place after 1845.

The upper reaches of the valley—the lands drained by the East (Pepacton) and West Branches before they merge to create the Delaware River proper, were far and away the most populous portion of the region in the 1840s. The work of glaciers, so long before, had much to do with this. Scouring out wider vales, creating glacial lakes where sediment deposition eventually left bottomlands more fertile than most of the area, the most promising farmlands proved to lie along the Branches, becoming homes for dairy farms especially. Almost two-thirds of the Upper Delaware's population lived along the two Branch streams in 1845. Even there, opportunities to cash in on the forest cover differed with location.[29]

Above the village of Delhi (smack in the middle of Delaware County), the West Branch narrows to the point where the stream is unnavigable for all but the smallest craft, making rafting close to impossible. Sawmills were few and diminished in number with time. A few asheries and tanneries operated, but the opportunities to profit from the forest cover were few. Yet the pace of land improvement was exceedingly quick—economic opportunity was there, once the forest was chopped down.

The length of the West Branch below Delhi and nearly all the Pepacton Branch proved navigable, for colt rafts at least. Floated individually downstream, the colts were joined by raftsmen to assemble full rafts at a point close to the juncture of the Branches, later known (for just this reason) as Deposit. More than half the sawmills in the Upper Delaware functioned in the townships stretched along the navigable portions of the two Branches, the heart of the lumber industry in 1845. But again, settlers were vigorously "improving" the land; the forest they removed far outpaced the amounts the lumber and related industries could consume.

Downriver from the branches, on the northerly reaches of the Delaware proper, settlement lagged markedly. Although the first pioneering towns had taken shape at Cushetunk, at the heart of this stretch of the valley, the eighty years following demonstrated what an overly optimistic choice those Connecticut Yankees made. Between the junction of the East and West Branches at Point Mountain, near the village of Hancock, and Lackawaxen Creek, fifty-some miles to the south, populations grew slowly if at all from the 1820s through 1845. At an educated guess, population on the New York side between Hancock and Narrowsburg gained by a thousand people at most—a tenth of the growth in the East and West Branch towns. Precise growth is difficult to measure, as officials in Sullivan County saw no point in dividing their very large townships into smaller units along the river when almost no one lived there. The agricultural statistics for 1850 suggest that settlement proceeded at an even slower pace on the Pennsylvania side. Less than twenty-five percent of the available land in the townships fronting the river was taken up by farmers; the total population stood at 6,369 people. Of what land was settled, just 18,715 was considered "improved"—thirty percent.[30]

Topography was one element in the sluggish, nearly non-existent growth. Unlike the expansive valleys of the East and West Branches, the Delaware proper funnels through a narrow defile, flanked mostly by steep hills rising abruptly six hundred to a thousand feet above the valley floor on either side. The river flows swiftly, leaving few sedimentary deposits—fertile flats adequate to crop agriculture were few and far between. Broken by a maze of ravines cut by fast-flowing streams, there was water power to be harnessed, but with the only feasible transportation the unreliable river, there was not enough profit in sawmilling to make a concerted effort seem worthwhile. Just twenty-four sawmills operated on the New York side of the river as late as 1845.

Folks in Sullivan County blamed the low population and moribund growth on the lack of more adequate transportation. Apart from the river, the area's first connection to the outside world was the Newburgh-Cochecton turnpike, ponderously constructed between 1803 and 1809. Rather than running the length of the Upper Delaware Valley, connecting the tiny villages struggling to survive, builders cut the turnpike perpendicular to the river, linking the nondescript village of Cochecton precariously to the Hudson Valley. Continuing westward, the road eventually reached Ithaca, in the far more attractive Finger Lakes region. And that was the perceived source of the problem. Instead of bringing new settlers to the Delaware, the turnpike enabled people to bypass the valley in favor of more desirable lands in central New York. The toll road—one of several carved in the northeast to exploit a growing market economy—made Cochecton (population 896 in 1845) the most significant economic terminus along the river for the next forty years, while boosting the rest of the valley economy not at all. The road was of no use to lumbering interests; transporting planks across the Catskills by turnpike was fabulously expensive.[31]

No road of any kind paralleled the length of the valley during the first half of the nineteenth century. Several small local roads appeared, connecting points at short distance. But even these linked to new roads leading out of the region; Upper Delaware residents continued to depend on outside urban centers for their necessities. Local development went nowhere. Ironically, Sullivan County townships on the periphery of the watershed, interior towns such as Liberty, Rockland, and Callicoon, fared slightly better, lying closer to larger markets. Populations grew markedly after 1835, for reasons having much to do with events to the south.

Below Narrowsburg, the townships belonging to the Upper Delaware drainage become a special case for two reasons, one environmental, the other human construction. Recall for a moment the Upper Delaware's pre-history. Native peoples entering the region during the Early Archaic, eight to ten thousand years ago, carried their eating habits, including a fondness for nuts. Lots of nuts. Working in unconscious conjunction with the squirrels and blue jays, people fostered the spread of hardwood trees—nutbearing trees—northward, to the extent that the composition of the forest fundamentally changes in the southern portions of the Upper Delaware. The Northern forest—all those white pines, all those hemlocks, interspersed with small numbers of hardwoods—gives way to a forest association marked by a much larger percentage of hardwoods. An especially frustrating discovery for the few people who chose to settle there (the population in New York stood at 1,573 in 1825). Hardwoods were valuable, the raw material for fine furnishings and furniture, but they refused to float effectively. No way to get the nut trees to market. Settlement in Pennsylvania proved agonizingly glacial. On that side, the hardwoods come to dominate almost precisely at the border between Wayne and Pike Counties. Pike County townships in the Upper Delaware drainage, fully in the hardwood confines, supported a population of just 2,500 as late as 1850. Less than a quarter of the farmland was improved; forty-six sawmills operated in the whole of the County. Whatever means the settlers found to derive a cash income, lumber was not atop the list.[32]

Lumbering got an early start on the New York portion of the area. Quinlan's *History of Sullivan County* contends that in 1800 "the possession of farm lots was not considered desirable, and the real estate was held in large parcels by non-residents (principally citizens of Orange County), whose aim was to convert the timber into cash at the least possible expense to themselves." The meager population found the land too poor for farming, making woodcutting the occupation of choice. By 1825, the industry was fully established, with regular market contacts downriver and navigation routes well understood.[33]

Prospects altered somewhat in 1829, entirely the result of business decisions having nothing to do with hardwood trees, nothing to do with the scarcely breathing economy of the Upper Delaware. A canal opened, linking the lower townships of the valley with New York City. The number of sawmills operating in these southern townships doubled by 1835.

Entrepreneurs built the canal with a single purpose in mind: to move coal from mines in northeast Pennsylvania to ripening markets in Manhattan. The move to coal was a growing urban trend; local sources of cordwood were long exhausted, and supplies from the hinterland were becoming progressively expensive and difficult to obtain. Sensing an opportunity, two brothers, Maurice and William Wurts of Philadelphia, invested heavily in coal fields near Carbondale, Lackawanna County, lying forty miles from the Delaware.

The brothers expected to market the coal in their native city, only to discover that Philadelphia had already negotiated exclusive contracts with other suppliers. That left New York, if only they could get the coal delivered.

Looking at a topographic map of the lands between Carbondale and Manhattan would have intimidated anyone; the Wurts brothers were nothing if not determined. Moosic Mountain, a mightily steep hill, intervened between the coal field and the valley of Lackawaxen Creek, a stream at least flowing in the right direction, toward the Delaware. From there, all that intervened between riches and New York were the southern Catskills and the Shawangunk Mountains, drained by the thankfully navigable Hudson, the barely navigable Delaware, and the completely unnavigable (really treacherous) Neversink River, all lying in a haphazard jigsaw of terrain. That was the answer, then. They would build a canal. New York's Erie Canal, not yet fully open, was already promising success beyond the dreams of avarice, inspiring construction, and thoughts of construction, of additional watery ditches throughout the northeast. Why not another?

The engineers they consulted, including Benjamin Wright, chief engineer of the Erie Canal, may have thought the brothers nuts. Or perhaps not—a certain hubris grows with success. If engineers could organize construction of a ditch running more than two hundred miles from Albany to Lake Erie, maybe they could move mountains too. Or at least find a way through. The route the planners eventually chose transported the coal by land over Moosic Mountain and across sixteen miles of flatter terrain to the valley of the Lackawaxen, then via canal down the creek valley to the Delaware, along the river as far as Carpenter's Point, up the valley of the Neversink and finally overland to Kingston on the Hudson River. Reaching Kingston, flatboats could carry the coal to New York. Unlike the Erie and most other canals, this was to be a one-way trip, focused on the single purpose of delivering coal.

As the crow flies, the distance from the coal fields to Manhattan was ninety miles or so; travelling the torturous route of the canal, the distance was closer to one hundred-ninety. And distance alone does little to communicate just how nearly impossible the engineering challenge proved. The twenty-four miles of the Delaware River section alone required thirteen locks to accommodate a one hundred-thirty foot shift in elevation. The plan succeeded, creating a ditch four feet deep, twenty feet wide at the bottom, thirty feet at the top, 108 miles long.[34]

The western terminus of the canal could not be located any closer to the mines than the valley of Lackawaxen Creek, leaving Moosic Mountain and the sixteen miles beyond to solve. The engineers, headed by John B. Jervis, tamed the mountain with a series of inclined planes. Carts rode the planes up and down the hill, drawn by steam-powered winches. That left the sixteen miles. The first thought was horse-drawn carts riding on rails.

Bringing out pencils and paper, William Wurts figured maintaining the horses would cost $71.87 a day. Truly imaginative calculating suggested that a fleet of steam-powered locomotives would cost thirty dollars a day less. A radical thought for the 1820s—there were absolutely no locomotives anywhere in America, none much of anywhere except Great Britain. Jervis dispatched his young assistant, Horatio Allen, to England to explore the possibilities. Allen met with George Stephenson, resident locomotive genius, at Stourbridge, England. Stephenson allowed the idea of a sixteen mile run was more than workable; a bargain was struck. Allen purchased a locomotive made to order, along with several miles of strap iron. Examining the locomotive upon arrival in New York, enthusiasts thought the scary contraption possessed the "fierce-looking face of a lion." The first locomotive in America had a name: the Stourbridge Lion.

At Honesdale, Pennsylvania, just east of Moosic Mountain, the Wurts brothers laid wooden rails re-enforced with the strap iron. This was the age of wood. Whenever possible, wood was the building medium of choice; the strap iron was attached to the top of the rails to add strength. (This was a practice long continued in the United States, contributing to some very nasty railway accidents.) Engineers calculated the rails could support a burden of four tons. Regrettably, the Stourbridge Lion weighed seven and a half tons, considerably more than Jervis and the Wurts Brothers anticipated.

At least they tried. On August 8, 1829, a few weeks before the canal opened, Horatio Allen climbed aboard the Lion at Honesdale, intent on a three-mile test of the layout. He later recalled "believing that the road would prove safe, and preferring if we did go down, to go handsomely and without any evidence of timidity, I started with considerable velocity, passed the curve of the creek safely, and was soon out of hearing of the cheers of the large assemblage present." Allen chugged the three miles, reversed direction, and returned safely, disproving the fearful expectations of several. But the Lion's first run was also the last—the weight was too much for the iron-strapped wooden rails. The Wurts Brothers hitched up the horses; America's first experiment in railroading reached a premature ending.[35]

What happened at Honesdale was a harbinger. For the Wurts, the Stourbridge Lion was an experiment proved too expensive to continue; the brothers were entrepreneurs chasing money, not technological innovation. They glimpsed the future and turned away. Opening their canal in October, they delivered their coal, little imagining that in just twenty years' time a railroad would run the entire length of the Upper Delaware. Enormous change was coming.

Putting the canal in proper working order was hard enough. For the Delaware section, the surveyors originally thought to save expense by employing the river itself to carry the boats between the mouth of the Lackawaxen and Carpenter's Point twenty-four miles south, but that proved too dangerous. Better the reliable serenity of a canal alongside. The eastern (New York) bank was the flatter and more accessible, so the builders dug their canal on that side. To see their canal boats safely across the Delaware from Pennsylvania to the eastern bank, engineers constructed a wing dam across the river a short distance upstream, intended to create a quiet eddy where the canal boats could safely cross.

Not the best idea. Focused single-mindedly on a nearly impossible task, the builders forgot that other folks made a living navigating the river as well. All too quickly, extreme animosity blew up between the canal men and raftsmen coming downstream, as rafts wrecked at the thoughtlessly designed dam or collided with passing canal boats. Competing groups hurled insults, nasty names, and select missiles at one another; local taverns became the meeting ground for instructive brawls. More serious to the canal company were the lawsuits the collisions inspired, which proved expensive.[36]

The war continued for eighteen years, until the company produced one more engineering marvel: a suspension aqueduct extending from the Pennsylvania side to New York, literally carrying the canal over the river.[37] Completed in 1847, the aqueduct was the third project drawn up by John A. Roebling, most famous for designing the Brooklyn Bridge, where he employed the same suspension principles. (The aqueduct, converted to a highway bridge, remains in use.) The dam across the river remained to protect the aqueduct, but was rebuilt, designed this time to minimize rafting accidents.[38]

Deemed the Delaware and Hudson Canal, the system answered the hopes of the Wurts brothers, delivering their coal to New York, seven thousand tons the first year. But maintaining a canal (much less building one) was an expensive proposition; the company opened the locks to additional traffic. A study of the stockholders' reports reveals that D & H canal boats hauled stone, leather, tanning bark, and lumber bound for the New York market. In short, the canal appeared to be an answer to the Upper Delaware's most besetting problem, at least for the southerly towns—the Delaware and Hudson Canal offered a steady transportation alternative. By the 1850s, the canal was moving as much as twenty-five million board feet of lumber in a single year.[39]

Much of this came from outside the Upper Delaware drainage; the canal threaded through a large portion of the Catskills before reaching the Hudson. Just how much lumber originated along the Delaware can be calculated from the notebooks of John Lord, surveyor and manager of the canal during the 1830s and 1840s. For once a reasonably precise primary source, Lord's notebooks break down each year's shipments by canal sections, detailing just how much lumber shipped from the Delaware section. (Delaware River towns sent no leather or tanning bark along the canal at all—the State Census counted just one tannery operating so far south. With the lumber business in full operation so early, not enough hemlock remained to bother.)

Taking the typical year 1845 to illustrate what was happening; census records suggest that the southern towns cut a little more than two hundred acres of forest. Lord's notebook entries indicate that lumbermen shipped just seven percent of those trees by the canal to New York. A bit more than half the total loaded on the boats was hardwood, another quarter white pine. The story every year was much the same, from the canal's opening through 1850. Despite the promise of steady transportation the canal represented, the Delaware and Hudson was a minor factor in the continued deforestation of the valley over the first twenty-some years of the canal's existence. Too much trouble and cost. Transporting lumber by the canal meant identifying new markets, as well as paying a not inexpensive shipping fee. Most lumbermen proved unwilling to make the transition. Rafting to Trenton and Philadelphia remained the preferred means of marketing lumber from the southern towns.[40]

What emerges from John Lord's notebooks is a glimpse of specializing lumbermen, dealing largely in the more profitable pines and hardwoods, leaving the hemlock to others. The canal presented an opportunity to send upscale product to a new and waiting market. The pine reached its destination in much better shape than rafted timber, commanding a better price, and the hardwoods found a buyer by the only possible means. Relatively insignificant early in the years of the canal's existence, specialty lumbering employing the canal assumed a larger importance after 1850, when the more general lumber industry suffered a disastrous crash.

What the Delaware and Hudson Canal did inspire, right from the beginning, was dreams. Dreams are not often marketable, but sometimes they point the path to the future. Dreamers at the southern end of the Upper Delaware certainly hoped so. The desire to transform the woods was the desire to do away with the wild forever, create something more human in the space—something "civilized," something urban. With the lack of anything resembling adequate transportation, with agricultural potential so severely limited, the valley economy had been stuck at the starting point, scarcely removed from the wilderness—no local markets to support, or to depend on. Anything beyond the bare necessities meant a trip to New Jersey at least, or an arduous journey across the mountains to the Hudson. There was no lack of urban dreams along the Upper Delaware. Building the canal spawned the first of many hopes that a tiny hamlet might become a great metropolis.

This particular dream took shape in Deer Park, Orange County, New York, the very last of the townships lining the Upper Delaware. At a place where the river enters an abrupt bend to the southwest, where the boundaries of New York, Pennsylvania, and New Jersey meet, stood a tiny village known for a century as Carpenter's Point. In 1829, Carpenter's Point suddenly became Port Jervis, named for the canal's chief engineer. Located at an important juncture where the canal turned northeastward, following the valley of the Neversink, Carpenter's Point had quickly become the focus of canal business for the Delaware section. Could real economic growth, flocks of new people, be far behind?

Port Jervis grew slowly, not passing a thousand residents until after 1845. The economy remained firmly dependent on local conditions, specifically the sawmills and, to a lesser extent, stone quarrying. The presence of the canal created a few jobs and made the town more of a trade center than the run-of-the-mill hamlet, but Port Jervis was unable to attract new industry. Despite the presence of the canal, the Upper Delaware remained a backwater still.[41]

Such a series of innovations. Steam-powered inclined planes, an experimental railroad, a state-of-the-art suspension aqueduct, a ditch 108 miles long threaded through forbidding terrain, an inspiration for urban dreams—the Delaware and Hudson Canal was in so many senses an engineering marvel. Gazing back at the construction from the perspective of nearly two centuries after, none of that accomplishment strikes the eye quite so forcefully as one inescapable fact. The Delaware and Hudson, along with the Erie and all the miles of canal constructed from the east through the Midwest, represented humankind's determination to overcome the limits to progress imposed by the natural world.

From the first colonial settlements of the American continent, the most vexing problem had been transportation. Just two options presented themselves. People could build roads—often muddy paths impassable in rainy seasons, slow, impossible for the transport of anything much in bulk. More feasible were the rivers. Boats could carry so much more, were considerably quicker than horse-drawn carriages run overland. The drawback was location—rivers were what they were, often in inconvenient or limited locales, becoming unnavigable at maddening points, discouraging development. The Upper Delaware was an obvious case in point—a maddening river thwarting settlement, limiting growth, preventing market formation.

The canal represented a challenge to such limitations. A lengthy ditch such as the Delaware and Hudson or the Erie was a river that went where people wanted the water to go, safe and navigable the entire length. There were limits still; building a canal across a mountain was a bit much to ask—the Wurts brothers pushed the limits of topography about as far as they could be stretched. But they succeeded, overcoming the barrier of the Catskills, moving tons and tons of coal from northeast Pennsylvania to waiting markets in Manhattan. A century earlier, such a task would have been beyond consideration. By the early nineteenth century, people were venturing to reshape nature, build their own rivers, test the limits nature imposed. Those limits were not yet overcome—a canal froze just as a river froze, rendering the route unusable for three months each year at least. But plainly the limits were weakened. A door swung open. Successful canals did much to shape the subsequent challenge to nature in America. If engineers could bend the limits, was it not possible to eliminate them completely? The Stourbridge Lion provided a clue.[42]

As matters stood in 1845 or so, the forests of the Upper Delaware were, in the parlance of modern ecologists, considerably disturbed. The demands of agriculture, coupled to the human determination to remake the landscape, resulted in the removal of at least one-fourth of the trees. More, really—the "cut and run" approach of the landowners in the southern towns was not counted in the "improved acreage" statistics provided by the New York State Census. However much deforestation occurred, the event was something unparalleled in the history of the land since the retreat of the glaciers eighteen thousand years before. Over the long millennia, patches of the Upper Delaware forests had endured repeated climate change, windstorm, epidemic disease, species invasion, fires both natural and human set. But the work of the axe was a disturbance unequalled, a disruption of the ecosystem bound to impart severe, probably permanent effects.[43]

In 1845, the disturbance was still contained. The human population was small, economic opportunity almost negligible. Sawmills, tanneries, asheries, and the occasional craftsman consumed what they could, but there was little reason to much expand. Lack of reliable transportation barred the way. A question perhaps worth asking is whether the Upper Delaware might have reached some kind of ecological balance, where settlers cleared away the last of the lands conducive to agricultural expansion in difficult terrain, where regrowth in the uplands kept pace with the limited industrial consumption. Severely disturbed but standing still, the forests—and the web of life therein— might adapt and survive.

The answer is most assuredly no—for two critical reasons. The first was the human determination thing. Forests were wild places, the antithesis of civilization. The impulse to reshape nature, control the wild, was very much a part of the American "go ahead" mentality so prevalent in the first half of the nineteenth century. Forested lands given over to bucolic field and pasture, these were essential signs of American progress. A cow struggling to graze on a nearly vertical pasture was an improvement over a tangled forest covering the slope.

The second reason was technology and need. America was growing by great leaps and bounds in 1845; urban centers cried out for a long list of resources ranging from food to fuel to building material to water. Newly developing industry demanded ever more, drawing heavily from a rich resource base to sustain and promote the manufacture of iron and textile. Dead trees were needed to feed the great American maw. If the harvest of available forest resources proved a challenge, technology would provide the necessary solutions.[44]

A coarse-grained disturbance would accelerate.

FIVE

Manhattan Offers
a Revisioning

While the tiny population of the Upper Delaware struggled night and day to transform their forest holdings to cropland, convert their trees to ready cash, a contemplative handful in New York City—not a hundred miles away—wrestled with the fundamental notion of how best to comprehend the wild American landscape. With the utilitarian approach so evident all around them, these few intuited the need for alternative perspective. Surely the mysterious woodlands, the quiet river valleys, the craggy mountain tops so pristine, so close, spoke to something more, values measured not in dollars and cents. More a sense than even an idea, the challenge was to find suitable means to properly express this awareness, give definition to a possibility. As much as anything, this small community of like-minded individuals knew something was missing, something was wrong in this newly free nation called America. Their struggle to communicate what they sensed gave birth to the vague, nebulous, often contradictory complex of values now labeled American environmentalism. It is not usual to contend that the cradle of our environmental values was the great City of New York. Manhattan was the stage where ideas took shape, slowly grew.

New York City entered the nineteenth century with an equivocal reputation. High-handed British occupation and a devastating fire during the Revolutionary War destroyed much of the old Colonial town; the city renewed itself from scratch when independence arrived. Fed by waves of new immigrants, the population grew rapidly, reaching 123,706 by 1820. Extremes of wealth and poverty were everywhere visible in the newly constructed urban areas; Manhattan was at once dynamic, vibrant, exciting, and loathsome. The water supply was scarcely adequate and not a little dangerous, cholera outbreaks a regular summer occurrence. Public sanitation did not exist. Settlement in 1817 reached as far north as 10th Street; in thirty years people would be building homes on 30th. Plans adopted in 1811 laid out a grid extending one hundred-ten streets up the island. The city exemplified the spirit of the new republic—aggressive, avaricious, materialistic. The elites of Boston and Philadelphia (already grasping their money) looked askance at greedy New York's "go ahead" spirit, finding all that drive vulgar in the extreme.[1]

One native New Yorker viewing all this growth with misgiving was a young writer named Washington Irving. Born in 1783 (the year the British finally left New York), Irving began his writing career by submitting observant letters to the New York *Morning Chronicle*. His talent recognized, he eventually became the first American to earn a living solely from his pen. Publication of *A History of New York*, initially issued as the work of Dutch historian "Diedrich Knickerbocker," secured Irving's popularity. This was the first history of the city, a narrative of the Dutch occupation that ended in 1684. Underlying the narrative was a lament, a longing for a lost age when life was better on Manhattan Island. Irving found a "sweet and holy calm" in the Dutch city lost to the past, a peace utterly foreign to his own New York. The note would sound again in his most famous stories.[2]

In his own eyes, perhaps Irving's greatest accomplishment was to become the first American writer to earn real respect among European reviewers. He became a master of the craft, fully capable of competing with the renowned English authors. His triumph underscored the cultural dilemma facing talented Americans in the early nineteenth century—to truly achieve, an artist needed to affect, to mimic, European values. Politically free, the American republic lived in cultural thrall.

Washington Irving did not mind. Leaving New York for England in 1815, intent on salvaging his family's shipping company (unsuccessfully), Irving remained abroad for seventeen years, basking in his literary reputation, producing his most renowned and popular work, *The Sketch Book of Geoffrey Crayon, Gent.* Comprised mainly of travel stories and fictions grounded in Europe, the book was published first in Britain, appearing in the United States in 1819. Irving set just two of the stories in his native America, both in the Hudson River Valley: "Rip Van Winkle" and "The Legend of Sleepy Hollow." The tales ensured his enduring fame; American readers took pride in Irving's determination to create an American literature, independent of the British tradition. Washington Irving intended nothing of the kind. After his eventual return to America, Irving was often asked just where in the Catskill Mountains was the setting for the Rip Van Winkle story. His reply: nowhere in particular. Which was true. Irving had derived both his American stories from German folk tales. He had never walked in the mountains, viewing them only from a boat on the Hudson.[3]

Intended or not, the stories did much to encourage the desire for a more purely American artistic expression, reflective of American experiences, American values. A highly ironic consequence, as Irving was himself consciously out of step with the values of material progress so prevalent in the United States, in Manhattan particularly. (He is credited with inventing the phrase "the almighty dollar.") In "The Legend of Sleepy Hollow," Irving imagined that a "drowsy, dreamy influence seems to hang over the land," a land filled with legends of haunting and spirits. The sounds of forest creatures at dusk prodded the imagination. A colonial world, utterly foreign to Manhattan. And "Rip Van Winkle" echoed his distaste for modern New York. After twenty years asleep, Rip returns to his village to discover "the very character of the people seemed changed. There was a busy, bustling, disputatious tone about it instead of ... drowsy tranquility." The lament for a world that was lost.[4]

No matter. What mattered to discerning readers was not the lost tranquility of the Colonial Dutch, but Irving's celebration of a wild America that existed yet, not that far away from bustling New York. Climbing into the mountains, Rip Van Winkle "looked down into a deep mountain glen, wild, lonely and shagged, the bottom filled with fragments from the impending cliffs and scarcely lighted by the reflected rays of the setting sun." He saw that "every change of weather, indeed every hour of the day, produces some change in the magical hues and shapes of these mountains...." Looking outward, he "saw at a distance the lordly Hudson, far, far below him, moving on its silent but majestic course...."[5]

Washington Irving, studiously committing his art to an intellectual romanticism all the rage in the Europe he loved best, had created an American romance. In Irving's Catskills, wilderness nurtured something more than money.

James Fenimore Cooper was already celebrated nationally when he moved to New York City in 1822. Born in Burlington, New Jersey, Cooper lived his youth in the frontier village of Cooperstown, established by his father as the center of a speculative real estate venture. Located on south shore of Otsego Lake, headwaters of the Susquehanna, Cooperstown retained a memorably wild flavor into the nineteenth century; Iroquois Indians came through town frequently. Cooper "passed his childhood, with the vast forest around him, stretching up the mountains that overlook the lake ... a region in which the bear and the wolf yet hunted, and the panther, more formidable than either, lurked in the thickets...." Inheritor of some small wealth, Cooper tried his hand at writing at the age of thirty, believing he could better the lame pap his wife was reading. His initial try, *Precaution*, published anonymously in 1820, really wasn't better, but his second book, *The Spy*, a fictional rendering of the apprehension of Major André during the Revolution, struck a patriotic chord with the American reading public. A career was begun.[6]

Swelled with confidence, Cooper quickly established himself as a figure of note in Manhattan. His next book, written in the city, was a fiction loosely based on his father's venture at Cooperstown. *The Pioneers* spoke to the enticing spell of America's wilderness, the wonders of the secret forest, the tragedy of its evanescence. "Ah! the game is becoming hard to find, indeed, Judge," Natty Bumppo warns "with your clearings and betterments...." The Judge's daughter is amazed to watch the settlements seemingly "enlarging under her eye, while she was gazing, in mute wonder, at the alterations that a few short years had made in the aspect of the country." The Judge too voices concern. "The wastefulness of the settlers with the noble trees of this country is shocking." Witnessing a wanton pigeon shoot, Natty Bumppo echoes the sentiment: "I don't relish to see these wasty ways that you all are practysing, as if the least thing wasn't made for use, and not to destroy."[7]

The Pioneers marked the first appearance of Cooper's most compelling character, "Leatherstocking"—Natty Bumppo. A grizzled older man as introduced, Natty Bumppo was drawn as the child of white parents, brought up among the Delaware Indians, educated by Moravian missionaries. As Cooper's biographer emphasizes, "there was nothing like Natty Bumppo in all American literature—or other literature to date." In *The Last of the Mohicans*, the second of the Leatherstocking Tales (1826), a much younger character is seen "without guile," trusted for his "sturdy honesty." "The eye of the hunter, or scout, or whatever he might be, was small, quick, keen, and restless, roving while he spoke, on every side of him, as if in quest of game, or distrusting the approach of some lurking enemy." Natty Bumppo was the product of uniquely American conditions, a man of the forests, rugged and self-reliant. His creator drew him out of his own vision of the American Indian, a vision of strength. Cooper's understanding of Indians may have been too often mistaken or wrong, but it was a source of powerful inspiration. The Leatherstocking Tales were expressions of the power to be found in American wilderness. To Cooper, the evidence of God was "so clear in the wilderness." Settlements "deform his works." The early Tales were the best sellers of their time.[8]

Cooper acknowledged his literary debts. The title page of *The Pioneers* featured the quotation from a poem entitled "The Backwoodsman," published by James Berke Paulding five years before. Paulding had been an early writing associate of Washington Irving, producing short-lived satires of big city life in New York. Unlike Irving, Paulding firmly rejected European literary tropes, contending America was ready to embrace a more unique national literature, featuring native themes and experiences. Though he tried, Paulding was himself unable to deliver much. "The Backwoodsman" sort of told the story of a man determined to make a new life for himself on the frontier. The published result was almost unreadable, and the literary critics howled. Paulding opted for a career in politics, eventually becoming Secretary of the Navy. But his idea was sound, as James Fenimore Cooper soon demonstrated.

With Washington Irving living abroad, James Fenimore Cooper was by far America's leading literary figure, a position he relished to the fullest. He was, in fact, full of himself. Making the most of his fame, Cooper on his arrival in Manhattan set about making himself the center of the City's growing artistic circle. At a weekly gathering on Broadway he called "The Lunch," Cooper brought together the leading writers, artists, and businessmen of his day. New members were brought into the circle by vote: a bowl was passed from hand to hand; a bit of bread added was a positive vote for a nominee, a lump of cheese a negative. The Lunch became better known as the Bread and Cheese Club, though there was certainly more than that on the menu. Cooper's culinary tastes matched his outsized personality; The Lunch included fine wines, pastries, kidney pudding, stewed oysters.

Members recalled that the purpose behind the gathering was "Irony and raillery. May they be the serious pursuits of the Nation." But there were far more serious discussions afoot. Smarting under a cultural regime too much governed by British attitudes and tastes, the Bread and Cheese Club considered the possibilities of prospective American alternatives. Adding strength to the dominant opinions voiced by the author of the Leatherstocking Tales were several members who would point the direction, prominent among them Thomas Cole, Asher Durand, Samuel F.B. Morse, William Putnam, and William Cullen Bryant. Washington Irving was voted membership in 1826, the last year of the gathering's existence. When Cooper departed for Europe, the artists from his group, along with writers such as Bryant, formed their own "Sketch Club," carrying on the discussion with much lighter fare.[9]

Forceful as it was, Cooper's own influence faded very quickly. In *The Pioneers*, one of his characters makes the point that "Old England, after all, is the country to go to, after your models and fashion pieces." James Fenimore Cooper heeded that call in 1826, one more American artist acknowledging the pull of Europe's supposed cultural superiority. He said he wanted a better education for his children. Cooper remained abroad for seven years, while his own country altered tenor, becoming more consciously democratic with the election of Andrew Jackson. Viewed increasingly as an elitist, Cooper returned to New York to file legal actions against his detractors, gaining him satisfaction but costing dearly in funds. Returning to Cooperstown after a year in the city, he set himself up as a country squire, penning books that failed to restore his popularity, struggling to make ends meet. The search for independent cultural expression passed to others.[10]

William Cullen Bryant was voted unanimously to the Bread and Cheese Club when he moved to New York City in 1825. He and Cooper shared a broad perspective, seeing nature as the inspiration for proper ethical behavior. (Cooper would quote a portion of a Bryant poem in *The Last of the Mohicans*.) Aged 31, Bryant was already famous, America's most celebrated poet, known and acknowledged even in Britain. Born in western Massachusetts, Bryant drew on images of the Berkshire Mountains to compose early poems. He published the short poem "To a Waterfowl" at the age of twenty-one. In the same year, he wrote and published the first version of his most famous work, "Thanotopsis," a rumination on death and the affirmation of life. By 1817, his poems were appearing in the highly regarded *North American Review*, along with a series of essays examining the state of American poetry. If a native literature was taking shape, Bryant was at the heart of the development.[11]

Nature was a central theme in Bryant's verse, the inspiration for vital thought. In a second, expanded version of "Thanotopsis," published in 1821, Bryant wrote:

> To him who in the love of Nature holds
> Communion with her visible forms, she speaks
> A various language; for his gayer hours
> She has a voice of gladness, and a smile
> And eloquence of beauty, and she glides
> Into his darker musings, with a mild
> And healing sympathy, that steals away
> Their sharpness, ere he is aware...[12]

Bryant may have been very much a national figure by 1821, but poetry did not pay his bills. Trained in the law, William Cullen Bryant was a practicing attorney, and he was bored. Seeking a change from New England, Bryant visited Manhattan three times before choosing to move permanently, accepting a position as editor of a new literary journal, the *New York Review and Atheneum Magazine*. The journal would be the first to publish the poetry of Longfellow, and the art criticism of Samuel F.B. Morse, but failed after just two and a half years. Bryant became an assistant editor for the New York *Evening Post*, developing a cosmopolitan perspective for a journal strongly supportive of Jacksonian democracy. Literary journals would continue to cite Bryant as the nation's leading poet, even as they assailed his editorial hack work.[13]

Like Irving and Cooper, Bryant was drawn irresistibly to the flame of British cultural convention. The poetry, so well regarded by American critics, adhered strictly to English conventions, English expectations of meter and form. Publishing his first volume of poems in America in 1831, he wrote to Washington Irving, asking the highly regarded author to arrange a British edition, which appeared in 1832. Two years later, Bryant sailed for Europe himself, planning a year of "cultural travel." A second journey in 1845 left Bryant impressed with the London system of public parks.[14]

As a member of Cooper's Lunch gathering, Bryant often felt himself a little overwhelmed by the abrupt personality of the famous author, believing Cooper "a little giddy with great success his works have met with." This was an experience shared by a young artist invited to join the Bread and Cheese Club at much the same time. William Cullen Bryant and Thomas Cole, each shy by nature, became close friends. Cole's landscapes and Bryant's poetry were in many ways the representations of a shared vision of nature.[15]

Cole was born in England. Emigrating with his family to Philadelphia in 1818 at the age of seventeen, he followed his parents in a number of failed enterprises before taking up painting in Steubenville, Ohio. Self-taught, he began with a portrait business, followed a wandering path in the hope of escaping desperate poverty. Back in Philadelphia, he viewed the landscape paintings of Thomas Doughty and felt he could do better, if there was a market. Some chance. In 1825, still broke, Cole journeyed to New York to rejoin his family, opening a studio at his father's house on Greenwich Street. Here he devoted himself to portraits and historical subjects, demonstrating talent enough to earn a living.[16]

Painters at the time were in a difficult position, prisoners to the dictates of a wealthy elite who paid the commissions. Subject matter was most often chosen for them by privileged individuals wishing to express their own tastes, rather than bow to any inspiration the hireling artist might suggest. Landscape ranked very low in preference; classical tradition, defined by English convention, demanded portraits, religious paintings, historical compositions—"intellectual" works.[17] Cole was fortunate enough to earn a respectable commission from City merchant George M. Bruen, money enough to fund a journey to the Catskill Mountains in 1826. Returning to Manhattan with a series of sketches, he quickly produced three landscapes. A bookstore owner agreed to display the works in the window of his shop on Broadway.

There they stood for weeks, largely unnoticed, until Colonel John Trumbell happened by. Trumbell was America's most powerful, most influential artist, the painter of that still famous (if inaccurate) historical scene, the signing of the Declaration of Independence. Trumbell not only marched into the bookshop and bought Cole's *Kaaterskill Falls*, he brought the painting to the attention of two of his most important friends in the art world, William Dunlap and Asher Brown Durand (both members of the Bread and Cheese Club). They quickly bought the two remaining works. More importantly, they spread the word. American art was about to find new direction.[18]

William Dunlap was the publicist. Art critic for the New York *Mirror*, Dunlap was long and lavish in his enthusiasm for Cole's assays in landscape. Here was a bold departure from the uninspired, insipid devotion to European convention. The paintings were genius. By 1834, Dunlap produced a two volume *History of the Rise and Progress of the Arts of Design in the United States*. He related the story of Cole's discovery in full. The excitement was general. One newspaper critic noted that "the boldness of the scenery itself, the autumnal tints which are spread over the forest, and the wild appearance of the heavens, give it a character and stamp that we never see in the works of foreign schools."[19]

Thomas Cole readily grasped his opportunity. Over the next four years, he produced another twenty-five Hudson Valley scenes, composed from sketches drawn while on a series of expeditions. (Much of the dramatic landscape he and subsequent artists found so inspiring was a product of the glacial retreat twelve thousand years in the past.[20]) Breaking new ground in America, he was still far from a revolutionary, adhering to European landscape traditions in fundamental ways. In three essays published in 1782, Englishman William Gilpin defined the principles of the picturesque romantic art Cole sought to emulate. A true landscape was to be something more than the faithful reproduction of pretty scenery. Gilpin emphasized the need to compose, to combine features from isolated places to produce an effect, suggestive of the beautiful or, preferably, the sublime. A painting imparting to the viewer a sense of the sublime captured an elusive condition of mind, stimulated by views of bleak wilderness pregnant with hidden powers, threatening conditions. The sublime picturesque was an expression of God in his most frightful majesty. The beautiful picturesque, imaginative still, was to be a more peaceful, idyllic representation of nature in repose. Faithful to Gilpin's dictums, Cole never painted directly from nature, working from field sketches in the quiet of his Manhattan studio, never painting a scene precisely as it appeared in nature. His pictures were composites, a river valley from one location, a mountain peak from another, a stately tree from a third, woven together to express the picture of perfect Nature resident in his mind. Writing to Asher Durand, Cole confessed that "I never succeed in painting scenes, however beautiful, immediately on returning from them. I must wait for time to draw a veil over the common details, the unessential parts, which shall leave the great features, whether the beautiful or the sublime, dominant in the mind."[21]

Fully aware of the roots of the audience's growing interest in American scenes, Cole was careful to consider the influence of Washington Irving and James Fenimore Cooper as he constructed his pictures. Kaaterskill Falls, setting for his initial triumphant landscape, was described by Natty Bumppo. (Cole's friend, William Cullen Bryant, composed a narrative poem using the Falls as a setting.) Cole even wrote to Irving, hoping to collaborate on a series of stories and pictures. As his reputation grew, Cole was commissioned to paint scenes directly out of Cooper's works, a kind of combination of landscape and the more "intellectual" historical painting, even if the history was fictional. Asked by a Baltimore merchant to reproduce the famous Indian trial scene from *The Last of the Mohicans*, Cole changed the setting completely, moving the council from Lake George in the Adirondacks to the Mountains of New Hampshire, aiming for a more theatrical effect. Taxed by his patron over the qualities of the sky and the precarious positioning of some boulders, Cole assured the merchant that the scene was real enough.[22]

Like Cooper, Thomas Cole firmly believed God was embodied in the wilderness. English by birth, he had witnessed the industrial blight overtaking his native landscape, realized much the same was in store for America. His wilds became an Eden, an idyllic landscape offering a soothing escape from the mad grasp of material progress. The vision, echoing the literary musings if Irving and Cooper, would be shared by a host of landscape painters in the decades to follow. A "school" of landscape artists took shape. Shared convention eliminated all traces of industrial growth in virtually every picture. Common symbols imparted a subtle communication of ideals—a deer in the painting evoked the wilds; a cow suggested approaching civilization; a mullein the European invasion of America; a tree standing tall at the forefront the sacred connection between heaven and earth.[23]

Cole stood at the forefront, both as an artist with the daring and will to innovate, and as a full participant in the revolution among artists fomented in New York. As much as anything, the struggle was about opportunity. With few notable exceptions, American art in the first decades of the republic was nothing to write home about. Wedded to European expectations, American artists were separated from European models by three thousand miles of ocean. There were no art exhibitions worth mentioning, no masterpieces in America to study. Inferior copies and sad plaster casts offered little chance for refining technique. The nation's one training facility was the American Academy of Fine Arts located in New York, capriciously operated by John Trumbell, one more elitist full of himself. Insisting on the European traditions, controlling access to the exceedingly limited models, Trumbell so alienated Cole, Morse, Durand and others, they walked out. Meeting at Morse's home, thirty artists agreed to establish the New York Drawing Society to advance their cause. Further spats with Trumbell brought a complete break; Samuel F.B. Morse in 1826 became the founding president of the National Academy of Design, the first association run entirely by the artists, most of them from greater New York. (William Cullen Bryant was named the Academy's "Professor of Mythology and Antiquities.") A hundred and seventy works were exhibited at the Academy's first show, including contributions from Cole and Asher Durand. The National Academy of Design exhibition became an annual event, providing the public the opportunity to view the new departures in the nation's artwork, including ever-increasing numbers of landscape paintings.[24]

Creative as the growing movement was, the landscape painters remained oddly conscious of the dictums laid down by European classical artists. Sir Joshua Reynolds had ranked landscape art very low on the scale of artistic endeavors, so it had to be true. Even if an artist was to spend his time pursuing this lower art form, he was not to limit himself to a replication of the scenery—art was to communicate higher truth. For Thomas Cole, landscape was allegory, the artist's sincere effort to communicate biblical, historical, and moral truths. "Simple nature is not quite sufficient," he wrote. "We want human interest, incident and action, to render the effect of landscape complete." Mindful of the classical European dictums defining true art, Cole grew increasingly disenchanted with the landscape art that sparked his career, a trend accelerated by a three year sojourn to Europe. William Cullen Bryant wrote a sonnet dedicated to Cole on his departure. Like Irving and Cooper, Thomas Cole was one more creative artist unable to free himself from the European mold.[25]

Returning to New York in 1832, Cole found a patron for what became his most celebrated series of paintings, *The Course of Empire*—five works depicting the same location through time, the first a view of near wilderness, followed by a sequence of rising civilization, ending in ruin. (Fenimore Cooper praised the series as "the work of the highest genius this country has ever produced.") Cole was determined to be remembered as something more than a mere landscape painter. By the time of his death in 1848, declaring he was no longer a "leaf painter," he refused to do landscapes. "I am not the painter I should have been had there been a higher taste," he insisted.[26]

Yet he drew comfort from the wilder country, cared about the fate of the land. Tiring of the bustle of Manhattan following his return from Europe, Cole left the City to take up residence in Catskill, a village near the Hudson, in 1833. Here he married, found organized Christianity, turned more pastoral in his themes, more overtly determined to portray religious truth. He walked in the mountains long and often, drawing inspiration from the scenery. Until. Speaking before the New York Lyceum in 1835, Cole argued that "the most distinctive, and perhaps the most impressive, characteristic of American scenery is its wildness," warning that soon it would "pass away." In a letter written the following year, he reported "I took a walk last evening, up the valley of the Catskills, where they are now constructing a railroad. This was once my favorite walk; but now the charm of solitude and quietness is gone." In 1838, he authored a poem, "The Lament of the Forest," grieving a woodland lost in "A few short years." His painting, "River in the Catskills," executed in 1843, bore the appearance of one more landscape, but was actually "a deliberate attack on the conventions of pastoral landscape painting and consequently on a pervasive, if often contested, ideology that lauded improvement and material progress." Striving for a more prestigious legacy, Cole could not turn his back on a wilderness that spoke to him so eloquently.[27]

None of this would have mattered very much if the public had remained unaware. Irving, Bryant, and Cooper provided a popular literary image celebrating unaffected nature, but that popularity hinged heavily on foreign opinion—Americans liked the books because the Brits thought they were pretty good. As Asher Durand's son put the problem, "What could infant America do—a colonial dependence of England, using the same language, taught by its thinkers, and imitating its customs—but remain artistically in the orthodox fashion?" Visual image was a necessary ingredient to any education of public opinion.[28]

Positive perceptions of the natural world took hold in large part because Cooper, Bryant, Cole, and the others made their case at a nexus point in the history of New York, city and state. In 1825, the year Cole's first landscapes appeared in the Broadway bookstore window, the Erie Canal opened, connecting the City to the Great Lakes, providing shipping access to the granaries of the Midwest. Business boomed. When Andrew Jackson vetoed the recharter of the Second Bank of the United States, the nation's business center shifted from Philadelphia to Manhattan. New York was the place to be.[29]

The canal provided unmatched opportunities for tourism. People could now travel up the Hudson River to Albany, hop a canal boat to reach Niagara Falls. An American version of the "Grand Tour" developed—viewing the Falls, the engineering of the canal, the haunts of Rip Van Winkle and Natty Bumppo, the sites of the Revolutionary War became nearly obligatory for the cultural traveler. Guide books began to appear—*A Visit to the Catskills* in 1828, four more over the next quarter century. The Catskill Mountain House, one hundred miles north of Manhattan, opened in 1824, a popular resort for artists and tourists alike. The surrounding scenery came to be seen as a pristine reflection of the country's moral value.[30]

An essential element in the growth of Hudson River tourism was the coming of cheap steamboat transportation. Back in 1807, Robert Fulton's *Clermont* made the journey from New York to Albany in an astonishing thirty-two hours. Granted a monopoly by the state, Fulton and financial partner Robert Livingston ran just three pricey boats up and down the river until 1824, when the U.S. Supreme Court declared the monopoly unconstitutional. In a short while, steamship traffic increased tenfold, while ticket prices declined by ninety percent or more. An excursion up the Hudson came within pocketbook reach of the common folk. One steamship company hired Thomas Cole to paint landscapes to be mounted on the boat, a visual taste of what the passenger could expect to see heading north.[31]

If a person was unwilling or unable to make the journey, he or she could bring a taste of the American wilderness directly into their home. As one young journalist observed, "We could wish the spreading of a sort of democratic artistic atmosphere, among the inhabitants of our republic." Technology provided the means. Lithographed prints of Catskill pictures originated by Cole, Durand, and others could be mass produced and sold cheaply, becoming popular domestic wall displays. A *Hudson River Portfolio* appeared in 1820, featuring a set of twenty landscape prints after watercolors by William Gray Wall. In 1830, William Cullen Bryant proposed the issue of an annual volume devoted to scenery. A single volume appeared, featuring a commentary by

Bryant with copies of paintings by Cole and others, engraved by Asher Durand.[32]

Even original paintings became more readily available. In 1842, a group of businessmen, sensing the growing market for native art, organized the American Art Union, exhibiting on Broadway, admission free. Submissions came from all across the country; people came to see in the thousands— school kids, ladies, merchants, whole families. Membership in the Union cost five dollars; at year's end the exhibited paintings were raffled off to the members. The scheme lasted eleven years, giving the National Academy of Design a real run for its money until the State of New York declared the Union an illegal lottery. Probably it was, but the exhibitions brought new art to the view of common folk.[33]

By the 1850s, landscapes had come to dominate the exhibitions sponsored by the National Academy of Design. The landscape market was grown large enough to segment by then. A subjective approach, employed by artists such as Sanford Gifford, John F. Kensett, and Worthington Whittredge, attempted to stamp a distinctive and personal viewpoint on a particular scene, while the objectivists—latecomers including Frederic Church (Thomas Cole's only pupil) and Albert Bierstadt, chose to portray the natural world as chosen scenes appeared before them. What these artists shared was a disinclination to shape their landscapes to suggest allegorical values. No moral or religious suggestions, nothing of the human experience. Nature as it existed was message enough. Perhaps the most striking practitioner of this Nature as nature approach was the second president of the National Academy of Design, Asher Brown Durand.[34]

Asher Durand had been a pivotal figure in the development of a national art since the early 1820s. Born in Jefferson Village, New Jersey, in 1796, Durand entered the art world as an engraver, an essential skill in the early republic. His big break came when Colonel John Trumbell hired him to engrave his painting of the Declaration of Independence, paying him three thousand dollars. The job took three years; completed in 1823, the work insured Durand the reputation as the best engraver in the United States, earning him membership in Cooper's Bread and Cheese Club. Two years later he took part in the discovery of Thomas Cole's work. Durand was a visible and active member of the growing art community, taking part in the organization of the New York Drawing Society and the National Academy of Design.

Engraving demands a deft touch and a careful understanding of subject, but the task can be deadly dull to an original mind. He branched out, exhibiting three paintings at the National Academy of Design in 1827, demonstrating a versatile talent by showing a portrait, a historical subject, and a landscape. Samuel F.B. Morse wrote a laudatory review before heading off to invent the telegraph. By 1835, Durand had endured enough. Profoundly shook by the sudden deaths of his wife and child, he took a calculated risk, foregoing the engraver's art for a painting career. Thomas Cole wrote to encourage him: "You must come to live in the country. Nature is a sovereign remedy." Commissioned to do a series of presidential portraits, Durand chose to remain in Manhattan, concentrating on historical subjects. Acknowledging the legacy of Washington Irving, Durand painted *Dance on the Battery in the Presence of Peter Stuyvesant*, an image drawn from the Knickerbocker *History of New York*, and *Rip van Winkle Introduced to the Crew of Hendrick Hudson in the Catskill Mountains*. Later he would paint Cooper's Leatherstocking crossing a stream in *Kaaterskill Clove*.[35]

In 1837, Durand accepted Cole's invitation to join him on a sketching journey to the Adirondacks. Half joking that he would become a "trespasser" for Cole's patrons, Durand at first struggled with the breadth and subtlety of landscape art. When the pictures he sent to the National Academy of Design exhibitions sold readily, Durand threw over portraiture, committing himself fully to landscapes. By 1846, Asher Durand was the central figure in Manhattan's art world, becoming president of the National Academy of Design.[36]

Perhaps the saddest commission Durand ever undertook was painting "Kindred Spirits," a landscape featuring Thomas Cole looking out over the Catskill Clove in the company of William Cullen Bryant, a painting requested to commemorate Cole's unexpected death. Bryant and Cole had walked the Catskill forests frequently, drawing quiet inspiration from the spectacular views and one another's quiet company. Durand would subsequently execute a series of paintings based on Bryant's poems, including "Thanatopsis."[37]

Asher Durand began his career trusting he would not prove a "poacher" on Thomas Cole's ground; by the time of his friend's death, Durand was breaking new ground. Like everything else, oil painting was experiencing the benefits of new technology that simplified the technical aspects of the task. Portable easels and pre-mixed paints in tubes created the opportunity to move out of the studio, paint a finished canvas out of doors, directly from nature—"plein aire." Durand was the first to do so, an innovation that came to shape his approach to the entire art. Composition remained at the heart of his work; his "practice was, while faithfully painting what he saw, not to paint all that he saw." Unlike Thomas Cole, Durand saw that the artist need not interpret nature as allegory—a faithful expression of what was there could become true art.[38]

Durand was echoing the thoughts of John Ruskin, English landscape artist. In *Modern Painters*, a five-volume series of essays much admired in the United States, Ruskin argued the necessity of a greater realism as "an unparalleled means for depicting nature as it might have been at the time of Creation." In his own "Letters on Landscape Painting," published in the art journal *The Crayon* in 1855, Durand emphasized the healing power of landscape, the best antidote to the suffocations of urban life. Enough with European traditions—wild nature was to be found in America, not in England. (Following the path of Irving, Cooper, Cole, Bryant, and so many others, Durand journeyed to Europe in 1841, endured a "year of toilsome exile." Never again.) Durand stressed the value of seeing and painting real nature, rather than any abstract ideal. No extremes, no sublime. Reality. He had become the spokesman for a school seeing the portrayal of nature as spiritual endeavor.[39]

The shift was a subtle yet important modification in outlook. Cooper saw the presence of God "so clear in the wilderness." Bryant found in nature an inspiration for philosophical insight and proper virtue; Cole saw a power to encourage the spirit. Andrew Jackson Downing would be assured that natural beauty was a gift from the Creator. Each looked at nature as an essential source of something apart from the objects in front of them—something critical to human aspirations, yet apart from what they saw. More than humanizing their landscapes, they allowed themselves to shape nature's definitions, force nature to serve the yearnings of "higher art." The works of Durand and Church offered a glimpse of an alternative vision, where nature might assume a value for what it was—a material world people needed and enjoyed.[40]

The perception of Nature as a unity embodying God assumed more nuanced meaning with the growing popularity of Alexander von Humboldt's *Kosmos*, published in three volumes of English translations between 1845 and 1850. Humboldt had travelled extensively, spending five years in South America, seeking to define the parameters of the unity he saw, "to depict in a single work the entire material universe." *Cosmos: A Sketch of a Physical Description of the Universe* demonstrated that the climate and topography of the earth functioned as an integrated whole, an ordered system that gave and supported life on the Earth. Here was a scientific examination of the forces governing global conditions, a treatise that attempted to explain how everything works. Throughout the Western World, educated people found the analysis captivating.[41]

One especially fascinated soul was Thomas Cole's pupil. Frederic Edwin Church. Born in 1826, the son of a merchant, Church exhibited at an early age both a striking artistic talent and a complete lack of interest in his father's business. Agreeing to take the young man on in 1844, Cole encouraged Church to work out of doors, sketch extensively. The pupil was apt. Producing more than a dozen surpassing landscapes in a year and a half, Church exhibited at the National Academy of Design in 1845, took up on his own a year later. Frederic Church would fill the void left by Cole's death in 1847.

Inspired by Humboldt's writings, Church in 1853 decided to retrace the great scientist's tracks, journeying to South America to sketch and paint the Andes Mountains so vividly described in *Cosmos*. One spectacular product of the journey was *The Andes of Equador*, exhibited in 1855. Two years later came his mesmerizing interpretation of Niagara (scenery that had defeated Cole and many others), a vast painting that enthralled Ruskin in London. A second sojourn in South America resulted in "The Heart of the Andes," shown in 1859. What had begun as a small collection of artists attempting to capture a wildness close by and rapidly disappearing had become, in the hands of Church, Bierstadt and others, an international quest to capture the soul of the wilderness. What would be later disparagingly labeled "The Hudson River School" had ventured well beyond the river.[42]

One painter worth considering stood apart from the Manhattan landscape tradition. In 1839, William Cullen Bryant wrote an editorial for his *Evening Post*, lamenting George Catlin's decision to transport his vast gallery of Native American art to Europe. Catlin had little choice; he was desperately poor—American audiences were unprepared to support his task.[43]

Catlin was born in 1796 at Wilkes-Barre, Pennsylvania (scene of Teedyuscung's murder and two later massacres). He demonstrated an early interest and talent in art, but there was no money in that, so he pursued a law practice. No go. Acquiring a reputation as a decent portrait painter, Catlin established himself as an artist in Philadelphia, where he became fascinated with Plains Indians visiting the city in 1823. Traveling the northeast in search of paying work, he struck gold in Albany, New York, painting portraits of Governor DeWitt Clinton and other officials, landing the commission for a series of paintings celebrating the Erie Canal, marrying into a well-off family, undertaking his first portraits of Indians—Senecas, Oneidas, Tuscaroras, Mohegans (apparently Cooper's was not the last). Moving on to Virginia, he painted James Madison, John Marshall, and James Monroe, earning enough to finance his dream—a westward journey to paint the Natives of the Plains.[44]

Arriving in St. Louis in 1830, Catlin painted a portrait of territorial governor William Clark, who aided him with his plans. For the next six years, George Catlin traveled the American West, as far north as the sources of the Mississippi, west to the Rockies, southwest into Mexican territory. Here he found "a people who don't live for the love of money." Painting mostly on canvases 28 by 23 inches, Catlin assembled six hundred portraits and painted scenes, together with artifacts amounting to eight tons of material. This he transported east at his own expense—he had no sponsor—setting up exhibitions of what might best be labeled documentary art in a few smaller cities before attempting the big time. His Indian Gallery came to Manhattan in 1838, a combination of exhibits and lectures he provided out of his experiences.[45]

The reception was mixed, to put it kindly. The pictures fascinated, the lectures intrigued, but very few were willing to believe Catlin was not broadcasting a fantasy. James Fenimore Cooper may have been well disposed if ill-informed about Indians; Washington Irving may have contended that the

Native Americans had been grievously wronged, but most people saw them as evil savages, blessedly doomed to disappear. Even William Cullen Bryant believed that. The show earned money in New York, but not enough. Moving on to Washington, D.C., Catlin hoped to persuade Congress to purchase his collection, employ it as the basis for a National Museum. What a hope. The only option remaining was across the sea. When Asher Durand journeyed to Europe in 1841, Catlin's wife was on the same ship, sailing the Atlantic to join her husband in London. Poverty and horribly poor luck plagued Catlin abroad; the death of his wife in 1845 brought him a never-ending sorrow.[46]

A grim story; a footnote to the story of Manhattan art in antebellum America, but for one thing. George Catlin was the first individual to advocate the creation of national parks in America. In 1841, seeking to drum up greater interest in his life's work, Catlin penned *Letters and Notes on the Manners, Customs, and Conditions of the North American Indians*, published in London in two volumes, at eight hundred pages. Here he imagined the Indians "as they might in future be seen (by some great protecting policy of government) preserved in their pristine beauty and wildness, in a magnificent park, where the world could see for ages to come, the native Indian in his classic attire...." It was an idea thirty years ahead of its time. In 1841, America's eastern cities had no parks to speak of, much less the wild west. When the National Parks did come into existence after the Civil War, the first thing officialdom saw to was evicting the Indians who had lived there for millennia. Parks urban and wild took shapes vastly different from the vision George Catlin entertained, but it was a vision of some significance. A dream for a park begged a larger, more fundamental question: what was to become of America's wilderness? Opposing notions reflected a growing equivocation. On the one hand stood manifest destiny, the quest for more—more land, more resources, more opportunities, more wealth. On the other hovered the impulse to protect, to preserve what was uniquely American, the wilderness untamed.[47]

Parks were very much on the mind of one practitioner who had little time or use for the wilds. Landscape architect Andrew Jackson Downing was one artist happy to see the wilderness disappear—all that tangled growth, so unorganized. What America needed was more private homes devoted to planned, ordered landscapes, emblematic of American values. An ambiguous ambition at best.[48]

Downing was born in 1815 in Newburgh, New York, fifty miles above Manhattan. His father operated a nursery on the family property; Downing showed a strong interest in botany from adolescence. Wealthy estates lined the Hudson to Newburgh and beyond by the 1830s; the nursery thrived. Downing took to experimentation on the four-and-a-half-acre family property, gravitating from there to a consulting business that steadily grew into the self-taught profession of landscape gardening. Making careful study of the works of English antecedents, he sought to graft the values, the structures, the philosophies of planned landscape to American conditions, cultural and social. Initially, he had precious little to work from.[49]

His first go at expressing ideas emerged with the appearance of his *Treatise on the Theory and Practice of Landscape Gardening, Adapted to North America*, published in 1841, the first American work on the subject. "Adapted" was exactly the word to choose. Downing was long on philosophical intentions, short on the actual means of implementation. One more expression of the drive for a national literature, his treatise was aimed at an American audience, contending that British works on landscape art were "worse than useless." The climate was considerably different, and besides, a country property should reflect the owner's patriotism and pride of home. Like so many writers and authors down in Manhattan, Downing was troubled by the hectic atmosphere of the city, felt the country home should serve as a refuge. Believing that the days of uneducated, unrefined American values were receding into the past, he argued the time had come for Americans to demonstrate some real taste.

Wealthy Americans, that is. Given his business aims, Downing could not help but write for a wealthy, elitist audience, people with vast acreages in need of skilled artistic shaping. There was not much to be done with a few square feet of lawn in the village. Despite his patriotic, anti–English tone, Downing could not help but advocate a set of values somewhat out of tune with the wave of Jacksonian democracy overtaking American political culture, whatever his namesake represented.

He was beholden to the Brits for his landscape tenets. Despite his American orientation, he advocated the extensive use of foreign trees, plants and shrubs in the place of American species, and employed English standards of planning with little alteration. Application did little to meet intention. Downing despaired of American holdings ever matching the great landscape manors of England—there was no hereditary aristocracy to guarantee survival from generation to generation. Although he quoted William Cullen Bryant's poetry in a few passages, most of his illustrative quotations were drawn from British authors. European values transplanted to American landscapes was the best he could envision.

The *Treatise* was reissued in new editions in 1844 and 1849, reflecting both the public interest in the subject and the evolution of Downing's perspective. By 1844, he had decided that the United States represented a "new starting ground" for landscape artists. He began arguing for a greater use of native trees and shrubs, elms especially, though the goal was not to copy nature, but to bring order to the inherent wildness, eliminate aesthetic defect. The 1849 edition, influenced by a reading of Ruskin, remained a treatise for the wealthy—only the elites could possibly implement the carefully ordered landscapes Downing prescribed. The preferred aesthetics remained English, much the same classifications employed by landscape artists such as Cole. Downing tending to the picturesque at the expense of the sublime. Like Asher Durand, he saw pastoral settings as healthy therapy to troubled minds.[50]

Downing journeyed to England in 1850, two purposes in mind. A first-hand tour of noted English landscape properties might enhance his under-standing of the values he promoted. And, he hoped to locate an architect. Several of his clients had expressed the desire to build or refurbish a country home to better blend with the aesthetic Downing advocated; a house designer should prove a valuable addition to the business. In London, he came across a series of landscape watercolors executed by Calvert Vaux, an architect apprenticed at the age of nine. Impressed, Downing sought out the English-man, urged him to emigrate, form a partnership in America. Vaux, twenty-six years old, agreed. The firm flourished. Downing and Vaux are credited with developing the idea of the front porch, a transition point between inside and outside worlds.

A man with a lucrative business and a growing reputation, Andrew Jack-son Downing was professionally situated to serve families with large fortunes to spend; his work did not come cheap. But at heart, he was more egalitarian than he seemed, believing his work could do much to define and uplift Amer-ican cultural values generally. He shared the ideals expressed in the works of Cooper, Cole, Durand, and so many others—that God was present and visible in nature. Nature was the antidote to the crowded horror of urban life. Thoughtful in his appreciation of Thomas Cole's landscape paintings, Down-ing came to emulate Asher Durand in his working methods, developing his designs out of doors on site.[51]

A new journal appeared in New York beginning in 1846. *The Horticul-turist*, edited by Downing, became his vehicle to express a more democratic sentiment in keeping with the age. Here his disdain for European values could be expressed more freely; he edited the journal to "talk American." "No two languages can be more different than the gardening tongues of England and America," he advised his readers, encouraging them to distrust foreign notions, and above all, to participate in the shaping of American scenery. Even the owners of tiny properties could attend to aesthetic qualities, choos-ing decorative plants with care and good taste. Responding to letters, his columns dispensed good advice to urban dweller and poor country farmer equally. In editorials, he scolded town officials across America for lining their streets with foreign trees. "Select the finest indigenous tree or trees"; he stressed "such as the soil and climate of the place will bring to the highest perfection." More to the point he was coming to appreciate, Downing fought the general prejudice against trees: "Woodman, spare that tree." Forest destruction was pointless waste, making no sense economically or aestheti-cally; old trees possessed a value.[52]

Andrew Jackson Downing died in 1852, victim of a steamboat accident and fire on the Hudson River. His legacy was considerable. William Cullen Bryant was one ardent follower, devoting himself to landscape design at his new estate near Roslyn, on the north shore of Long Island, beginning in 1843. Before his death, Downing and Bryant would lend support to one another on a larger, far more significant, more democratic undertaking: the creation of a large public park on Manhattan Island. Downing's work assisted to set in motion a chain of events that in several ways shaped the practical development of environmental values in America.[53]

Cultural orientations were shifting a bit by the 1840s and 1850s. Irving and Cooper were deceased, their popularity faded; Cole was gone, too. Bryant's place as America's poet was giving way to new voices—Longfellow, Whittier, James Russell Lowell. Ralph Waldo Emerson in 1836 echoed the call for a distinctly American literature; his own works, along with the novels of Nathaniel Hawthorne, drew national attention. New England transcendentalism, eschewing the material world defined by the senses in favor of an intuitive insight into the universal reality of God was assuming an essential role in the shaping of American values. The transcendentalists sought inspiration in nature, seeing the wilderness as symbolic ("emblematic") of some greater truth.[54]

One son of New England formed a slender yet critical bond with the juggernaut of Manhattan. Having reached a blind alley in his life, Henry David Thoreau in 1843 agreed to move to Staten Island, where he would serve as tutor to the children of William Emerson, powerful City attorney, Waldo's brother. Thoreau was at this time wholly committed to the transcendental interpretation of things, writing ephemeral essays and journal entries, acting as substitute editor for *The Dial* (the short-lived transcendental journal) while Emerson was away. Nature writing was far from his mind.

Staten Island proved an unhappy choice. Thoreau and William Emerson sharply disagreed on the proper education for the oldest boy; Thoreau was very homesick. He most enjoyed solitary rambles to wilder parts of the island, admiring the vegetation and the vistas of the sea. Visits to Manhattan left him cold, but he did forge one link that proved essential to his later success. He had first encountered Horace Greeley, dynamic editor of New York's *Tribune* (and fierce competitor of William Cullen Bryant) in Massachusetts the preceding winter, following a lyceum engagement. Renewing the acquaintance in New York, Greeley offered to serve as literary agent for the frustrated young author. It would be a pleasant change to receive actual payment for published pieces, an experience Thoreau had not much enjoyed.

Greeley would prove instrumental in popularizing the transcendental ethos in New York. The *Tribune*'s columns offered publicity and lavish praise for Emerson's works, assisting his rise to become one of America's most popular lecturers. In 1844, Greeley offered Margaret Fuller (the first editor of *The Dial*) the position of literary editor at his newspaper. Fuller spent two years at the *Tribune*, contributing three pieces a week, before sailing to Europe. Greeley also wrote the Introduction for her book *Woman in the Nineteenth Century* (1845), a thoughtful and provoking defense of women's rights. As transcendentalism outgrew New England origins to become a national expression of ideas, Horace Greeley stood in the front lines.[55]

If ever there was an author firmly associated with a specific space, that author was Henry Thoreau, the place New England. Thoreau left Staten Island behind in December 1843. But he did send his essays to Greeley, beginning with "Thomas Carlyle and His Works," a critical examination of the writings offered by Emerson's English friend. Greeley praised the essay, placed it with *Graham's Magazine*, asked for more. In 1848, fresh from his Walden experiment, Thoreau submitted "Ktaadn," detailing an exploration of the Maine wilderness. The essay proved a critical breakthrough for Thoreau. Distancing himself from transcendental suspicions that material nature might not be real, he perceived wilderness in the raw, a powerful, tangible, definable force in the world. Greeley saw to publication of "Ktaadn" in five installments in *Sartain's Union Magazine*, and publicized the piece. Soon after, Thoreau sent along the draft of a lyceum lecture entitled "Life in the Woods"—the tentative beginning of *Walden*. Much to Thoreau's surprise, Horace Greeley published the essay in the *Tribune*. When the finished product saw publication in 1854, Greeley praised *Walden* heavily in his columns.[56]

By the 1850s, Thoreau had committed himself to a largely scientific approach to nature, training himself expertly in botany and ornithology. Yet he retained an artist's perspective, seeking the most evocative constructions to convey just what he saw. His efforts mirrored the methods of painters such as Church and especially Durand, who sought to present nature objectively and as it was, not as a simile for some human experience. Like the landscape artists, Thoreau studied Ruskin's ideas, wrote like a painter.[57]

Two years following the publication of *Walden*, Thoreau met Walt Whitman at the home he shared with his parents in Brooklyn. Bronson Alcott, the philosopher who brought the two together, recalled that it was "like two beasts, each wondering what the other would do, whether to snap or run." Each seemed to think, "Well, you're almost as great as I am." At least they appreciated one another. Neither experienced much appreciation in his own lifetime.[58]

Walt Whitman was born in 1819 in West Hills, a village on Long Island. He began writing poetry in his teens, submitting verses anonymously to journals while trying to find a living as a teacher or a compositor. Moving to Brooklyn in 1841, he began a career as a journalist, becoming the editor of the Brooklyn *Daily Eagle*, an organ of the Democratic Party, one more competitor with Bryant and Greeley. By 1850, he was writing the first version of *Leaves of Grass*, the verses that fractured the conventions of classical English poetry, introduced a truly American voice. Whitman was said to be the poet of democracy. *Leaves of Grass* came as an enormous shock to sensibilities conditioned by English tastes; contemporary readers most often failed to understand or appreciate the startling verse. Ralph Waldo Emerson wrote that he liked the work, but took it back when criticism and complaints reached his ears.[59]

Whitman believed William Cullen Bryant the most skilled of the American poets, sought him out for long walks around Manhattan, discussing poetic forms. Whitman's praise was pointed criticism—Bryant was the best of that classical school wedded to British expectations; Bryant was, by Whitman's measure, scholarly. Longfellow, Whittier, too much the same. All that labor, all that worry over matters of meter and rhyme. Let go. There was a song out there, waiting to be sung. Like Bryant, Whitman was troubled by the impact of urbanization, but his response was different, fundamental, American. Whitman drew his identity from the voice of the common man. The second edition of *Leaves of Grass*, published in 1856, a third in 1860 included "Chants Democratic"—"I hear America singing." Whitman was the first to listen.[60]

Like Frederic Church, Walt Whitman was drawn to the three volumes of *Cosmos*, Humboldt's "Sketch of a Physical Description of the Universe." The picture of nature as a "harmoniously ordered whole" spoke to Whitman's sense of identity with everyday nature—he seized on the word to communicate the idea in "Song of Myself," eventually evolving into an image of "Walt Whitman, a kosmos, of Manhattan the son." Whitman in fact shared a lot of ground with the landscape artists, Asher Durand especially: "All he does is good."[61]

Whitman's close association with nature, wild and tame, his minute observations, found shape in the first edition of *Leaves of Grass*. Consider a verse from the earliest published version of "Song of Myself."

> Oxen that rattle the yoke or halt in the shade, what is it that you
>   express in your eyes?
> It seems to me more than all the print I have read in my life.
> My tread scares the wood-drake and wood-duck on my distant
>   and daylong ramble,
> They rise together, then slowly circle around.
> ... I believe in those winged purposes,
> And acknowledge the red yellow and white playing within me,
> And consider the green and violet and the tufted crown
>   intentional;
> And do not call the tortoise unworthy because she is not
>   something else,

And the mocking bird in the swamp never studied the gamut,
   yet trills pretty well to me,
And the look of the bay mare shames silliness out of me.

The wild gander leads his flock through the cool night,
Ya-honk he says, and sounds it down to me like an invitation;
The pert may suppose it meaningless, but I listen closer,
I find its purpose and place up there toward the November sky.[62]

Meeting in 1856, Whitman presented Thoreau a copy of the first edition of *Leaves of Grass*. Thoreau gave Whitman a copy of his own first book, *A Week on the Concord and Merrimac Rivers*. He had several copies to spare.

Among the many rural people writing to Andrew Jackson Downing at *The Horticulturalist* to seek advice was a young farmer from Guilford, Connecticut, who wanted to know what kinds of fruit trees worked best along the coast. Downing suggested apple trees. Not that the advice mattered much. Frederick Law Olmsted gave up the farm soon after, seeking more promising pastures.[63]

Olmsted was the son of a New England fabric merchant, wealthy and tolerant of his oldest child's uncertain ambitions. Olmsted was twenty-two when his father bought him the farm that proved intractable; four years later he purchased him another, one hundred twenty-five acres on Staten Island. Perhaps the young man would find his calling, settle down at last. At least he had interesting neighbors. William Cullen Bryant lived close by, and publisher George Putnam. A stimulating atmosphere. And the ferment of Manhattan was just a short ferry trip away. A farmer's life was just too dull. By 1850, Frederick Law Olmsted was off on a walking tour of England. Returning home, Putnam offered a contract to write about the journey. Olmsted's first book appeared in 1852.[64]

Perhaps a writing career was better suited to his temperament. In 1851, he journeyed up the Hudson to meet Andrew Jackson Downing. Downing agreed to provide Olmsted writing projects for *The Horticulturist*, and introduced him to his new partner, architect Calvert Vaux. Moving on, Olmsted struck a deal with the newly established *New York Times* in 1852, agreeing to undertake a tour of the slaveholding South, report on conditions in the slavocracy. His articles, published in the *Times* and quickly collected into book form, did much to awaken Northern antipathy to the slave system, further polarizing the nation's sections. They also made Olmsted a confirmed abolitionist.

Olmsted sold the Staten Island farm to his brother in 1855. Moving to Manhattan, he became a partner at *Putnam's Monthly Magazine*, which published, among other things, pieces by Herman Melville and Henry David Thoreau. But writing too had its limits as an attraction, while the business side of publishing held little appeal at all. Restless and in need of funds,

Olmsted landed a job superintending the clearing of green space on Manhattan Island between 59th and 110th Streets. (Washington Irving was among his supporters for the position.) Plans for a new public park were under way.[65]

Urban parks were a novel idea in America—none of the major cities possessed a public park of any size into the 1850s. The cities were growing so rapidly—New York alone accounted for twenty percent of the nation's urban growth, reaching a population of more than 800,000 by 1860—and real estate so valuable, the thought of leaving open space was utterly alien. Melville (who grew up reading Cooper's Leatherstocking adventures) encapsulated the image of the cityscape in words given one of his characters: "Think'st thou, Pierre, the time will ever come when all the earth shall be paved?" A horrifying thought, and not altogether an impossible one, at least on Manhattan Island.[66]

William Cullen Bryant, much impressed by the parks he visited in London, wrote a letter to the New York *Evening Post* as early as 1833, sounding the idea of a Manhattan park. Eleven years brought no tangible response, so he tried again, printing an editorial advocating "A New Public Park" in his own newspaper, specifically urging public acquisition of Jones's Wood. Andrew Jackson Downing picked up on the idea, writing his own editorial in *The Horticulturist* supporting a large open park for the City of New York. London had large parks, Paris, Berlin, Vienna; why not Manhattan? Asher Durand, who knew both Bryant and Downing, was well aware of Downing's ideas regarding the therapeutic potential in pastoral nature. The idea was powerful. Bryant followed with yet another editorial, this time touching off a campaign that pressured the city government enough to exercise the right of eminent domain, condemn scrappy properties at the upper end of Manhattan Island. In 1857, Frederick Law Olmsted took charge of clearing the property.[67]

A nasty job it was. Not only was the proposed parkland a tangled maze of rocky outcrops and scrubwood, it was also home to the dregs of the Manhattan economy—rag pickers, bone collectors, transients. Evicting the squatters took something like a cavalry charge; then came the backbreaking work of crushing stones, clearing underbrush. Keeping watch, the city's journalists were impressed with Olmsted's work, not least because he refused all bribes, an unusual stand in the corruption-ridden city.[68]

While the clearing went forward, the design for the park became the subject of competing visions, intense controversy. Was this to be an urban affair, filled with museums and public buildings, a grid of lanes suitable for carriage races, or a quiet, rural idyll, a peaceful haven in the midst of the teeming city? Calvert Vaux, finding the original plan tasteless and inadequate, proposed a planning competition to honor the memory of his deceased partner, Andrew Jackson Downing. When officials agreed, declaring a competition in 1857, Vaux approached Olmsted, proposing a partnership. Not that Vaux perceived any great landscape design skills in Olmsted; what he wanted was his partner's exact knowledge of the land's topography, something of a mystery to most everyone else. Their design, the "Greensward Plan," won them two thousand dollars and the privilege of implementing their vision. The Greensward Plan would create a pastoral landscape in the center of the city, a respite from the urban madness, with winding lanes, hidden grottos, lakes for skating, small streams, overarching trees. The plan was much in keeping with the perception begun with Washington Irving and James Fenimore Cooper, embodied in the works of Thomas Cole, Asher Durand, Frederic Church. Nature was a salve to the urban soul, a retreat to a tranquil space where the spirit grew nearer the Creation. Olmsted became the architect in chief, paid $2,500 a year, Vaux his assistant at five dollars a day. Olmsted had found his calling at last. Calvert Vaux was partnered with a lion. From the beginning, there was struggle; city fathers wanted a zoo, a museum, cushy jobs for political hacks. Olmsted fought them all. Invited to view Central Park at its opening in 1858, Horace Greeley observed, "They have let it alone a good deal more than I thought they would." Precisely the sentiment the Greensward Plan aimed to inspire.[69]

Even as the park took shape, the comforting image of nature so long cherished by so many was to undergo a jolting challenge. While Olmsted and Vaux developed their serene vision, while Durand and Church continued to paint an ordered nature, while Whitman saw in himself and in America Humboldt's cosmos, Charles Darwin was in the process of advancing a soberingly different interpretation of nature. His theory of biological change through time, labeled "descent with modification," argued that life was altered and sustained not through harmony, but competition. The better adapted to meet life's challenges survived; the weaker fell away. Darwin's was a mechanistic view of nature, not nearly so ordered or tranquil as the cosmos envisioned by Alexander von Humboldt.[70]

One of the first Americans to grasp the significance of Darwin's *On the Origin of Species* was Henry David Thoreau. Now firmly interwoven into the natural world surrounding Concord, Massachusetts, Thoreau had become considerably expert in the realms of natural history, reading everything he could find pertinent to his study, including Darwin's earlier travel works. Combining book studies with daily field research, Thoreau reached beyond the collector's habit of identifying plants and animals, sought to achieve an understanding of how the various aspects of nature functioned together, why oaks grew when a farmer cut down a pine grove. What we might now describe as an ecological view. Reading Darwin's descriptions of natural selection, which hinged so much on the dispersal of seeds across the earth, Thoreau recognized that his studies were yielding highly pertinent information. He began an even more intensively organized research program while summarizing his preliminary work in an essay delivered at the Middlesex County (Massachusetts) Cattle Show in 1860. A copy of his talk went to Greeley in New York.

Recognizing the essay's theoretical and practical import, Greeley published "On the Succession of Forest Trees" immediately in the New York *Weekly Tribune*. Four additional journals followed suit, including the *New England Farmer* in February 1861 and *Century* Magazine soon after, making the essay by far the product of his pen most widely read in Thoreau's lifetime.[71]

For good reason. Thoreau disparaged the ill-considered tree-cutting practices of New England farmers, which not only wasted trees, but more often than not hindered subsequent growth. With a minimal comprehension of the patterns of forest reproduction—the importance of soils, the roles of winds and animals, squirrels especially—a farmer could manage his wood lot selectively, encourage a more rapid and productive growth, guarantee his wood supply into an indefinite future. Forest management was not only possible, but profitable.[72]

Greeley gladly published the essay, but he remained skeptical of the conclusions, writing privately to "friend Thoreau" to defend the principle of spontaneous generation—the common notion that living things could spring from properly conditioned circumstances with no seed at all—literally, instant life. Magic. His letter cited what he believed were two personally witnessed instances of spontaneous generation. Thoreau wrote back to politely inform Greeley that the journalist could not possibly be more wrong. "There are several plants peculiarly fitted to reclothe the earth when laid bare by whatever cause," he noted. Belief in spontaneous generation rose from a lack of careful observation—plants supposedly never present in a forest were there all the while, patiently awaiting a change in conditions to spring forth. Scorched earth would be rapidly reseeded by the wind. Every plant, everywhere, sprang from a seed somehow planted there. Diligent observation would disclose the mechanism.[73]

Greeley was far from alone defending his faith in spontaneous generation. Ralph Waldo Emerson was a firm believer. More significantly, so was Louis Agassiz, the leading American scientist of his day. Small wonder Agassiz became so staunch an opponent of Darwin's descent with modification; natural selection withered any possibility of spontaneous generation. A critical moment in the unfolding of scientific knowledge had arrived. Shedding uninformed conjecture, coming to grips with the realities of biology, comprehension pointed a path to scientific management—a foundation for the principles of forest ecology. "On the Succession of Forest Trees" was a small ray of light shed on the rampaging darkness of willy-nilly forest consumption. More importantly, the debate was a small skirmish in a fundamental revolution. Darwin's theory conclusively demonstrated the critical relationship between organisms and their environments, opening the door to ecological under-standing.[74]

And so, on the eve of the American Civil War, the fibers of an American environmental consciousness were largely in place. Often the threads were the merest gossamer, ephemeral expressions of delight at nature's beauty, a faint hope that America's proper image of itself rested in untamed wilds upriver, westward from wherever that might be. So nebulous a sentiment could not help but prove contradictory in intent and interpretation, give rise to all manner of responses to the obvious sickness in American life—worship of the almighty dollar. Washington Irving laid bare the problem, longing for a bucolic New York less ridden with greed. Almost inadvertently he pointed the antidote, depicting serene beauty hiding in the Catskills. James Fenimore Cooper echoed the image, made the trackless forests the setting for romantic adventure, lamenting the advance of settlers bent on destroying nature's bounty. William Cullen Bryant found evidence of the Creation in the wilds. So did Thomas Cole, wringing the emotions in his search for the sublime beauty in landscape. An entire generation of artists followed his lead. Popular exhibition and technology brought picturesque expressions of the wild within reach of everyone, inspiring a reverence for nature coupled to a desire to experience at least a hint of real nature—Hudson River treks became Amer-ica's "Grand Tour."

What to do? Even as respect for nature grew, the wilds were melting away, target of unstoppable progress—land cleared and "improved," needful populations demanding lumber, canals and railroads making access (and deforestation) ever easier. How best to translate a sentiment, an idea so vague as to be almost indefinable, into useful action? Awkwardly different responses began to emerge, unavoidably discrepant in goals and application. At such an early stage, disparities were difficult to see, much less resolve. Regard for nature was such a simple, such a noble expression, any practical idea was welcome in the search for a cultural identity constructed on wilderness. Refined definition could come later.

The place to begin was a proper definition of American character, as well as a better perception of whatever nature might be. Durand and Church looked at the natural world with eyes different from Cole's, seeing in nature something real, something expressive of itself, rather than symbolic of some-thing else. Henry Thoreau reached the same conclusion. Walt Whitman heard America singing with a voice all its own, glimpsing the subtle realities of the natural world. Seeing himself as a quintessential American, a cosmos, his voice could for the moment blend with a more impulsive desire to rearrange nature, make it a little better. Andrew Jackson Downing heard a unique America too, carefully designed country estates reflecting an uplifted taste separated from Europe, an example to the common folk. Perhaps a managed nature could be imported to the City, provide emotional relief to gasping residents too much driven by greed. Bryant and Downing demanded; Olmsted and Vaux brought their vision to life, a rural beauty at Manhattan's center. But managed nature was not Cole's nature sublime, though that was difficult to see. At "Ktaadn," Thoreau appreciated the raw potential of wild nature; the perception did not discourage him from investigating nature's ways with an eye to managed improvement. What was best? Nature preserved, protected from harm? Nature managed, precisely understood, better utilized in a money-driven world? Contradictory impulses, not obvious in antebellum Manhattan.

New York City was home to more than eight hundred thousand people by 1860, yet in some ways the vast metropolis still functioned as a small village. The people who spoke for the trees lived in a community of forged connections: Irving new Cooper who knew and recognized Cole, who was friends with Bryant, who found common ground with Downing, who hired Vaux, who partnered with Olmsted. Bryant befriended Whitman, who exchanged books with Thoreau. The City was a meeting place, a ferment of ideas, a cross fertilization of disparate yet sympathetic ideas, a market for their expression.

A hundred miles away, consumption of the remaining forests intensified.

SIX

A Disturbance Beyond Measure

The future that brushed reality at Honesdale, Pennsylvania, in 1829 quickly assumed shape in places nearby. The idea of a carefully gauged and constructed track for carts drawn by draft animals or some other motive force—a rail road—was inspiring. Linked to the promise of steam to power a land vehicle, a railroad became the compelling answer to the most pressing problem of the day: how to weave a sprawling and rapidly expanding nation into an efficient commercial whole. Effective transportation over large distances had become imperative; the faster, the better. The Erie Canal, opened in 1825, epitomized the prospect—a network linking the agrarian Midwest to a major Eastern center, laying bare the path to untold wealth. New York City boomed; Baltimore and Philadelphia rightly feared they might wither in the falling dust. Both cities wanted their own canals; each soon recognized the task impossible. Some kind of railroad, then.

Baltimore was the first to investigate the prospect of an extensive rail line. Incorporated two years after the Erie Canal opened, the Baltimore and Ohio Railroad Company envisioned a rail road connecting the city to some yet-to-be-determined point on the Ohio River. An immense task, fraught with all kinds of unanticipated engineering problems—no one knew how to build a railroad extended over hundreds of miles through difficult terrain. The project proceeded slowly, the first few miles opening in 1830, one year after the Stourbridge Lion adventure. Like the Wurts brothers, the Baltimore and Ohio employed wooden rails strengthened with strap iron, but created a firmer bed using stringers fashioned from solid granite. Engineers exercised considerable thought and care, and faced ongoing frustration. Bridges were a particular problem; early stone structures just washed away. Construction took twenty-three years to reach Wheeling, Virginia.[1]

Philadelphia was every bit as anxious to tap into some portion of the trade monopolized by New York's canal. The City begged the State of

Pennsylvania to build a competing artificial river, a project much discussed but deemed unworkable. The State instead encouraged a project called the Main Line of Public Works, a system of canals where feasible, short rail lines here and there, inclined planes powered by winches to bridge the frequent and forbidding hills. The resulting crazy quilt of transportation modes, unavoidably featuring innumerable halts for transfer of goods from one mode to another, began rickety operations in 1834. Without much success. Barge traffic on the Erie Canal may have been slow, but Pennsylvania's Main Line proved painfully slow. And expensive. Noting the Baltimore example, the State incorporated the Pennsylvania Railroad in 1846, and managed to construct a line linking Philadelphia and Pittsburgh by 1854. Extensive railroads took time.[2]

The State of New York was hardly standing still while competing cities did their best to horn in on their canal business. The Erie dramatically reconfigured the State's demographic geography, creating large towns where not much existed before, smothering the dreams of villages unconnected to the waterway. Short rail lines sprang up quickly, linking inconveniently located centers to the canal. The Schenectady and Albany, incorporated in 1826, opened for business in 1831. A host of similar lines followed; New York soon possessed a welter of short lines, several with different gauges and different rolling stock, making transfers awkward and time-consuming. Albany financier Erastus Corning took control of ten such lines in 1853, binding them together to create the first railroad octopus in the State, the New York Central. By 1867, Cornelius Vanderbilt would be running the show.[3]

All of which serves to demonstrate that the old adage about necessity being the mother of invention bears some truth. New York's new-fangled artificial river, much doubted and maligned during planning and construction, had proved a wonder. Not just an engineering marvel, but an irresistible market force, a magic wand generating millions. Hoping to cash in, other states dreamed of their own water highways, dreams dashed against the harsh realities of Northeastern topography. New York's Ontario Lake Plain was the only place flat enough to locate a canal. Alternatives became a necessity in a "Go Ahead" world.

The railroads, adopted in some desperation, proved not simply an option, but a vast improvement. Learning from experience (much of it harsh; early railway accidents make for gruesome reading), engineers eventually mastered the problems of moving mountains, spanning rivers. And goods began to move, move much faster than any canal boat could promise, move through all four seasons of the year. If "Go Ahead" was the nation's motto prior to the Civil War, the railroad was the vehicle for getting there.

A fact that naturally inspired still more competition. If railroads were better than canals, more railroads connecting more remote and distant places were better still. So we come to the New York and Erie, the railroad that transformed the economic life of the Upper Delaware. The railroad connected the valley to the wonderful world of urban commerce, encouraged a small rural population to invest themselves in the larger world of trade. Unfortunately, all they had to offer were the trees, aggravating an ongoing disturbance of the forests. Disaster followed.

Cognizant of the railway schemes developing in Maryland and Pennsylvania, the New York State Legislature incorporated the New York and Erie Rail-Road Company in 1832, committing to construction of a line spanning the state. The line was to be an alternative to the canal, linking Lake Erie to New York via a route through the state's southern counties, providing a boost to their economies. From the beginning, the planning was a bit odd, with a western terminus located at Dunkirk, a small village on Lake Erie lacking much commercial potential, and an eastern stopping point at Piermont, on the Hudson River in Rockland County, fifteen miles north of Manhattan. A railroad that began next to nowhere and ended up in much the same place.[4]

Real work came slowly in this brave new world of railroad engineering and finance. The company initiated surveys in 1834, finally began actual construction two years after that, completing the line from Piermont to Goshen, fifty-eight miles inland in Orange County. Then began a long interim marked by dithering indecision and financial chicanery, setting the tone for the company's future. Twice between 1834 and 1845, the State was forced to bail the Corporation out of financial troubles, while not a single train traveled farther than Goshen. New company commissioners took over in 1845 to resolve a scandal. They quickly set about generating a financial ruckus of their own.

According to the original company surveys, the New York and Erie was supposed to extend almost due northward from Goshen into the interior of Sullivan County, sweeping through the towns of Liberty and Monticello before bending westward to strike the Delaware River at Callicoon, some fifty miles above Port Jervis. The rails would then parallel the river northward as far as Tompkins Township in Delaware County, where the line would bend westward into Broome County. Adhering to the plan, laborers graded the proposed sections between Callicoon and Tompkins in 1836, the last work to be completed over a period mounting to thirteen years.[5]

For any number of reasons practical or dubious, the new commissioners determined the route had to be changed. The line they now proposed would run from Goshen to the struggling little town of Port Jervis, bridge the Delaware River into Pennsylvania to avoid the Delaware and Hudson Canal (the company obtained a permanent injunction), proceed northward twenty miles, then bridge the river back to New York at Big Eddy. The rails would continue upstream, eventually reaching the long-completed grading dug beyond Callicoon. The new plan ensured a great many new complications, not least the permissions needed from the State of Pennsylvania for those twenty miles north of Port Jervis.

Howls of rage there were. Speculators had bet heavily on the original line, sewing up land along the route, expecting to enjoy a real estate killing. Accusing the new commissioners of treachery, the investors renewed accusations of financial scandal. James Quinlan's *History of Sullivan County* (1873) enshrines a few choice comments detailing the episode ("falsehood and treachery"), leading the reader to suspect he was one of the speculators undone. While the lawsuits unfolded, laborers constructed the grades between Goshen and Port Jervis. Work along the Delaware sections trespassing on the twenty miles of Pennsylvania began in 1849. (The company agreed to pay Pennsylvania ten thousand dollars a year for the privilege.) Construction provided one more lively moment in the history of railroading.[6]

The boatmen operating on the Delaware and Hudson Canal must have been a surly bunch. Tavern brawls punctuated their exchanges with the raftsmen; now they managed to get on the wrong side of the railroad workers as well. Twenty-some years earlier, the Delaware and Hudson engineers had chosen to dig on the New York side of the Delaware, the flatter and much easier path. The New York and Erie planners were stuck with the Pennsylvania bank, a sheer rock sheet facing the river. (For whatever reason, the railroad commissioners must have been desperate to avoid the interior route.) To shatter enough rock to construct the necessary grades, workers (mostly German and Irish immigrants) employed frequent and potent charges of gunpowder. Soon they were timing the explosions to occur when canal boats passed on the opposite bank, showering the boatmen with dust and gravel. Eventually the boatmen hid a large gang in one of the boats, launching an attack when the railroad workers set off another charge. Several beating deaths ensued. The sheriffs of Sullivan County, New York and Wayne County, Pennsylvania had to send armed deputies to quell the riot. Another riot blew up when a hotel keeper at Big Eddy told the railroad workers they deserved an upcoming cut in their pay. The man barely escaped with his neck. Such was railroad building in the wild East. Construction was not entirely smooth either. Engineers discovered that the original grades cut between Callicoon and Tompkins were located too low on the river bank, flooding out every spring. The entire stretch had to be re-dug.[7]

The developing railway at least made local lumbermen very happy. Construction of seventy miles of track opened an enormous market for railway ties fashioned from hemlock. Buying from numerous sawmills, mainly in Tompkins, the New York and Erie eventually purchased 373,483 board feet of hemlock timber, paying the handsome price of nine to ten dollars per thousand feet. The going rate for the same timber at Philadelphia was six dollars.[8]

Despite the ongoing rash of problems dramatic and irritating, laborers completed the Delaware section by the winter of 1849; the first locomotive running the length of the line at an average speed of six miles per hour, maximum eight. (The decision to run locomotives was recent—until nearly the last minute officials were envisioning horse-drawn vehicles.) For the first time in its history, a dependable means of transportation ran the length of the Upper Delaware Valley. Two years later, the entire line from Lake Erie to New York was complete—464 miles, at that time, the longest continuous rail line in the United States. President Milliard Fillmore and his entire cabinet were aboard for the first run, in April 1851. Speeds on the Pennsylvania stretch above Port Jervis approached sixty miles an hour. Daniel Webster, the Secretary of State, had himself tied to a platform car so he could better enjoy the scenery. With all the speechifying en route, the journey took two days.[9]

By the next December, trains were plowing through major snowstorms to reach Dunkirk on a daily basis. The Erie Canal was closed for the season, frozen solid. The Delaware and Hudson as well. The railroad had overcome the limits of winter—the doors of unrestricted commerce lay wide open.

Originally, the New York and Erie established nine stations on the New York side of the Upper Delaware, another five in the twenty-mile stretch across the river in Pennsylvania. Settlements on the wrong side of the river built bridges to gain access to the railroad or shriveled and died. Most of the station towns had been quaint little hamlets before 1849; now they grew into respectable villages with one hundred to five hundred inhabitants. Some of the new residents were the German and Irish immigrants who had labored to construct the railroad; they found new work in the Upper Delaware's vitalized extractive industries. Trees awaited the axe in all directions. Bluestone quarrying—one more extractive industry, supplying flagstone for the construction boom ongoing in Manhattan—flourished as well. Quarries near Pond Eddy, Pennsylvania, employed upwards of six hundred laborers by the 1870s, while stonecutters worked both sides of the river above Callicoon.[10]

Attracting new people to the region, the railway infused blood into the local economy. Between 1845, prior to the railroad, and 1855, six years into the road's existence, the population of the towns lining the New York side of the Upper Delaware doubled almost exactly, rising from 10,207 to 20,437. (Population on the Pennsylvania side stood at 6,369 in 1850.) Some of the newcomers ventured into agriculture, and more went to work as hired laborers, but a few new commercial enterprises started up, slightly diversifying the market structure. No longer would a raftsman have to buy sewing needles in Trenton.[11]

One business entity less than delighted by the construction of the New York and Erie was the Delaware and Hudson Canal Company. Hearing the footsteps coming, the company began a program of improvements as early as 1842, deepening the canal by two feet, increasing boat capacity to forty tons. They dug down another six inches in 1844, and grew still more serious as railroad construction approached. Workers lined the banks of the Delaware section with stone to discourage an ongoing leakage problem, and increased the bottom and top widths to further increase capacity to one hundred forty tons. A losing battle, once the railroad began operating. From the start, trains were twice as fast as the boats; the ratio grew wider as locomotives became more powerful. And the canal linked the region only to New York City, while an ever-growing rail network offered access to markets throughout the Northeast, and soon the Midwest. After the Civil War the canal company began to build railroads themselves, gradually forsaking dependence on the waterway. Abandoned, the Delaware section of the canal, deemed a health hazard, was drained early in the twentieth century by the new owners—the Erie Railroad.[12]

Just as the Delaware and Hudson Canal had inspired dreams of urban growth twenty years before, so too the New York and Erie. When the railroad company altered plans to run their trains through Port Jervis, the struggling village finally prospered for real, attracting new industry, growing into a respectable manufacturing town of 3,023 people by 1855, close to nine thousand by 1880. The New York State Legislature incorporated Port Jervis as an official village in 1853. Yet the town remained very much tied to the traditionally limited economy of the region. New industries included a saw factory established in 1855; a sash, blind, and door manufacturer opened before 1865. Industry remained too much dependent on the tree supply.[13]

With the advent of the railroad, still more unlikely places contracted the urban bug. Big Eddy, the village close by the bridge bringing the trains from Pennsylvania back to New York, was one. During construction, the railroad company let it be known they intended to establish a major train yard somewhere in the Delaware section for maintenance and repair of rolling stock. The location would become a central terminal for the line, undoubtedly attracting large business to whatever community they chose. Dollar signs glowing in their eyes, the hamlet fathers at Big Eddy acted quickly, changing the town's name to the more urban-sounding "Narrowsburgh," and buying up all the flat and low-sloping ground in the neighborhood. Too greedy. After careful investigation, railroad officials determined land prices in Narrowsburgh were way out of line, opting for Port Jervis instead. Narrowsburgh's moment of light faded away, leaving one more tiny timber town. In 1855, the village population stood at 277.[14]

The Big Eddy experience was a single moment driven by avarice, very small compared to the schizophrenic behavior of Long Eddy, twenty-four miles upstream. Not even designated a station on the railroad (close by stood the station at Basket), village dreamers convinced themselves and others that theirs was the ideal location for urban growth. By 1867, the village won approval from the State to incorporate as the City of Douglass. Proponents of the scheme believed that ten years would see Douglass City a commercial center rivaling Binghamton or Elmira, New York. Crucial to their hopes was development of the Long Eddy Hydraulic and Manufacturing Company, capitalized by village residents at twenty-five thousand dollars. The plan was to build a dam across the Delaware, harness the power of the river to drive any number of factory wheels. Despite the angry protests of raftsmen, the company constructed the dam. Twice. The river proved mightier on each occasion, washing the hopeful structures away with the spring freshets. By 1871 the project was collapsed, undone by wasted capital, inadequate dams, lawsuits, rumors of financial misdealing. Douglass City dis-incorporated, becoming Long Eddy once more.[15]

Nor were the fits of urban scheming the only ill-advised projects to grow out of the railroad's new presence in the valley. If the railway represented the promise of distant markets, delivering product to the railway stations was crucial. New and better roads there had to be—good, well-surfaced roads. Not an easy equation in the middle of the nineteenth century. Experience demonstrated that clay was prone to quagmire, while cobblestones were too rough and uneven to support heavy cargoes. Engineers viewed macadam, a new invention, very expensive to justify for a very short anticipated lifespan. The obvious answer was plank roads, certainly an answer fit to the character of the Upper Delaware. Planks were cheap and plentiful, created a wonderfully smooth road surface, sturdy and long lasting—at least in theory. Originated in Russia, another country harboring a vast frontier filled with evergreens, the plank road idea reached the United States in the late 1840s, winning immediate favor. A plank road craze gripped the Northeast.[16]

Plank roads were plainly a good idea if you were in the business of selling planks. The sudden demand for good sound boards gave birth to an entirely new market for lumbermen, one that showed every sign of becoming perpetual. The news was especially good for Upper Delaware operators, as the developing market was local, and hemlock was regarded as the superior building material, holding a nail well. Uriah Gregory, mill owner on a tributary to the West Branch of the Delaware lying in Sanford Township, Broome County, left papers listing orders for construction lumber throughout the Northeast. In 1853, one of his regular housing customers wrote Gregory to plead, "Now, do not let the *Plank Road* crowd my order out this year." Construction of the railroad transformed the fortunes of the lumbermen, whether they ever loaded a board on a train or not.[17]

Between 1849 and 1852, workers constructed at least seventy-eight miles of plank roads in the New York portions of the Upper Delaware, and more in Pennsylvania. (At least one in Wayne County got bogged down in an 1849 lawsuit.) The various county histories in New York list four such roads, including a twenty-six mile construction stretching from Walton to Hancock to connect the West Branch to the railroad, and a twenty-seven mile road joining the Mongaup River Valley to the station at Port Jervis, twenty-seven miles to the southwest. The State of Pennsylvania chartered a plank road extending nineteen miles from Honesdale to Mast Hope, on the Delaware, in 1850. Another, running fourteen miles from Honesdale to Narrowsburg, opened in 1851 with a whole day celebration featuring speeches and parades.[18]

To grasp some idea of the lumber involved, picture workers beginning with construction of a weblike understructure, perhaps ten feet long. Overlaying the base came a layer of the three-inch planks, nailed crosswise. At a minimum, that's 630 board feet per ten-foot section. With 528 sections per mile, the boards add up pretty quickly. Estimated conservatively, the four plank roads constructed in the New York side of the valley consumed at least twenty-six million board feet of hemlock, the production of 244 flutter mills. That translates to 613 acres of hemlock forest sawn into boards to build local roads.[19]

All for a chimera.

Heavy use of the first plank roads revealed that the boards did not hold up nearly so well as predicted. Stories from Russia and a large dollop of optimism gave rise to an estimate that the roads would last a good ten years without major repair or replacement. But horses' hooves, iron carriage wheels, and considerable damp weather were not a healthy formula for an outdoor construction entirely of wood. The roads were severely compromised in five years' time. Nationwide, the plank road boom was over by 1857. No new roads appeared in the Upper Delaware after 1852. In his *History of Sullivan County*, Quinlan reported that "In not a single case were the planks relaid, and when the road was not abandoned, it was reconstructed of other material." (The Monticello and Port Jervis Railroad, constructed beginning in 1868, did a far more efficient job of serving much the same communities as the abandoned Mongaup plank road.) The local market for hemlock planks came to an abrupt halt. By that time, several owners were already invested heavily in increasing the productivity of their mills.[20]

The future must have glowed gleamingly bright for an Upper Delaware lumberman in 1852. Six roads constructed, and several more in the discussion stage. So much local consumption went a long way to solving the lumberman's most vexing problem: market delivery. Loading boards on a train or sending a raft downriver were unnecessary; local consumption absorbed so much of the supply. Opportunity was beating down the door. The only thing separating mill operators from untold wealth was their limited production capacity; a matter immediately taken under consideration. The lure of easy profits based on greater local demand led lumbermen to consider the efficiency of the milldam, the waterwheel, the gearing, the saw, everything. When the bottom dropped out of the dream all too soon, the railroad stood close by. What sawmills could not raft to Trenton or Philadelphia, they could load on a train bound for Binghamton, Elmira, or Manhattan. An article in the *New York Times* in 1872 noted that "The annual exports from these regions at present is not far short of 200,000,000 feet. This is not all sent to market by the river. No inconsiderable amount from Wayne County is shipped by Delaware and Hudson Canal, and Erie ... Railroads." J. H. French, in a *Gazetteer of the State of New York* published as early as 1860, warned that "Lumber was formerly rafted in large quantities to Philadelphia; but, although still extensively exported by R.R., the quantity is diminishing."[21]

Fueled by construction of the New York and Erie, energized by the plank road movement, lumbering in the Upper Delaware exhibited a notable shift in orientation by 1855. While the total number of sawmills on the New York side actually decreased by a handful, numbers dramatically increased in several towns touched by the railroad. Away from the rail line, and perhaps already beginning to show signs of disappearing forest cover, the towns grouped along the East and West Branches of the Delaware saw thirty-two mills (out of 146) end production. This despite the determined construction of that twenty-six mile plank road connecting Walton (halfway up the West Branch) to the railway station at Hancock.

At the southern end of the valley, a similar abandonment developed as the hemlock gave out. No fewer than sixty-four mills were sawing away in 1835 at the peak of the consumption; the number had dropped to twenty-seven ten years later, just seventeen by 1855. Much of the marketable lumber had disappeared from the southern towns before the railroad arrived to assist. The remaining mills mostly specialized in hardwood lumber for the Manhattan furniture industry, shipped to New York on the Delaware and Hudson Canal.

Taken all in all, there were fifty fewer sawmills operating in those portions of the valley little influenced by the presence of a new transportation system. In the six New York towns with direct access to the railroad, fifty-five new mills appeared. Bearing in mind that these new mills were far more efficient than their predecessors, forest consumption was bound to accelerate. Business boomed.[22]

No precise records exist to track to track the considerable range of changes in sawmill technology. With the exception of a single case, it is impossible to cite just when any particular idea was introduced to the region. In 1825, there were flutter mills and more flutter mills based on a technology wholly of wood; fifty years later a bewildering array of newer designs operated, all making the sawing of a tree faster and easier. The cumulative effect off all the change was considerable. By 1850, production at newer sawmills was double what the flutters could do; by 1870 the yield per mill had nearly tripled, probably the peak to be achieved with the hydraulic energy the rivers and streams provided. A newer mill could consume eight acres of trees in a year.[23]

Technological change in the Upper Delaware lumber industry followed an essential human pattern: faced with natural limitations, inventors and millwrights experimented, seeking the means to get more out of the basic machinery. Problems beset mill operators at four points in the process: the milldam, where leakage and small volumes could lead to power shortages; the mill wheel, where too much or too little water meant a work stoppage; the saw, where low speed and wobble slowed the operation and produced too much "kerf" (point of contact between blade and log, reduced to sawdust); and the log feed, where excessive movement contributed to the kerf problem. New developments in the middle years of the nineteenth century addressed each of these issues.

There is little to say regarding the increase in mill dam efficiency. As much as anything, this was a matter of knowledge gained from experience. Every mill stream was a little different, so was the dam designed to capture the water. But observation taught which locations on which streams served best, while more careful attention to dam construction, perhaps employing less porous materials, made for improvement. New dams, or old dams reconstructed, held back more water and fed the mill wheel more efficiently, increasing the mill's season of operation. Here was one way an operator could boost production without resorting to the large expense of fancier machinery.

The challenge of holding the log steady while feeding the saw was a serious one, contributing not only to excessive kerf but the occasional bloody accident. The response was an iron carriage anchored to the mill floor, running twice the length of a typical log, equipped with clamps to hold the timber in place and guide it mechanically through the saw. A carriage saved raw material and fingers, but also increased the initial capital cost of running a mill, tending to make the enterprise more an industrial venture than an adjunct to agriculture. Mills employing carriages began to behave as a fulltime business, separated from the agricultural past.[24]

Considerable innovation came to the heart of the venture, the saw. The basic up-and-down saw underwent a variety of changes, at least three of which were employed in the Upper Delaware. The most important of these was introduction of the sash saw, in which the blade, rather than standing stark, was enclosed in a gate, dubbed a "sash" because of the resemblance to a window. The sash checked the degree of saw wobble, reducing kerf. An alternative innovation, the Muley saw, took an opposing tack to the problem. Rather than setting the saw in a gate, this approach attached the saw to a pair of guide carriages called Muley-heads, set above and below. The heads induced a reciprocating motion that increased saw speed while maintaining position, checking the tendency to wobble. Finally there was the gig saw, a thin blade with a rapid reciprocating motion, used extensively in finesse work.[25]

Apart from the variations on the long-employed up-and-down saw, several mills developed the simple expedient of powering more than one blade at a time. By mounting a pair of saws in the place of one, the lumberman theoretically doubled his speed sawing a single log. And if two saws could work in tandem, why not five? The gang saw was born, much in evidence by 1860.[26]

Efficiency was the watchword.

That being so, the most significant innovation was a rotating blade—the circular saw. The concept seems so obvious it is difficult to believe circular saws were not there from the beginning, but the blades in fact won favor slowly. Developed in Britain about 1790, the concept arrived in America after the War of 1812. There were teething problems—round blades proved expensive to manufacture, and dulled all too quickly. In 1826, a circular saw with inserted removable teeth appeared, enabling operators to exchange teeth and maintain a much sharper cutting edge. Disadvantages remained. Circular saws wobbled on the shaft to an even greater degree than the up-and-down variety, generating prodigious mountains of sawdust. And detachable teeth did fly off occasionally, inflicting serious injury. But circular saws noticeably increased efficiency, and that outweighed any other consideration. One C. C. Murray is credited as the first to employ a circular saw in the Upper Delaware, introducing the round blade at a mill on the Pennsylvania side near Narrowsburg in 1849—the one technological shift to be dated precisely. The date is an important one, coinciding with construction of the New York and Erie and the beginnings of the plank road mania. "This was soon followed by others in various sections, until they numbered in the hundreds," an unidentified lumberman recalled. "The adoption of these ... gave a great impetus to the lumber trade, and brought into the region ten-fold more capital." Perhaps more accurately, Pennsylvania historian Alfred Mathews stated that fifty circular saws operated in Wayne County in 1870.[27]

The milldam, the log feed, the saw. Innovations in each of these areas fed the desire for greater output. The lion's share of the considerable production increase came at the fourth locus of the industrial process—the power source. The water wheel. After 1845, a bewildering array of inventions aimed at strengthening the efficiency of the wheel, lessening the amount of water required, would lengthen the average mill's period of operation by two or three times. New-fashioned wheels also generated greater power, speeding up the sawing.

Before 1840, the vast majority of mills were the undershot-flutter variety, though others were employed. These included breast wheels and overshot wheels, and perhaps the occasional pitchback or float wheel. Less in evidence (for saw mills at least) were tub wheels—very simple, very inefficient machinery, suited more to smaller grist mills or bark mills. All the different designs were familiar to wheelwrights early in the nineteenth century, as inventors in Europe and America began to tinker with the basic concepts, aiming to build a better wheel. Who could guess the lowly tub wheel held the key to the future?

The first step in the long line of innovations was called the reaction wheel, somewhat smaller than the typical water wheel of the period, designed along the lines of the trusty tub. Tub wheels were fundamentally different from their fellows. As the name suggests, these were wheels mounted within an enclosing wooden tub, with openings at key points to allow the water to enter and discharge. Most unusually, they rotated on a plane horizontal to the fall of water, the opposite of the more widespread vertical-standing flutters and overshot wheels. The strange horizontal orientation lessened the chances of the wheel drowning at high water, but produced negligible power. Building on the tub enclosure idea, reaction wheels were an attempt to improve the performance by injecting jets of water from above to drive the wheel paddles before exhausting through a side opening. Not much of an improvement.

The next step appeared in 1827. Experimenting with the reaction wheel, two brothers living in eastern Ohio, Zebulon and Austin Parker, accidentally invented the "helical sluice," a water feed imparting a swirling action to the entering water jet. Striking the wheel buckets at an angle, the swirling action surprisingly doubled the power output. Obtaining a series of patents, the brothers charged millwrights across the nation a fee to copy their idea. They made money, though this refinement did not really amount to much, either.

Experimentation continued—an international effort. While the Parkers experimented with their helical sluice in Ohio, Monsieur Benoit Fourneyron was building wheels in Paris that would evolve into the first recognizable water turbines. Beginning from the horizontal tub concept, Fourneyron by 1834 constructed an enclosed wheel with curved blades that took in water from the top and expelled the flow through the sides—an "outward flow" turbine. Articles appearing in Philadelphia's *Journal of the Franklin Institute* brought the technical aspects of Fourneyron's research to America.[28]

By that time, Samuel Howd, a wheelwright from Geneva, New York, was also experimenting with tub wheels. Howd developed a wheel in 1838 with water introduced from the top and discharged through the center, rather than the outside. Patenting his idea, Howe sold copies of the engineering plans to licensed builders in several locations. He was just a little too far ahead of his time. Howd abandoned the center discharge four years later, turning to Fourneyron's outward flow design. Other engineers were doing the same. A variety of outward flow proto-turbine designs appeared, including the Johnson (1838), Rose (1839), and Rich (1842), and probably the Ferguson (1837) and Hotchkiss (1844)—all developed in New York State. The old wooden tub wheel was unrecognizable in these newer forms, streamlined, with curved paddles and a helical sluice, constructed wholly from shining iron.[29]

The central discharge wheel remained an intriguing possibility, one taken up by Uriah A. Boyden of the Appleton Company of Lowell, Massachusetts, along with James B. Francis, Superintendent of Locks and Canals on the Merrimac River. Their research was important—Lowell was the first true industrial center in the United States; the demand for greater power was a constant. While Boyden fiddled with Fourneyron's outward flow concept, Francis studied inward flow. Combining their ideas, they produced what became known as the "American mixed flow turbine," which soon powered the textile mills at Lowell. Francis patented a standardized American turbine in 1859, a prototype for the variety of mixed-flow machines soon to appear. Several companies sprang into existence to take advantage of the idea—some reputable, a few fly-by-night. Some of their products appeared in the Upper Delaware, including the Conkle, the Gibb, the Teed, and the Robinson. Typical was the Gibb. Manufactured by George C. Gibb of Stamford, Delaware County, beginning in 1869, the Gibb turbine was designed "to see how much power could be got out of a small amount of water." He claimed an efficiency of 91.5 percent. Who could prove otherwise? Gibb turbine water wheels were the most prevalent of all technologies at work in Delaware and Sullivan Counties.[30]

One year after James B. Francis patented his mix-flow turbine, yet another technology appeared, designed specifically for use on smaller millstreams. Researching in Vermont, J.W. Truax developed a propeller arrangement, affixed with screw-shaped blades. Named the "Green Mountain Turbine," a few of these appeared in the Upper Delaware as well. Racing to cash in on a suddenly expanded market, lumbermen were more than anxious to try new designs to better utilize the power of water to saw more wood.

Whatever the intricacy of the design, the beauty and appeal of the turbine was the prospect of deriving maximum power from a minimum of water. Compared to the huge overshot wheels, turbines were tiny—surprisingly so. (You could store several in your basement.) Unlike the big wheels, the encased turbine featured a sluice directing and regulating the water flow. That quality made the wheel immune to drowning—water could splash overtop without affecting performance in the least. That, and the fact that far greater power could be got from a minimal jet of water meant a far longer season of operation. The mill pond remained close to full volume for months on end, while the log cutting—one saw, two saws, five saws, circular saws, carried on well into summer, and renewed in the fall.

While a great many Upper Delaware sawmills embraced the efficiencies of turbine technology, wheelwrights continued to experiment with the more traditional vertical variety as well, trying new materials, reconfigured designs. Cast-iron overshot wheels—stronger, more powerful—displaced the wooden flutters. Far more complicated arrangements appeared. D. Reynolds, an inventor from Napanock, New York, introduced a scroll-cased vertical wheel with a central water discharge, a variation on the flutter wheel employing concepts borrowed from the turbine designs. A large turbine, mounted sideways. So ended the long career of the old-fashioned wheel. The picturesque flutter, water gently splashing from a wooden sluice to power a stark single saw, all but disappeared. Sawmills were busy places after 1850, employing four or five laborers, operating for months at a time.

The new technologies fulfilled the promise of greater production. They also proved costly to maintain, let alone purchase. By 1860, most milling equipment was arriving from distant factories ready to install, diminishing the role of the local millwright, leaving the lumberman more dependent on outside expertise. This was expensive, demanding a considerable outlay of initial capital. As the newer mills took hold, the smaller-scale operations—the sawmill at the edge of the farm—began to die out. Lumbering had become an intensified business. Describing a mill near Hancock, a late-nineteenth-century traveler cataloged the essential qualities the industry had evolved:

> The logs were hauled from the mountain-side lumber districts by teams, or in season floated down stream. The buildings, 3 in number, for sheltering workmen and machinery, were erected in what had been a mountain gulley. The possibility of a washout was prevented by a stout dam of earth and timbers, braced by rocks, built above. This dam stopped in its course a tiny mountain rivulet, whose channel, diverted from its bed higher up, was led around to the right by a circuitous route and then carried *over* its natural bed, and 30 feet above it, by means of a trestle-supported wooden chute, to a log flume, 4 feet square, into which the water tumbled, operating an overshot wheel. Huge piles of sawdust and lumber scraps lay scattered about.[31]

That an accelerated pace of production occurred after 1845 is plain from the industrial data gathered by the State and Federal census marshals at five year intervals. Tracking the specifics of change is not so simple; the census takers made no attempt to record the numbers of different power sources in use until 1880. (Officials gathered that data but never did analyze the result to any useful degree.) Comparisons over time are beyond hope, but the figures gathered in 1880 convey some idea of the relative efficiency provided by the various wheel technologies.[32]

Sifting through the vagaries of mixed flow, outward flow, horizontal and vertical orientations, propellers, and so on, water wheel technology can be divided into four rough categories embodying the often imprecise records gathered by the census marshals. Some officials adopted categories such as "turbine," "rose wheel," or "flutter," to list the power sources in use at local mills. Other employed specific manufacturing names to specify the power source. Organizing the conflicting descriptions into an elemental framework, waterwheel deployment on the New York side of the Upper Delaware in 1880 operated along these lines:

Table 6.1: Wheel Technologies and Average Production, 1880

Technology	Number	Average Production (board feet/mill)
Mixed Flow Turbine	92	323,000
Outward Flow Turbine	29	177,000
Propeller Turbine	6	377,000
Vertical Wheel	27	301,000
Steam Engine	1	500,000
TOTAL:	154	297,000

Source: United States Census, Products of Industry, Manuscript Schedules (unpublished), 1880.

Mixed flow turbines, patterned from the Lowell manufacturing success, were obviously the more popular choice, powering three wheels of every five in operation. Producing three to four times the lumber a flutter could manage, mixed flow turbine-powered mills were especially prevalent in the towns lining the northern sections of the Delaware, where the New York and Erie ran—some indication of the response to the railroad's convenience. Mixed flow turbines were also popular in the upper reaches of the West Branch, where lumbering had virtually died out after the 1850s. A revitalization followed construction of new railroads connecting the interior towns of Delaware County to the outside world. The New York, Ontario, and Western, constructed in 1873, included stations in Walton, Hamden and Delhi; the Ulster and Delaware, built two years after, joined the townships of Roxbury and Stamford to the Hudson River at Kingston. Similar activity opened the interior of Wayne County. The Pennsylvania Coal Company constructed a line along the Lackawaxen River in 1862–63, connecting Hawley to the Delaware. More lines extended the reach of the railroads well into the coal country west of Honesdale; the new lines were leased to the Erie. New markets appeared. Lumbering began anew. The new mills opted for the machinery of choice.

Outward flow turbines did not fare so well. Developed in advance of the mixed flow variety, they may have been the thing when technological upgrades commenced in the 1840s (they were an obvious advance over the old flutters), but they were outpaced by 1880. Most of the survivors operated along the East Branch in Delaware County, where the railroads did not reach, and rafting remained the sole means of delivering sawed lumber to customers.

Production could not match the newer vertical wheels, much less the competing turbine designs, but there was little need to invest in more production.
Rafting season was short.

Scattered here and there, Green Mountain propeller turbines proved
especially efficient. Appearing a bit late in the game, census marshals found
just six at work in 1880. Three functioned at the southern end of the valley,
in the vicinity of Port Jervis. Probably they were expensive. Port Jervis boasted
the valley's most expansive economy, after all.

Four flutter wheels survived to 1880, presumably the most efficient (or
at least long lasting) of the more than three hundred once in operation. Their
distant cousins, the cast iron vertical wheels were all variations of the recent
overshot design. These were attractive wheels, producing lumber almost at
the rate of a fixed flow turbine, while proving easier to install and maintain.
As sawmills diminished in number in the last years of the nineteenth century,
vertical wheels often outlasted their turbine competitors. Hanford Mill in
East Meredith, Delaware County, one of the very few to survive into the
twenty-first century, utilized at least two different turbines during the structure's long existence, but eventually turned to a large iron overshot wheel,
still in operation.[33]

There was a steam engine. Just one. Steam-powered mills sporadically
appeared in the valley between 1850 and 1880. From the census records, three
were operating on the New York side in 1860, four in 1870. One opened in
Damascus, Pennsylvania, in 1882. They never lasted too long in any one place.
There can be such a thing as too much efficiency. Working rapidly through
the entire year, a steam-powered mill could cut through any local stand of
trees all too quickly, forcing an inconvenient move. Expensive to adopt,
expensive to maintain, a steam engine was not, to most operators, a sufficiently attractive option. By century's end, steam would be driving the enormous consumption of forest in the Adirondack region. Not so the Upper
Delaware, where the trees were gone before steam came much into use.

Located in Sanford, Broome County, along the West Branch of the
Delaware, the one steam-powered mill at work in 1880 sawed five times the
production of any flutter mill, easily outpacing every other mill in the valley.
(Suggestively, this mill enjoyed more ready access to a large urban market,
sitting close to the growing city of Binghamton.) Why not a general exodus
to the greater efficiencies of steam? The reasons seem to lie in technological
burden, coupled to misleading expectations of technological progress.

The power and potential of steam were well understood in 1850. Steam-
boats were plying the Hudson River as early as 1807; more than one hundred
made regular scheduled journeys up and down the river by the 1840s. (No
steamboat ever ventured into the too-shallow Upper Delaware; the ships carried far too much draft.) Steam locomotives traversed the New York and Erie

railroad line on a daily basis beginning in 1849. But there were obstacles to importing steam engines for use in the local lumber industry, expense being the largest. If a turbine represented a steep initial cost, a steam engine was ridiculous. And turbines were quite small and relatively light; a "portable" steam engine weighed eight to ten tons—no frolic to haul up a hillside. And a steam-driven millseat would have to change frequently—operating year round, a steam-powered mill would consume twelve acres of trees every year.

A steam mill affected the traditional rhythms of the lumber business as operated in the Upper Delaware. A mill powered by water was forced to shut down in winter, and in periods of dry weather. During the layovers, the sawyer and the mill hands were out in the woods, cutting trees, preparing to float them to the mill. At a steam mill, that interregnum did not exist. There needed to be two sets of employees, one in the woods, another at the mill sawing boards. With the high production rate, each group would have to be large, larger than customary. More expense. A lumberman invested in a steam mill was running a factory operation.

Another factor to consider: turbines had no tendency to explode. The very first Congressional Investigation into public safety back in 1833 studied the disturbing tendency of steam engines to blow up, really hurting folks. Responding to several tragic accidents, Congress actually adopted legislation regulating the steamboat industry in 1838, a highly unusual step at the time.[34]

Still, there was all that power, crying out for use. A too facile apprehension of that magical word "progress" might lead the observer to conclude the Upper Delaware was technologically backwards, sticking to water when a vastly superior power source was available. Better to say the lumbermen were practical and realistic, retaining a fully adequate technology well-suited to local conditions. (The manufacturers at Lowell employed much the same approach.) Riddled with fast-flowing tributaries large and small, the valley harbored water sources sufficient to power at least four hundred sawmills, together with grist mills and tanneries. The water was free, the wheels to harness the energy relatively cheap and adequate to a purpose limited by additional factors. On average, a steam engine cost more than one hundred dollars per horsepower per year to operate, while a waterwheel cost roughly thirty dollars. If the steam engine broke, repair was bound to involve aggravating grief with manufacturers located at some distant city. Why change?[35]

The truth was, the lumbermen of the Upper Delaware did not fully harness the power potential of the water available before they ran out of raw material. By 1880, the valley's forest resources were visibly melting away. The last statistic in Table 6.1 is the most telling. The number of sawmills functioning in 1880 on the New York side was down to one hundred fifty-four. In 1855, 323 sawmills were sawing away; 197 in 1870. Across the river in

Pennsylvania, sawmills consumed more than one hundred million board feet of timber in 1870; ninety percent of the logs were hemlock. Ten years later, just ninety mills operated in all of Wayne County (some of these in the Susquehanna watershed); only twenty-one in the whole of Pike County. By 1884, just twenty-seven mills continued sawing in Wayne County, producing twelve million board feet—an eighty-seven percent reduction in fifteen years. The heyday of the sawmills was past before the steam engine could make much impact. As the trees disappeared, the lumber business withered.[36]

Though much of the blame would be attributed to the lumbermen, they were by no means the sole actors in the wasting of the trees. A force far more demanding and greedy was at work.

Published in 1871, Hamilton Child's *Gazetteer of Sullivan County* states that the first large-scale tannery in the county opened at Cochecton, a station on the New York and Erie Railroad, in 1850. Hardly a coincidence. The presence of the railway made a large industrial tannery possible, offering a steady supply of raw material for the tanning, access to markets for the finished product, a supply of laborers to grind the bark, work the hides, tend to the vats. Large tanneries multiplied quickly. French's *Gazetteer* noted in 1860 that "Since the completion of the R. R., tanneries have sprung up in favored localities, and will continue until the supply of bark is exhausted."[37]

The industrial tanning process was not vastly different from the small-time operations pursued by a few of the region's more ambitious farmers earlier in the century. The difference was scale. Farm-based tanneries worked a few hides in season, depending largely on the local deer and cattle populations to find the necessary skins. The tannin required came from hemlock bark crushed using a horse or a small water-powered mill. Employing the same basic formula, tanning factories gravitating to the region crushed tons of bark each year, treated thousands of hides, producing leather, jobs, and an aromatic ambiance that worked deep into the sinuses.[38]

Hemlock trees were the critical element attracting tanners to the Upper Delaware. Industrial tanners had begun operations in the Catskill Mountain hemlock forests as early as 1810. The hides, imported from Central and South America, came to the mountains from the southern end of New York City, shipped up the Hudson River in tens of thousands—far easier to send the hides to the hemlock than the other way around. Tanned, the leather came back to workers in a Manhattan area known as "The Swamp," notorious for foul smells and toxic wastes. In the space of forty years, the big tanning concerns seriously compromised the hemlock supply in the mountains. Time to move on. The coming of the New York and Erie provided tanners convenient access to a relatively untouched hemlock concentration. Tanning migrated westward, setting up shop in the Upper Delaware.[39]

The transformation of tanning in some ways mirrored the shifts in the lumber industry. The New York State Census counted forty tanneries at work in 1845; ten years later, forty-nine were in operation. The numbers disguise fundamental change. Smaller tanneries along the East and West Branches gave up the ghost; twenty remained of the earlier twenty-eight. At the south end of the valley, where the hemlock was disappearing, a single establishment soldiered on. Where the industry grew like Topsy was in the northern and western towns of Sullivan County, close to the railroad tracks and in the more populated portions of the interior. The new establishments were true factory complexes, sprawled bleakly across the landscape, employing ten to twenty laborers on site, gangs of men sent to the woods to cut bark every spring. Many of the employees were immigrants, men drawn to the region to build the railroad, finding more permanent work in a noxious operation. Around the tanneries, villages grew.[40]

Industrial tanning meant changes in scale, rather than method. The factories still employed lime to remove fat from the hides, pummeled the hides on wooden beams to promote suppleness, ground hemlock bark to brew the tanning liquor, soaked the skins in vats for long periods. The stench was still compelling, the vats a lot bigger and more numerous, the bark mill a more energy-consuming operation. The steam engine found a home at a tanning factory—not as an exclusive source of power, but an adjunct, a last resort when the water ran out. When water power was available, tanners found a waterwheel sufficiently powerful, and much cheaper. As summer approached and the milldam emptied, the factory cranked up the steam and went on working. Always in production, the new tanneries required a seemingly endless supply of hemlock bark.[41]

Hamilton Child, working hard on his *Gazetteer of Sullivan County*, took the opportunity in 1871 to visit a tannery operated by W. Kiersted and Company, located in Bethel Township. Child was told the Kiersted tannery had contracted in 1847 for the rights to ten thousand acres of hemlock forest in the interior of Sullivan County. The contract was for thirty years, with a renewal option. Child went on to record that the tannery chewed, on average, three thousand cords of bark a year. (Kiersted also operated a sawmill, suggesting he at least utilized some of the hemlock cut by his peelers. Despite the size of his timber consumption operation, Kiersted listed himself as a farmer in the 1870 Census.) Calculated, Kiersted and Company in twenty-four years had harvested four thousand acres of bark from their contracted forest. Another six years, the hemlock would be half gone. Renewing their option for another thirty, nothing would be left.[42]

The figures are chilling. In 1835, a typical tannery consumed 452 cords of bark each year—twenty-five acres. That sounds like a lot until you see that tanneries in 1850 averaged 1,338 cords—almost seventy-five acres. By 1860, consumption averaged more than one hundred-one acres apiece. After that, the hemlock depletion really got out of hand. The rule of thumb grew to one square mile of hemlocks each year for each factory.

The peak of tanning operations in the Upper Delaware came in the Civil War years, 1861–65. Sullivan County historian James Quinlan claimed that there was "more sole leather made in [Sullivan] County than in any territory of equal extent in the world." The region took pride in the boast that the Union Army marched in boots fashioned from locally manufactured leather. The Federal Ordnance Department awarded huge contracts to the industrial tanneries lining the Upper Delaware in New York and Pennsylvania, making the region the tanning headquarters for the entire United States. Hemlock fell in earnest. By war's end, the resource was noticeably diminished; by 1870 a quarter of the tanneries on the New York side had departed. Several continued westward. Eighteen tanneries of various capacities operated in Wayne County, Pennsylvania, in 1869, practically one in every township. By 1880, the Federal Census found five industrial tanneries remained in Wayne County, including (allegedly) the largest in the nation. By 1884, the number was down to four. In New York, the tanneries remaining in New York continued to grind at a relentless pace, nearly one hundred acres of hemlock each and every year. Tanners foresaw the last stands of hemlock disappearing by 1890. The unrelenting demand for hemlock was a slow-moving, voracious monster crawling the landscape from east to west, leaving behind a broken forest.[43]

The business of cutting bark was a seasonal endeavor. Gangs of "peelers" entered the woods in late spring when the sap ceased to flow, weakening the membranes between bark and wood. Establishing camps for work that would last a month or so, the peelers marched into the surrounding woods, each piling up as much as two cords of bark a day. Some gangs chopped down the hemlocks, employing some of the lumber shorn to build shelters and feed fires, leaving the remainder to rot on the forest floor. Others left the hemlocks standing, stripping the bark from the base of the tree as far as the first branch, leaving the tree to waste away and fall with the wind. Either way, the waste was enormous. After stacking the sheets in the woods to dry, peelers eventually transported the bark to the tannery in wagons.[44]

Naturalist John Burroughs, walking in the southern Catskills in 1893, recorded that "The ravages of the barkpeelers were still visible, now in a space thickly strewn with the soft and decayed trunks of hemlock-trees, and overgrown with wild cherry, then in huge mossy logs scattered through the beech and maple woods." Burroughs encountered evidence of peeler activity in several of his treks—the rotting logs, the decaying shelters where he occasionally escaped the rain. The scars to be seen in the woods were frequent and inescapable.[45]

The consequences of the bark frenzy did not end with hemlocks decaying in the woods. In his "1886 Report to the State Forest Commission on the Catskill Preserve," forest inspector Charles C. Carpenter (in his long-winded way) observed that

> Thirty years ago this Catskill region was in places a dense hemlock wilderness and the business of tanning was the leading industry, at least in Sullivan County and other parts of the Catskill counties, but the avarice of the tanners got ahead of their judgment, and the timber was slaughtered for the bark alone.... [T]he woods became filled with the dry trunks and drier tops then the fire caught in these old 'peelings,' and the old story of total denudation was repeated.... Some places have never recovered from the effect of the fire and never will, for the soil that sustains the life of the tree has been consumed or washed away.... A thousand years will not re-clothe these denuded mountain-sides with forest.

Carpenter estimated that in addition to the vast acreage devastated directly by the peelers, several million acres more fell to the resulting forest fires. Fires were especially bad throughout the State of New York in 1903, and again in 1908.[46]

Taken together, the tanners and the lumbermen did an appalling number on the forests in just thirty years' time. And that was not the end of it. Farming continued to slowly expand in tandem. After 1845, agricultural endeavor on the New York side of the Upper Delaware "improved" another 218,000 acres of forest; by 1875, nearly half the land available had been converted to agricultural use. In Pennsylvania, thirty percent of the Upper Delaware drainage was enclosed as farmland in 1850–36.5 percent of that was "improved." Thirty years later, slightly more than two-thirds of the land had been converted to farms, more than half of that improved. Population in the Pennsylvania drainage grew by seventy-seven percent, to 32,919 people. That much "improvement" ran ominously close to the valley's limits—portions of the conversion were not so much improved as compromised. Clearcutting the steeper hillsides to create pasture unleashed erosion problems, jeopardizing the bottomlands. Soon would come a reversal—improved land figures would diminish over the last years of the century as land farmed far too optimistically was abandoned to nature. Despite the improvement, which now amounted to more than half the total landscape, census marshals reckoned still that 316,000 acres of forest remained in New York in 1880. A pipe estimate. With more than 150 sawmills and 19 industrial tanneries still in operation, much of the forest they enumerated was severely compromised, the mature trees gone to the mills, the hemlocks shorn in the woods, awaiting the spark from a passing train. At least two-thirds of the original forest cover was gone.[47]

The contrast between the forest consumption taking place through 1845 and that coming after is the difference between night and day. The human determination to tame the forest, eliminate the wilderness, "improve" the land was constant. The locus, the ways and means, the effects altered mightily. Before 1845, agriculture drove the deforestation urge, fueled the desire to clear the land, create a fenced-in world of fields and pastures. One tree of every five felled may have fed a sawmill, an ashery, a tannery, but that was incidental, a way to derive a little extra cash from all the determined chopping. Most of the cleared trees were simply burned. Corn and contented cows were the intention.

Then came the railroad, drawing forest industry to the sound of the locomotive bell. Clearing the land for agriculture continued on; farmers burned twenty cords of wood to stay warm, consigned unwanted trees to the local sawmill or tannery, rafted logs downriver. Demanding as that relentless cutting continued to be, the effect on the forest was minimal compared to the demands of a newly vitalized forest industry. Sawmills moved to the railroads and grew bigger; industrial tanners came to claim the hemlocks, employing steam and dozens of laborers to import "Go Ahead" to the Upper Delaware. Precise numbers are difficult to pin down—how much of the lumber sawed at the mills came from peelers who took the bark first? How many of the rafts still floating downstream in the 1870s were sent from smaller sawmills, delivering orders to New Jersey? Sifting the imprecision, a reasonable guess is that four percent of the trees floated downstream as rafts, another twenty percent got burned as firewood. The tanneries and the sawmills consumed the remainder—three-quarters of the trees cut or killed each year. In thirty years, forest industries tore through at least a quarter million acres of trees on the New York side of the Upper Delaware. And they were not prepared to stop, or even slow down. The unidentified lumberman writing for the *New York Times* in 1872 estimated the timber would last "for at least another decade." Charles Carpenter described that deforestation as "reckless waste … the noble forests mowed down to satisfy the cupidity of man…." It is impossibly hard to disagree.[48]

Pretty much the hardwoods were all that remained. And industry had their eyes on the oaks, the maples, the hickories, the beeches, the ash, the chestnuts, too. As the tanners pulled up stakes to head westward, acid factories assumed their niche. The factories were tree kilns, huge ovens where workers subjected four-foot sections of large tree trunks to extreme heat, reducing the wood to charcoal while the saps and resins boiled off. The first appeared in the Upper Delaware in 1878, the investment of a Binghamton businessman, one Eugene F. King. The process he introduced was a relatively new innovation imported from Scotland—just seven acid factories functioned in the United States. Located at the northern end of the Delaware Valley near the railway station at Basket, King called his factory "Acadelia"—city of acid. Soon, two additional factories appeared close by. At least two more located in the interior of Sullivan County. Forest historian Michael Kudish has identified the locations of seven more in the upper reaches of the East Branch, accessing the Delaware and Northern or the New York, Ontario and Western Railroad. At least two set up shop close to Milanville, on the Pennsylvania side. Three more appeared in Buckingham township, Wayne County, between 1880 and 1882, another in Scott township. Each lasted roughly ten years before moving on to new locations—nearby stands of hardwood were gone.[49]

Along with the acid, the factories produced a stench that made a tannery seem like a spring meadow. Beeches were the preferred trees for the roasting, but any hardwood could be made to produce saleable chemicals. The factories burned anywhere from fifteen to thirty cords of wood each day just to fuel the furnace. Like the tanners, the factories sent gangs of cutters into the remains of the forest, seeking firewood and the largest hardwood trunks for the boiling. Employing lime to clear the fluids boiled off, acid factories produced "wood alcohol, acetate of lime, charcoal, creosote, and wood ashes," all valuable to the chemical industry. Explosives and embalming fluids were the end products to be derived from the acids. The factories lasted until the 1920s, when markets for wood acids largely disappeared, displaced by petroleum-based synthetics. The dramatic increase in explosions and embalming occasioned by the First World War had much to do with that. Most of the hardwood stands in the Upper Delaware stood ravaged by then, leaving very few mature trees at all. Michael Kudish estimates than eighty to ninety percent of the first growth forest in the Catskills was gone by 1885. Evergreen Kalmia shrubs—American laurel—blanketed Sullivan County hillsides, providing at least the illusion of greenery where trees once stood.[50]

The rapid rise and fall of the acid factories was emblematic of the harsh truth facing the Upper Delaware economy. The trees were pretty much it. Apart from the industries dependent on the trees, the only manufactories outside Port Jervis listed in French's *Gazetteer* (1860) were two small iron foundries located in Delhi and Thompson, and woolen mills in Delhi and Hamden. A few minor productions, glass and such, appeared momentarily. When the forests disappeared, the slim hopes of prosperity vanished alongside. The bluestone quarries continued on for a few decades, absorbing some of the labor force let go when the tanneries shut down, but they too were an extractive industry living on borrowed time; the introduction of Portland cement would finish them by 1920.[51]

Port Jervis remained the only community of any consequence; the population at the turn of the century stood at 10,507. The urban dreams elsewhere fizzled, leaving washed-out dams and unused flats. By 1900 fewer than one hundred sawmills operated in Delaware and Sullivan Counties, just three tanneries. The valley population, in decline since 1860, was fifteen percent beneath the peak by century's end. Farm abandonment was underway.

Attempting to tame hillsides too steep, valleys too narrow and subject to flood, farmers found they had bitten off too much. Abandonment was marked in Stamford, far up the East Branch, as early as 1865; in Deer Park and Lumberland in the southern reaches of the valley by 1875. Farms disappeared in several towns along both the East and West Branches by the late 1870s as erosion washed away what soils there were. The 1880 Census counted 31,965 acres on the Pennsylvania side as "old fields not growing wood"—lands improved, only to be abandoned as unworkable. The trickle became a flood in the twentieth century; farmers were abandoning even the larger farms by 1928, a trend accelerated by the Great Depression. Overused, the Upper Delaware was used up.[52]

As a fragile economy shriveled, there was the matter of assigning blame. Lumbermen came in for the largest share of that if the gazetteers and local newspapers are any indication. The standard story accused the lumbermen of indiscriminant cutting, resulting in over-fast consumption leaving barren hills and shot resources. The worst of it was, there wasn't even any benefit to be seen from all the activity. In his Delaware County history, David Murray noted that "no man ... in the valley of the Delaware, ever became wealthy by the business of lumbering."[53]

With considerable justification, the lumbermen placed the responsibility on the tanners. An article appearing in the Port Jervis *Evening Gazette* for April 30, 1888, contended that "It was the tanneries that thinned the forests...." The article was the work of "an Old Delaware River Man" who objected to the aspersions on his trade. Observing that sawmill operators at least cut and used whole trees, he argued "Not so the bark peeler however. At one time the number of men engaged at this business far exceeded the lumbermen, and wherever they traveled they left waste and ruin in their track." The consequence was soft and decaying trees "of no value to the lumberman."[54]

Reading Murray's book—a collection of township histories written by local people, the reader can sense a degree of shame. "The forests that sheltered the Indians and the game on which they lived have almost gone," one author wrote. "The streams of water once sheltered from evaporation by the abundant and overhanging trees have dwindled into insignificance. The lumber which used to give work to the chopper, and a rush of business every spring to the rafts man, is gone."[55]

The need to finger a culprit was understandable enough, but more than a little disingenuous. The reality was, the entire population of the valley was inextricably tied to the devastation. The woodlands were the sole means of making money. The farmers wanted the trees removed to graze cattle and sheep, raise crops. The lumbermen, the tanners, the acid manufacturers needed acres upon acres of forest to drive industries wholly dependent on turning trees into something useful. The remainder of the population—the civic employees, the professional people (doctors, lawyers, teachers, journalists), the market capitalists all relied on the continued existence of the extractive economy. When nothing was left to extract, all were diminished.

The one group possibly exempted from the blame was the hotel keepers. The coming of the railroad did initiate the possibility of a tourist trade—*Harper's New York and Erie Rail-Road Guide Book,* published in 1856 (with illustrations) emphasized the scenic appeal of the route, and mentioned several inviting hostelries located near the Delaware River stations. The one reason tourists might deign to visit the Upper Delaware was to view whatever was left of the wild scenery—the railroad was offering a new alternative to that boat trip up the Hudson to the Catskills. The *Guide* at several points offered such admonishments as "let the tourist, artist, and sportsman find it, and they will find its attractions doubly pleasant while enjoying the excellent accommodations of the hotel kept by Mr. Faulkner." Plainly a pitch aimed at the cultural shift coming of age in Manhattan, the astonishing notion that the wilderness was something more than money waiting for the taking. To some extent the advertisement paid off—a few tourists did make the train trip, fishermen especially, pursuing trout in upcountry streams not yet overheated by deforestation or polluted by the tanneries. But not many artists painted the Upper Delaware, nor did anyone author a poem worth remembering. Probably too late. Romantics would have to find wilder streams than the Upper Delaware had become.[56]

The hotel operators perhaps wanted or needed the woods, but they were a small minority, a contrary voice in a valley population fixed on seeing trees as natural resources to be consumed. And even a hotel owner could harbor mixed feelings. A Mr. Corwin, who owned the largest hotel in Narrowsburgh, saved a few large trees on his property, but cut the majority to create a meadow leading down to the river. Virtually no one wanted to leave the trees alone.[57]

Whoever was at fault—the farmers who tried to improve too much, the tanners supplying the leather industry in Manhattan, the lumbermen pursuing dollar signs offered by the coming railroad, the acid manufacturer determined to squeeze the last pennies from a diminished woodland—the consequences were stark. The first and most obvious was the loss of the forest's role in regulating water flow. In his *History of Wayne, Pike, and Monroe Counties, Pennsylvania,* Alfred Mathews noted that "the destruction of the hemlock woods in this county has materially affected the water supply, many large streams having become almost dry within the past decade." More ominous was the opposite effect: sudden floods. When the trees first began to disappear, no one had much of an inkling regarding a forest's role on flood control. James Quinlan's *History of Sullivan County* maintained that extensive woodlands enhanced flooding, as they attracted more rain to the region. But as the trees disappeared, floods became a monotonously repeated event. Small creek beds, so attractive to the sawmills and the tanneries, were often the first places to lose forest cover, making them especially vulnerable to flood. Root systems gone, there was nothing to absorb spring runoff, autumn rains. Extensive flooding along narrow streams descending from the hills soon resulted in heavy property damage and loss of life. Historic photographs of rafting on the Delaware reveal extremely roiled, muddy water, suggesting the inevitable erosion taking place. County histories make mention of floods in the Upper Delaware drainage in 1853, 1855, 1857, 1863, 1867, and 1869. There were undoubtedly more. By the turn of the century, with the trees largely disappeared, the Delaware itself took to swelling uncontrollably. In four successive years beginning in 1901, floods demolished bridges, washed away railroad cuts, drowned portions of towns. One small hamlet on the Pennsylvania side completely flooded away. So bad was the problem, officials in 1908 discussed construction of a dam at Narrowsburg to bring the river under control. That dam was never built, but dams constructed on the East and West Branches in the middle of the twentieth century (to supply fresh water to the City of New York) did much to ease flooding downstream.[58]

But the repercussions of the catastrophic forest disturbance ran far deeper than simple flooding. Destruction of this magnitude impairs the functioning of the entire forest ecosystem. Even a small disturbance will result in greater fluctuation in soil temperature, moisture retention, exposure to light. The landscape lies open to the ravages of wind, drying, blowing away unanchored soil, buffeting any surviving trees. Drier on top, the soil is wetter a few inches down—root systems to absorb the moisture are gone. Soil nitrates leach into unchecked streams and rising groundwater. The nitrogen cycle so essential to plant life is severely disrupted—plant uptake is interrupted just as the slash left behind decomposes rapidly. With the forest canopy so radically opened or completely gone, days become warmer, nights cooler. Winters will be colder without the insulation the forest provides, and summers hotter. The more profound and thorough the disturbance, the longer the recovery; soil nutrient depletion alone can take decades to rebuild. Animal populations will suffer—insects, small mammals, songbirds. The disturbance in the Upper Delaware was not small; this was a coarse-grained hatchet job about as deep and profound as they come. A hurricane lasting a century.[59]

In a single marathon sentence, Charles Carpenter's "Report to the State Forest Commission" described precisely what happened. The hills and mountains,

> once deprived of the mass of clinging roots, moss, and leaf mold, with a network of branches above or a canopy of leaves to break the force of driving rain storms, is shorn of its power to withstand this force of nature, and the loose masses of loam, sand or other earth overlaying in many instances only to a shallow depth, the smooth faces of the rock, become detached through the action of frost, are washed

into the streams threading the valleys below and are carried away to enrich some other section.

Carpenter took the long road to summarize a degree of devastation almost beyond natural repair.[60]

Abandonment of long-standing farms revealed long lasting effects equally severe. The land might be forsaken, left to nature to reclaim, but that would not occur any time soon. Seeds or saplings that might have survived the initial clearing in the 1820s had long since disappeared, leaving abandoned fields dependent on the contingent lottery of natural succession—whatever and whenever wind and animals might deliver in the way of encouraging a renewed forest. Small animals would claim the land initially as grass took over the forsaken fields—meadow voles, jumping mice. As vegetation litter accumulated with the years, deer mice would come, red squirrels, short-tailed shrews, leaving their spores. Nutrients long absorbed to sustain crops would re-anchor in the soil. Seeds carried by the wind might become the progenitors of a regenerated woodland. White pines, much appreciating open space, were especially aggressive in such lands as lay open in the Upper Delaware. No one was going to make much money from these pines; their growth too often proved stunted and haphazard—mature pines were gnarled, laden with deeply knotted wood. Once the pines got going, providing a canopy, squirrels and jays might possibly contribute hardwoods seeds to the mix. Or, just as likely, the incoming pioneers might be aspens, gray birch, pin cherries, paper birch—what any self-respecting forester might label "trash trees." So much depended on chance, the fortune and behavior of so many individual species, each seeking an opportunity to find the conditions favorable to their own survival and growth. A long ways down the road, some kind of woodland would take shape, subject to the same contingent whims of fortune. The probability of that forest bearing more than a superficial resemblance to the stands existing in 1750 was slim at best.[61]

Whatever the pattern of renewal, ecologists recognize that the more severe the disturbance, the more slowly the vegetation manifests any signs of recovery. And it would be difficult to imagine a disturbance more sustained and severe than what happened on the Upper Delaware.

SEVEN

Nature
Disturbed, Preserved, Conserved

Much can change in the space of a few years—especially when a country is torn apart by prolonged, savage warfare. The War of the Rebellion swept away much of the cultural spirit taking shape over the first half of the nineteenth century, leaving in its stead a host of familiar questions still more troubling. The war accelerated those aspects of American life repellent to Washington Irving, James Fenimore Cooper, and so many others. Capitalist greed was not merely ascendant; the "go ahead" mentality seemed poised to swallow the remaining natural assets. How to cope with an octopus that grabbed at every resource, trampled every evidence of finer feeling? Fed by the war machine, railroads multiplied, forests disappeared, America's lakes and rivers choked. The population grew steadily more urban, fostering a rift between town and country, rendering the traditional values quaint, if not meaningless.

Consumption of the forests provided stark evidence of what was happening, visual and statistical. Between 1600 and 1850, the American people chopped down forty percent of their forest cover—more than one hundred million acres. New York State led the nation in lumber production in 1850. Thirty years later, despite the opening of more remote sources with the construction of the railroads, the state dropped to fourth. Twenty years following, the rank dropped to seventeenth of forty-four. Maine was the focus for a brief while, until the lumbermen turned their attention to the vast forests of the Upper Great Lakes. The "cut and run" mentality held; very little thought was given to replanting, while acres on acres of clear-cut, littered with slash, spawned catastrophic fires that engulfed towns and cities. In New York, barren hillsides alternated between drought and erosive flood while lumbermen eyed the Adirondacks, the last relatively untapped source of timber.[1]

There was little left for artists to paint. Schroon Lake in the Adirondacks, site of one of the first sketching expeditions shared by Thomas Cole and

Asher Durand, scene of one of Cole's most spectacular landscapes, was devastated, victim of a charcoal industry that left a "blighted and hopeless land." Not that it mattered much to the world of art. Landscapes of the Cole and Durand variety were hopelessly passé, derided as "the Hudson River School," limited, unimaginative, parochial. So it goes in the world of art—one generation's genius is the laughingstock of the next. Durand struggled on until 1879, a living anachronism. Church, Bierstadt, Gifford found subjects in a world much wider than the Hudson River Valley. New styles displaced the old, heavily influenced by French values. Art as an expression of national identity was a notion disparaged.[2]

The scientific perspective was shifted still more profoundly. Humboldt's vision of a finely tuned, harmonious cosmos suffered most. The war, a ferocious competitive struggle if ever there was one, contributed. Reflecting Darwin's "descent with modification," nature was more readily viewed as a vast competition where "the fittest" survived—much like American society. Warfare blunted careful consideration of Darwin's evolutionary theories; there was much to be sorted out—the theoretically mechanistic nature of biological behavior, the role of religion, the meanings for human existence. *On the Origin of Species* was a critical step on the path to ecological understanding, vaguely comprehended as more philosophical issues intruded.[3]

A more immediate environmental outlook derived from a book actually published as the Civil War raged. George Perkins Marsh, son of Vermont, lawyer, congressman, diplomat, philologist, expert in a dozen languages, spent nine years abroad in the service of his government, mainly in Turkey, Greece, and Italy. The United States did not have much to say to those countries back then; the American minister had plenty of time to explore ancient ruins, examine old documents, study ruined landscapes. He reached some startling conclusions, which he published in an 1864 book entitled *Man and Nature*. Growing up in the Green Mountains, Marsh witnessed the consequence of clearcutting forest on steep hillsides: massive erosion, frequent floods. Carrying this knowledge to Europe, Marsh soon realized the desolated landscapes he encountered—the sterile wastes of the Anatolian Deserts, the ruined croplands flooded by the Pontine Marshes—were the products of human activity. In the remote past, those desert wastes had supported the first civilizations; the fetid marshlands had once fed Rome. Unheeding, uncontrolled exploitation ruined their productivity. Examples were easily multiplied, the conclusion inescapable. Human action could blight the most prolific landscapes. And, it could easily happen—was happening—in America.[4]

More than half of *Man and Nature* was devoted to discussion of forests, their role in shaping and protecting natural resources. Marsh in no sense advocated a "hands off" preservation of forests—the trees were critical resources to be harvested. But he saw that the forests served to protect and enhance another essential resource: fresh water. The forests were a vast sponge, soaking up rainfall, cleansing the water, regulating seasonal flow. Removing the trees promised a whipsaw of alternating flood and drought, coupled to an unavoidable loss in water volume.

Firmly believing humanity stood apart from nature, Marsh saw salvation in the power of human foresight, the ability to act outside the limitations of instinct. Much of the book's discussion was devoted to the proper means of protecting forest watersheds, arguing against the clearcutting so common, advocating the development of tree farms to provide sustainable yields. What Marsh recommended, at least forty years ahead of his time in America, was scientific forest management. Coupled to this, Marsh urged a careful study of natural conditions before embarking on any construction projects intended to alter the landscape. An environmental impact analysis.[5]

Man and Nature was not a best-seller by any stretch, but it was read, often by thoughtful individuals with influence on the direction of the future. With two-fifths of the nation's timber consumed in less than two centuries and the pace rapidly accelerating, drastic alterations in outlook would have to come soon.[6]

Several European states were already managing their forests, treating trees as one more crop to be harvested. Britain's continued quest for overseas empire was driven in part by the demand for timber; the island's forests were largely gone by the Fifteenth Century. France and Germany introduced silviculture practices early in the nineteenth century, determined to meet the demands created by industrializing economies. One European forester immigrated to the United States, where he encountered frustration, resistance, and a finally, a small measure of success.

Bernhard Eduard Fernow, born in Prussia in 1851, developed an interest in forestry reading German texts and the works of Linnaeus. Expected to manage his family's considerable forest estate, he instead fell for a visiting American woman and followed her to the United States in 1876. There he found not much call for his forest expertise—his first work was managing the holdings of a charcoal outfit in Pennsylvania. By taking on odd tasks here and there, lecturing extensively, he built up enough of a reputation to be named in 1881 the first director of the newly formed Division of Forestry at the U.S. Department of Agriculture. Fernow was one of very few people in America qualified for the position. The work was not demanding; there was little call for government advice when it came to chopping trees. Fernow produced pamphlets, experimented with cloud-seeding, advised the government on the framing of the Forest Reserve Act, which empowered the president to set aside portions of the public domain to ensure a supply of timber. The new reserves were naturally placed under the Department of the

Interior—where Fernow's Division of Forestry could exercise no management role.[7]

Creation of the Reserves was the latest in a small series of policy steps indicating interest in protecting a tiny slice of the nation's resources. In 1864, the United States granted the lands comprising the Yosemite Valley to the State of California for a wilderness park; in 1872, the government established Yellowstone to protect the weird assortment of natural wonders recently discovered—indications of a growing sentiment that the natural world might possibly possess some quality beyond the promise of natural resources for human consumption.[8]

At the forefront of the trend was none other than Frederick Law Olmsted, designer of New York City's Central Park. Grown tired of endless tangles with the city's hugely corrupt government, Olmsted left at the outbreak of the Civil War to assume direction of the United States Sanitary Commission, responsible for managing health conditions on the battlefront. Burned out by 1863, Olmsted took a position in California, managing the estate of bankrupted explorer John Charles Frémont. Finding himself close to the Yosemite Valley, Olmsted took a professional interest in the badly neglected park, delivering a treatise outlining the proper objectives for park management. Most importantly, government—state or federal—had to be responsible for a park's integrity; private entrepreneurs could not be trusted. The parks should be accessible to everyone—America was a democracy. And, the park had to be properly protected, insuring its survival for future generations. Three essential propositions, embodying a welter of conflicting ideas. How does a government manage a landscape open to all while guaranteeing survival for future generations?[9]

America was showing a few signs indicating that the thought begun with Irving and Cooper, visualized by Cole and Durand, celebrated by Bryant and Whitman, Emerson and Thoreau, was bearing meaningful fruit. Parks, urban and remote, were established to protect and promote natural beauty. Proper management of natural resources—forests and water especially—was at least considered. Faced with a juggernaut consumption of nature by a culture committed to the rapid acquisition of wealth, the problem for nature's defenders was to articulate a proper approach to protection. What was best? Were trees a crop like wheat or corn, to be harvested carefully, replanted, managed to provide quick and steady yields? Was it best to fence off the more spectacular spaces, keep the railroads and the axes away? Were these compatible notions, or antitheses? What was the duty of humankind to nature, to the survival of the human species? What decided priority? There were no clear answers, not even among those who fully devoted themselves to nature's good health.[10]

Strangely enough, the polarity of views among nature's friends was personified in two pivotal individuals born and raised in close proximity to the Delaware River. John Burroughs, born near Roxbury, New York, in 1837, fished in the East Branch of the Delaware as a child. Gifford Pinchot, born in 1865, spent much of his youth in Milford, Pike County, Pennsylvania, six miles south of Port Jervis, close to the Delaware. Burroughs would become one of the great popularizers of nature, penning a long series of books celebrating the simple attractions of the natural world. Pinchot parlayed his own love of nature into a notable career as a natural resources bureaucrat, advancing the principles of forest management, perhaps authoring the very word "conservation." Sharing a devotion to the natural world, their visions for nature's future could not have been more different.

John Burroughs grew up on a three-hundred-acre farm a couple of miles northeast of Roxbury, in the shadow of a Catskill peak known as "Old Clump." One of his closest childhood friends was Jay Gould, who would grow up to write a history of Delaware County before going off to New York to become one of the nation's most notorious "robber baron" financiers—the very personification of the "go ahead" mentality. Burroughs held much closer to the habits of his upbringing. As a child he earned spending money making maple sugar, learned to identify the birds in the neighborhood, and worked the farm with his parents and siblings. Much of the pocket money went for books—Burroughs felt little attraction to the agricultural life. At age seventeen he took a job teaching in a one-room schoolhouse on the other side of the mountains. This began a peregrination lasting nine years, in which he pursued a much-interrupted education, taught as far away as Illinois, married, and worked at the family farm at low water. In 1860, he published an essay in the *Atlantic Monthly* entitled "Expression," a piece on the craft of writing modeled after the works of his literary hero, Ralph Waldo Emerson. (Burroughs met Emerson at West Point in 1863 and enjoyed a pleasant conversation.) Derivative as the work was, the author set a tone, emphasizing "everyday speech, commoner illustrations." Find excitement in the commonplace.[11]

Managing to avoid the military draft, Burroughs reluctantly traveled to Washington in 1863, seeking steadier work. This he found at the Treasury Department, where he worked for nine years. More importantly, he managed to meet another of his literary heroes, Walt Whitman, who was serving as a nurse to wounded soldiers. The two became good friends, sharing long walks in the parklands still surrounding the capital, exchanging views on writing. Burroughs had continued his own efforts, writing newspaper pieces, honing his craft. Whitman urged him to "write about the things you know most, things you did in your boyhood in the Catskills." Very good advice. Burroughs renewed his study of birds, took up botany. Very soon, he was writing nature essays.

John Burroughs's first book was a critical review of Whitman's poetry (much assisted by the poet himself); his second was a collection of nature essays called *Wake Robin* (1871), the title suggested by Whitman. A career was born. Over the next fifty years, Burroughs would publish more than two dozen collections of essays devoted to his two great interests, literature and the natural world. The literary analyses stirred few hearts, but the nature essays were another matter. Writing nature made John Burroughs internationally loved and respected.[12]

After a journey to Europe on Treasury business in 1871, Burroughs resigned his post to take a bank job in Middletown, New York, short miles from his boyhood haunts. He completed construction of a house he called "Riverby" close to the west bank of the Hudson River in 1874, later adding a small cabin—"Slabsides"—a mile removed into woods he called "Whitmanland." The cabin was a peaceful, isolated spot where he could write in peace, free from the carping of his wife, who disparaged his writing career and wanted her husband to make something of himself. (Like Jay Gould, maybe.) Whitman visited Slabsides twice.[13]

Winter Sunshine, Burroughs's third book, included essays on England and nature explorations. Like his first essay collection, the volume sold well and earned laudatory reviews. Henry James saw him as "a sort of reduced but also more humorous, more available, and more sociable Thoreau." That pretty much nailed Burroughs's work. He was capable of touching essays, providing the reader an honest feel for the simple pleasures of the outdoors, an easily palatable lesson in the ways of nature. Yet there was inconsistency in quality, a lack of fire. Unlike Thoreau, Burroughs never produced a book among his two dozen that the reader could single out as great literature. Burroughs was a great popularizer of nature in a world increasingly urban.[14]

Burroughs wrote widely regarding a host of nature experiences, a few set in the Catskills, where he found time to explore from time to time. A pertinent example was a fifty-mile journey down the Pepacton (East) Branch of the Delaware River, described in an essay published in 1881. After building his own boat for the trip, perhaps the first boat to float the stream since the Indians departed, he embarked at Dry Brook, some twelve miles from his parents' farm. The journey downriver took four and half days, as he encountered drenching rains, inquisitive boys, a few natural curiosities (lamprey eel nests!), and an uncooperative stream. Geologists describe the Pepacton as a "fossil river" characterized by quiet pools amidst long stretches of woodland marsh. Burroughs found it "a stream of many minds." The boys he met along the way advised him of the best routes to maintain progress.

Nothing spectacular happened. That was not the point. Burroughs described what he saw—groves of willow, elm, hemlock, birch growing along the banks, high mountains impinging on either side, occasional flats of fifty acres or so. Not much in the way of farmland. The journey was enough to challenge his mettle, visit occasional discomfort, but most importantly a relaxing, refreshing interlude—boating, fishing, camping, finding pleasure in the glimpses of unhurried rural life. That was the heart of John Burroughs's gift, the antidote to too much "go ahead." (Jay Gould read all his books.[15])

The author made something of a shift in 1886 with the publication of *Signs and Seasons*, his seventh book of essays. Here he grew more philosophical, injecting less humor into his pieces. His aim was to provide an alternative world view, to slow the incessant drive for progress. The theme recurs in many of his essays. "I experience that serene exaltation of sentiment of which music, literature, and religion are but the faint types and symbols," he wrote. "Civilization seems to have done little more than to have scratched this rough, shaggy surface of the earth here and there." References to scripture occasionally appear in his essays, but in important ways, he was fashioning his own religious perspective from nature observation, echoing Bryant, Cole, so many others. "What power and effectiveness in Nature," Burroughs exulted, "and how rarely an artist catches her touch!"[16]

One of the pieces in *Signs and Seasons*, "Phases of Farm Life," echoed precisely the laments voiced by Washington Irving eighty years before. First came the pining for the lost golden age: "It is unquestionably true that farm life and farm scenes in this country are less picturesque than they were fifty or one hundred years ago." Progress is to blame, of course. The romance of pioneer life has been eradicated by machinery. Moreover, "the railroad has found its way through or near every settlement, and marvels and wonders are cheap." Worst of all is the urbanization; a "nation always begins to rot first in its great cities." (Visiting New York back in 1855, Burroughs noted that "a certain element of faith and charity seems to be missing from the city." Though he visited often, he hated the place.) The farm, dairy farms especially, retained a certain charm. The author even expressed nostalgia for the inventive wonders of Dutch architecture. Irving would have been tickled.[17]

As America's most popular nature writer during the latter half of the nineteenth century, Burroughs walked a fine line in his explications of nature's ways. Largely self-trained, he was firmly cognizant of the scientific aspect to his subject. Darwin's writings were a steady influence on his interpretations; he in fact insisted on a highly mechanistic view of natural behavior (more so than Darwin himself). To Burroughs, animal actions derived wholly from instinct, there was no learning, no reasoning out there. Birds built nest according to plans hard-wired into their brains; foxes did not plan ahead when escaping pursuing hunters. Incidents recorded in his essays underscored his scientist's approach—several times he mentions shooting birds to assist identification. (Thoreau had argued against the practice in *Walden*, which gained new popularity late in the century, due in part to Burroughs' efforts.[18])

Taking a hard line, Burroughs found himself embroiled in controversy when he published an essay in 1903 attacking other nature writers for "sham natural history," creating episodes he considered "sensational and improbable." His friend, President Theodore Roosevelt, supported him, writing an essay delineating the differences between scientific fact and fiction, but he too questioned Burroughs's extreme position, noting that animals certainly learned to avoid contact with people. A difficult question. Biologists, taken in by charlatans in the nineteenth century, always exercised enormous caution in considering any animal's capacity for thought. But ravens can solve puzzles, and beavers do build better dams as they gain experience. Where to draw the line?[19]

By those early years of the twentieth century, John Burroughs was one of the most celebrated writers in America, friend and travelling companion of Roosevelt, close acquaintance of preservation spokesman John Muir. Muir had done as much as anyone to publicize the wretched treatment California had provided Yosemite, spearheading efforts to make the neglected landscape a National Park, co-founding the Sierra Club as a watchdog group. Muir and Burroughs shared a disputatious friendship, traveling together, needling one another often. Muir was far more outspoken than his friend on the subject of nature preservation, but Burroughs had done his part, encouraging the growth of nature appreciation, making the natural world a peaceful, desirable space worth preserving.[20]

Gifford Pinchot loved nature, too. The Grand Canyon, the Rockies, Yosemite—the spectacular settings of the American West just floored him. But everyday nature—John Burroughs's nature—he studied with a different eye. An integral player in the great political and social movement called Progressivism, Pinchot saw forests and streams as necessary components to progress—properly managed. Blame it on the textbooks; most people understand Progressivism as a kind of radical reform movement. In some ways it was, but not the sort of reform anyone might expect. More than anything, Progressivism was a determination to apply the principles of scientific management to everything: capitalism, political affairs, population growth, urban problems, labor issues—everything, including the environment.[21]

Pinchot's grandparents emigrated from France to take up residence in northeastern Pennsylvania before the Civil War. Milford, Pennsylvania, close to the Delaware, became the center of a family mercantile operation that included substantial investment in clearcutting operations. The profits mounted until the 1840s, when the Erie Railroad bypassed the village, leaving the town a struggling backwater vainly hoping to rebuild the glory days. The children scattered to make their own fortunes. Gifford Pinchot's father, James, gravitated to New York, where he made sufficient money in the indoor furnishing trade to attract a rich man's daughter. That made him wealthy enough to retire in 1865, the year Gifford was born. The family established a summer home back in Milford, eventually constructing a palatial estate.

James Pinchot was much interested in the arts, playing a supportive role in the National Academy of Design, serving as patron to Hudson River landscape artists including Worthington Whittredge and Sanford Gifford, for whom his son was named. From an early age, Gifford was encouraged both in his love of nature and his sense of civic responsibility. No financial career for him. By the time he was ready for college, he had set his cap on becoming a forester. His brother gave him a copy of Marsh's *Man and Nature* as a twenty-first birthday present.[22]

There was a problem. No clear path existed in the United States to fulfill the ambition. No university in America offered anything resembling a program in a field as esoteric as forestry; anyone remotely connected to the profession, including U.S. Director of Forestry Bernhard Fernow, discouraged him when asked. So, Pinchot attended Yale, attended such science classes as seemed pertinent, and upon graduation in 1889, sailed for Europe to learn something from people versed in the field. In Britain he was made to understand that trees were a crop like any other—planted, cultivated, harvested, planted anew. On to France, where he enrolled in L'Ecole Nationale Forestière, the national forest academy, where he impatiently attempted to swallow an enormous amount of technical information in a very short, force-fed period. He benefited most from six weeks of practical field experience in Switzerland. After little more than a year altogether, he sailed for New York, by his own admission "half trained." He was "willing to try with what knowledge I have now." A little knowledge is known to be a dangerous thing.[23]

His first field job was in North Carolina. A longtime acquaintance of the family, one Frederick Law Olmsted, was wrestling with an enormous landscaping project in Asheville, the newly acquired home of George Washington Vanderbilt, heir to thirteen of the Vanderbilt millions. With no interest in finance, this Vanderbilt opted for the life of a country squire, and hired the nation's foremost landscape planner to wring an estate out of eighty thousand acres of exhausted forest. Recognizing an overwhelming challenge when he saw one, Olmsted counseled Vanderbilt to limit himself to a nice, scenic drive through the woods and forty acres of garden, with the rest given over to managed forest. Olmsted recommended Pinchot's half-trained expertise, and a career was begun. Gifford Pinchot joined Olmsted's staff at Vanderbilt's "Biltmore" in 1892, instituting management strategies designed to produce a sustained harvest while maintaining a healthy profit margin. He was not as successful as he claimed, but Biltmore is generally cited as the "nest egg" of American forestry. Vanderbilt recommended Pinchot to his friend William

Seward Webb, who owned 175,000 acres in New York's Adirondack region. Following what would become an established pattern, Pinchot submitted plans to stimulate sustained yield, concentrating on cutting that would encourage the growth of more profitable spruce. Trees were money, some more than others.[24]

Ambitious, adept at self-advertisement, well-connected to the centers of power, Pinchot made himself a visible success very quickly. Resource management was the salvation of the future, and Pinchot was prepared to educate the public. In 1896, he was named to a National Forest Commission charged with surveying and recommending policies for the country's newly established forest reserves. Touring the west, he struck up a friendship with fellow commission member John Muir. Muir, nationally renowned for his role in saving Yosemite, became for the moment something of a role model for Pinchot. Though Muir loved the wilds above all else, he remained ambivalent about the best course for the future of American resources. Was it possible to preserve the wilds while instituting scientific management practices? Not yet seeing the notions as incompatible, Muir's essays supported both. But soon he and Pinchot would famously fall out, initially when the young forester expressed a tolerance for sheep-grazing in the National Forests. (Muir considered sheep "hoofed locusts.") The real divide would come a few years later, when Pinchot supported construction of a dam inside Yosemite National Park. To Pinchot, resource management took precedence over natural preservation. America needed dams more than parks. Muir never forgave him.[25]

But, upward. When Bernhard Fernow left his post as head of the Division of Forestry to become the first dean of the New York State College of Forestry at Cornell in 1898 (a gig that ended really badly), Gifford Pinchot became his replacement. Soon he was in Albany, asked to consult with New York's governor, Theodore Roosevelt, on proper management of the state's waning timber resources. Three later, Theodore Roosevelt was President of the United States, and Pinchot was one of his closest advisors. Working together, they managed to place the National Forest Reserves under the control of the Division of Forestry while vastly expanding the reserves—in defiance of Congress. Pinchot now had the power to impose his resource management regime on a national scale, giving rise to a national policy the Roosevelt administration came to call "conservation." Pinchot firmly believed that conservation would reshape human behavior; natural resources would be managed with the common goal of providing for the common good. "Conservation of natural resources is the key to the future," he advised, asserting that the principle of "the greatest good for the greatest number" (an echo of English philosopher Jeremy Bentham) was the only logical guide to decision-making regarding nature.[26]

Pinchot is often portrayed as the villain of the piece when the nation's environmental history is interpreted. Certainly he endured a stormy career, earning the wrath of John Muir, eventually making Roosevelt's presidential successor, William Howard Taft, angry enough to fire him. The real question is, just what was his legacy? There are two answers. The more focused derives from a consideration of the policies he strove to implement. Recall that by his own accounting, Pinchot was just "half-trained" in the science of forestry, a complicated and difficult field. Recall also that the science of ecology was still very much in its infancy—no one much understood what was happening in the forests, how the multitudinous plant and animal species functioning individually for their own survival somehow produce and maintain an ecosystem, a whole greater than the sum of the parts. Gifford Pinchot was determined to manage something he very dimly understood.

In 1900, Pinchot released his second edition of *A Primer of Forestry*, a two volume handbook summarizing his (and presumably the nation's) knowledge of trees, their life cycles, their needs, their enemies. Leafing through Part II, the recommended conservation strategies are illustrated in straightforward language. Simplistic language, mirroring the suggested techniques. Baldly put, Pinchot sought to displace much of the original forest cover—all those unprofitable trash trees—with regular plantings of the few lucrative species suitable to the climate, a farm of even-aged, even-spaced, single species stands, a squadron of trees ready to march to the sawmill when they reach their prime, before they wither from old age, become a home for owls and woodpeckers. Employing a managed forest of lodgepole pines as his example, Pinchot sketched the recommended approach.[27]

> Now let us suppose that this land was taken in hand by the Government when the lodgepole pine first came in, and that the lodgepole reaches it maturity at 80 years. If the Government forest officers had divided such a forest into eighty parts, and then cut the timber from one part each year, after a time they would have had eighty divisions, each covered with even-aged forest, but differing among themselves from 1 to 80 years. Every year one part would reach the age of 80 years and would be cut, and evidently the other seventy-nine parts would always be stocked with trees from 1 to 79 years old.[28]

No consideration of the greater vulnerability to disease, to windstorms. No thought of biological diversity. Little mention of a forest's function beyond providing marketable timber. Build those houses. *A Primer of Forestry* is a sobering book. Again, a little knowledge can have grim consequences.

Pinchot's larger legacy is his role as the apostle of conservation. He was never so much a scientist as a publicist, and he was very good at that. In the nick of time, too—at the rate the nation's forests were disappearing, it was no small thing to advocate a change in direction. As the Progressives sought to dampen the "go ahead" mentality in politics and the economy, so too did the environmental aspect of the movement work to blunt the rapacious consumption of natural resources. As such, conservation was one of the more successful expressions of the management impulse. And Gifford Pinchot stood at the head of the legion of managers.[29]

How fared the Upper Delaware Valley in this welter of conflicting ideas? Largely shorn of forest cover, the immediate answer could be pithy and brief: the damage was done. But in the longer term, was the valley to see rank upon rank of even-age trees, marching toward Gifford Pinchot's future? Or perhaps the "power and effectiveness," the "serene exaltation of sentiment" John Burroughs found hiking the mountains, boating the Pepacton? Or even a blind repetition of the devastating coarse-grained disturbance that occupied the Upper Delaware's population for much of the nineteenth century. The ultimate answer, strangely enough, was preservation, achieved by the impulse of conservation. And conservation, protected by natural preservation.

The warnings of impending resource crisis found attentive listeners in New York. The immediate evidence was too plain to ignore. Lumber output was falling dramatically as barren hillsides became all too obvious, and the demand for fresh water was reaching a crisis point, in New York City especially. The forests of the Catskills and the Upper Delaware were diminished to the vanishing point; timber stands in western New York were melting away. Woodcutters cast covetous eyes on the last virgin stands in the Adirondacks, where lumber firms and charcoal kilns already nibbled along the edges. Manhattan Island faced a yearly struggle to supply enough fresh water to meet the pace of demand. Something had to give. As early as 1871, the *New York Times* published an editorial advocating preservation of the Adirondacks, primarily as a place of peace, a refuge from a world industrializing too rapidly.[30]

A few subsets of conflicting constituencies paid attention. Franklin B. Hough, a physician living at the edge of the great Adirondack forest, had trained himself in the science of timber management, making himself the nation's first native-born forester. Hough was very much in favor of the state assuming control of the forests, putting an end to the "cut and run" tactics of the lumber barons. Place the trees under state control, enforce scientific management, encourage a sustained yield. No park—Hough was opposed to the very idea. Nothing was as "unproductive and worthless" as a "pleasuring ground" where valuable resources stood unused.[31]

At the opposite pole stood Verplanck Colvin, son of an Albany attorney and legislator who made a career of exploring, surveying, and mapping the Adirondacks. Colvin pinpointed the source of the Hudson River at Lake "Tear of the Clouds"—a name that characterizes the romantic approach he brought to his very scientific work. Enamored of the mountains as a last refuge of outdoor adventure in the Northeast, Colvin pushed determinedly, even manically, for their preservation from the wasters, modeling his vision after

California's Yosemite Park. Colvin's reports and journal descriptions made for popular reading among the myriads trapped in the cities.[32]

Another perspective came from sports enthusiasts—hunters and fishermen very much alarmed by the steady loss of wildlife habitat. The ongoing forest destruction had uncovered long-shaded streams (including the Upper Delaware), exposing the waters to the warmth of the sun, making the streams uninhabitable for cold-water trout. Fly-fishing was disappearing, along with hunting, as "game hogs" sought to shoot everything left in sight. Sportsmen wanted protections—game laws, game refuges—to secure a recreational pastime that pumped money into rural economies.[33]

New York responded by establishing a Commission of State Parks in 1872. There were no state parks as yet; the commission's task was to consider the purchase of lands in the Adirondacks for creation of a public park. Franklin Hough and Verplanck Colvin both served. The Commission's report, issued in 1873, perhaps reflected Hough's point of view more directly, condemning the "cut and get out" practices, emphasizing the necessity of watershed protection. If New York was going to establish a park, it would be for utilitarian reasons.[34]

In the subsequent push for the park, water supply proved the galvanizing issue. New York was very sensitive about water, for two compelling reasons. The first, obviously, was New York City, where engineers had begun reaching beyond Manhattan's boundaries to find palatable water as early as early as 1837. The second consideration was the Erie Canal, the artificial waterway that had made New York the arbiter of the nation's economy. Though in many ways outmoded by the growth of the railroads, business leaders saw the canal still as a critical component of the economy, an alternative source of transportation that forced the railroads to keep their fares reasonably honest. Losing the canal would be surrender to a famously corrupt band of monopoly trusts.[35]

Beginning with George Perkins Marsh, discussion centered on the role of forests in securing a steady source of water. Verplanck Colvin described the Adirondacks as a great "hanging sponge"—the trees absorbing rainfall, holding water in the vast root network, allowing a gentle transpiration that released water into streams slowly and gradually, insuring a steady supply. Colvin was right; modern studies demonstrate that in a single summer, one hectare of forest transpires fifty tons of water. John Burroughs understood the function as well, noting in "Pepacton" that "There is one way, at least, in which the denuding the country of its forests has lessened the rainfall: in certain conditions of the atmosphere every tree is a great condenser of moisture; ... little showers are generated in their branches, and in the aggregate the amount of water precipitated in this way is considerable." Gifford Pinchot's *Primer of Forestry* would also acknowledge the role of forests in maintaining a water supply, though he left unclear the question whether a managed tree farm would serve the same function.

Forests were thought to generate anywhere from five to thirty inches of rain each year. With the trees gone, the danger of catastrophic flood increased dramatically (a deluge struck the Catskills in 1869), and conversely, so did the threat of wildfires. All while the Erie Canal went dry and Manhattan died of thirst.[36]

Manhattan pushed hardest. Support for the purchases envisioned by the State Park Commission came largely from New York City, where newspaper editorials, government studies, and popular rallies gave steady voice to the issue. Most New Yorkers firmly believed that the City's future depended on the health of the Hudson River, at that point the most obvious source of future water supply—despite potential problems with saltwater contamination, water pressure, and mounting industrial pollution. Opponents of the park idea pointed to the State's dwindling forests, the need for a continued lumber supply. Locking up the forests was not the answer. There was also the matter of dispersing state moneys to purchase lands for any public park. This was America; few concepts were more sacred than private property and the right to profit from the resources thereof. The government's job was to protect private property, not spend money to acquire some.[37]

In New York, the principle came to a test at Niagara Falls, one of the world's most spectacular places. Fenced off as private property, the Falls in the nineteenth century suffered from the usual mix of progress, greed, and really bad taste. Water power of that order was an open invitation to industry; turbines to harness the energy obscured views of the Falls almost completely. To catch even a glimpse, the visitor had to pay some private landowner who generally ran some tawdry carnival on the side, wanting more than anything to separate the tourist from his money. In 1869, Frederick Law Olmsted launched a campaign to make the Falls a public Park. Frederick Church, the Hudson River painter who had captured the cataract most eloquently, joined the crusade in 1877. The State Legislature passed a bill authorizing funds to purchase the lands in 1882, only to see the law vetoed by a private property–concerned governor. Two years later, the new governor, Grover Cleveland, signed. The State spent 1.5 million dollars to buy forty different parcels from twenty-five owners, razing 150 buildings. Olmsted and Calvert Vaux were commissioned to design a public park.[38]

So there was a precedent for landscape preservation in New York. Concerns over the health of the Hudson River, the Erie Canal, the ever-rising water consumption in Manhattan were fed by widespread drought in 1883. Just maybe all those disappeared trees were affecting rainfall. A new forest commission headed by Charles S. Sargent, forester at Harvard, recommended creation of a forest reserve, along with a law prohibiting sale or lease of state-owned lands in designated counties. In 1885, the State Legislature acted, establishing two reserves: 681,000 acres in the Adirondacks, 34,000 acres in Greene, Ulster, and Sullivan Counties: the Catskills. The first unintentional step toward protecting the Upper Delaware watershed.[39]

The political form of logrolling got the Catskills included. Tanners and lumbermen had pretty much worsted the region by 1885; there was very little forest to protect. When lumber companies in Ulster County skipped town without paying property taxes, local officials found themselves stuck with shorn, nearly worthless lands. (Forested lands generally sold for about a dollar an acre; cut-over, desiccated acres, unsuited for farming, brought perhaps a nickel.) In return for votes supporting the Adirondack Preserve, Ulster County legislators got the Catskill lands included. The following year, meeting concerns over lost property tax revenue, the legislature passed a law requiring the state to pay taxes to local governments like any other landowner. That made the reserves a much more palatable proposition.[40]

The State created a three-member Forest Commission to supervise operation of the reserves—an open invitation to chicanery. One of three appointed members proved to be a prominent lumberman, who naturally viewed the reserve as little more than a source of managed timber sales. Poorly protected, outright timber theft on the state lands quickly became a racket. More trees disappeared. Downstate, worries over the scarcely adequate water supply continued to grow.[41]

A far more ironclad solution to the problem emerged in 1894, when delegates met in New York City to revise the State's antiquated constitution. An amendment introduced by New York City attorney David McClure would constitutionally prohibit sale of preserve lands or the timber thereon. Enshrined in the new constitution approved by the State's voters, the amendment declared the reserves "shall be forever kept as wild forest lands." The effort to conserve timber and water resources culminated in the preservation of a vast forest wilderness. New York had created the first constitutionally protected wilderness in the nation. Not that anyone thought the provision would last too long. Politicians saw the amendment as a stopgap maneuver, a measure to provide protection for the water supply until some more workable solution could be hammered out. Twenty years maybe.[42]

But all those John Burroughs essays, along with John Muir's fulminations, Henry Thoreau's resurgence in popularity, and countless other influences reaching back to New York City before the Civil War, had an impact. New York's voters approved the amendment, and they exhibited a determination to get out and enjoy what their state had so torturously created. Yes, the reserves protected the watershed, saved the canal, preserved the forests, slowed erosion, guaranteed fresh water, but they also provided opportunities to see and enjoy the nature settings Burroughs brought to life in his books.

As the legacy of Franklin Hough twisted in anguish, his forest reserves, intended as managed landscapes, had somehow become parks—scenes of "unproductive and worthless" recreation. In protecting the Catskills, New Yorkers had opted for the "precipitous heights Irving sent Rip Van Winkle trudging with the burden imposed upon him by Hendrick Hudson's crew." The description, from a 1902 essay demanding greater funding for the parks, went on to note "Among these fastenesses, Cooper sent roaming Natty Bumppo, who so truly said 'None know how often the hand of God is seen in the wilderness but them that rove it.'" Irving and Cooper. The essay further cited the visions of Cole, Church, Durand, Gifford. In the midst of a prolonged discussion of the proper approach to resource conservation, advocates thought to recall voices that perceived something more in the mountains.[43]

The work was far from finished. The constitutional provision that the reserves remain "forever wild" had to be considered with a wry face, in the Catskills especially. Thoroughly mauled by bark peelers and lumbermen, dotted with marginal farms and steeply sloping pastures, bereft of key animal species such as deer, beaver, wolves, and cougar, the Catskills were not very wild at all. What the protections achieved was to create an opportunity for natural processes to reclaim the park with a minimum of human interference—to grow wild once more. Overcoming some reluctance to expend funds to acquire private lands within the reserve's boundaries, the legislature in 1904 established the Catskill State Park, drawing a "blue line" to demarcate the preserve's intended boundaries, now expanded to 576,120 acres, including much of the Delaware's East (Pepacton) Branch, as well as the mountain streams feeding the river—the first effort to protect any portion of the Delaware watershed. The park enclosed both public and private lands, making private property owners (who held the preponderance of the acreage) subject to regulations intended to encourage varying degrees of "wildness." Most important were rules restricting the use of fire to maintain farmlands.[44]

At least a few components of the natural world lost to progress and profit returned to the Upper Delaware region as the park took shape, a new century unfolded. The beaver were restored, and the deer, and even a lot of trees—all by human intervention.

In *The Last of the Mohicans*, James Fenimore Cooper's characters encounter a brook once managed by beaver, the animals gone almost a century by the time of the French and Indian War. "Everywhere along its banks were the mouldering relics of dead trees, in all stages of decay ... like the memorials of a former and long-departed generation." The beaver, hunted to vanishing in New York by Indians in need of European technologies, returned beginning in 1904, transplanted from Ontario by Harry V. Radford, a conservationist and sportsman. Radford began his campaign by persuading the

State Legislature to outlaw all forms of beaver trapping. With the Adirondacks safe for beaver, Radford introduced twenty onto mountain streams. By 1915, there were fifteen thousand opportunist rodents building dams within the park, enough to become a nuisance. Officials began transplanting the animals to recovering forest lands to the south. Throughout the state, populations rose. Beaver returned to the reaches of the Upper Delaware.[45]

Deer survived still in the Adirondacks, barely. Infamous "game hogs" bagged far too many, and the "sport" hunting of deer with packs of dogs remained popular and deadly. An effort to outlaw deer-hounding failed in 1889, but passed eight years later when people wrote from all over the State in support of an anti-hounding bill. Elbert Hubbard, the first to write a biography of John Burroughs, attributed the change of heart to the naturalist's works, popular reading for adults and schoolchildren alike. With hounding outlawed, the Adirondack population stabilized and began to grow. Migrating southward, deer re-inhabited much of the State, aided by the Forest Commission. Foresters in 1887 began rounding up the very few deer to be found in the Catskills, protecting them in a fenced one hundred acre deer park. In eight years, the park count mounted to ninety-five deer. The foresters released this population into the mountains, continuing the program for years afterward. With human hunters their only predators, the deer did very well.[46]

Soon there were new forests for the deer to inhabit. Fifty years after the lumber and tanning industries faltered, forest succession renewed the woodlands on steeper slopes, abandoned pasture and croplands. Not the mature forests of the past—full restoration would require two centuries at least—but a woods, comprised largely of fast-growing opportunists: birch and such. Human intervention encouraged the process. In 1931, New York Governor Franklin D. Roosevelt saw passage of the Hewitt Act, enabling the state to purchase lands lying outside Adirondack and Catskill Park blue lines but inside forest reserve counties. With the Great Depression, a lot of acreage came available, especially marginal farmland abandoned for taxes. Over the next ten years, the State bought up more than 400,000 acres, planting trees to return the land to forest. Conifers were the trees of choice: Norway spruce, white spruce, white pines, which explains a lot of even age evergreen stands gracing modern slopes and hilltops. State Forests and Wild Forest lands line much of the valleys on both the East and West Branch of the Delaware, largely planted out of camps established by the Civilian Conservation Corps, a relief force created during Roosevelt's first hundred days as president. The CCC established camps along the Upper Delaware at Deposit, Port Jervis, Margaretville, and Narrowsburg, along with several locations in the Catskill Park.[47]

So a measure of wild nature returned to the Upper Delaware region.

Beaver were restored, deer wandered back, trees began to grow. No wolves, no cougar, disturbingly few hemlocks; the picture remained far removed from what greeted the first Europeans to venture upriver back in the Seventeenth Century. (A few wolves might have kept the deer population from running amuck, but that was not about to happen. Not in dairy country.) What with blue lines, abandoned farms, returned animals, absent carnivores, reforested slopes, a new ecology was evolving in the Upper Delaware, a haphazard splicing of natural succession and intervention fit to redefined human wants. All that was necessary was to figure out what that ecology was, how the processes operated, what was desirable, what was going to happen despite human intentions. Human intent grew still more complicated in the twentieth century, when New York City added one more large component to the developing mosaic.

New York, historically beset with water woes, had always manifested a large thirst and a curious reluctance to introduce practical water-saving measures. Officials pointed with pride to the extraordinarily high level of per capita consumption, maintaining the figures demonstrated the city's cleanliness. In 1898, Manhattan entered into a union with Brooklyn, Staten Island, Queens, and the Bronx to create the five boroughs of Greater New York. The union made water supply more imperative than ever; Brooklyn had long fought a losing battle to provide adequate water.[48]

The quest for new sources intensified a long-standing conflict between city residents and rural neighbors. Initial struggles pitted the City against Westchester County, where the inhabitants severely resented New York tapping into their streams. This particular discord was resolved when New York agreed to include the more populated portions of Westchester in the City's system, a measure that bought peace, if only for a time. The Westchester streams were small; a growing City was going to require a much more plentiful supply.

At first glance, the Hudson was the obvious choice, and the prime impetus behind the ruckus that created the Adirondack and Catskill Parks. But the Hudson for nearly a century had been a dumping stream for much of America's first industrial wastes; unidentifiable pools of mucky black substances kept appearing. And the lower reaches of the river were really a saline estuary—depending on season, tide, and volume, a considerable portion of the water was salt. And the Hudson was pretty much level with Manhattan; feeding Hudson water into the system would require a hugely expensive system of pumps. Surely there were more attractive solutions.[49]

The State Legislature, frequently at odds with the City (that urban-rural thing), in 1895 awarded the rights to water flowing out of the Catskills to Ramapo, a private company looking to make a killing. Ten years later, when the City's Board of Water Supply firmly decided they needed and wanted that water, they set to work, maneuvering Ramapo out of their socks, persuading the legislature to create a regulatory body to facilitate state approval of city projects. The State Water Supply Commission, concluding that a well-watered New York was an urgent necessity in the better interests of the State, approved construction of a reservoir on the eastern slope of the Catskills.[50]

City officials painted word images of the Catskills as a wilderness with very few residents, justifying some high-handed decision making. Backed by the State Water Supply Commission, the City simply exercised the right of eminent domain to condemn rural properties, providing adequate or inadequate compensation, depending on who you asked. Rural sentiments were generally steamrolled. The first reservoir construction project initiated a pattern that was to be replicated five times in the next half century.

Beginning work in 1907, city engineers supervised a small army of workers who dammed Esopus Creek (a tributary of the Hudson) twelve miles west of Kingston, shaping the surrounding landscape to create the Ashokan Reservoir over a period of seven years. The molding was very thorough; workers removed tree stumps, orchards, fences, graves, houses, farms, entire villages. Above the water line, the City retained what forest existed and planted more trees, surrounding the artificial lake with a forest buffer covering thousands of acres. The completed Ashokan looked for all the world like a mountain lake, surrounded by wilderness. Picture postcards celebrated the new natural beauty. The City's Board of Water supply policed the area, enforcing regulations severely limiting hunting, hiking, boating, and farming, all in the name of protecting this quasi-natural purity. A Catskill Aqueduct carried the impounded water to New York, enabling the city to supply the needs of a population grown to 4,766,883.[51]

It was not enough. By the time the Ashokan began feeding water into the system, Board of Water Supply officials were computing how soon demand would exceed this new supply. After once again discussing and dismissing the Hudson River as a source, damming Schoharie Creek at Gilboa to feed the Ashokan, the City sought new resources westward, the other side of the Catskills, where the Delaware River rose. By 1922, New York was seriously considering tapping into the Delaware drainage, preferring such upland sources. No pumping, no salt, no pollution. Clean, rural water.

The State Water Supply Commission saw no problems with this fresh idea, but that counted for little in the face of the complications the Delaware posed. John Burroughs may have thought of the Delaware as "one of our minor rivers"; the fact was that the system poured through four states, becoming increasingly integral to local economies as the water surged southward. Philadelphia, another metropolis with large water demands, stood astride the Delaware, while several communities in New Jersey looked to the river. New York City's planning led to the formation of a three-state commission to decide how best to share the water. Friendly, but not terribly productive. When New York's state legislature approved a plan to build reservoirs on the Upper Delaware, New Jersey sued in Federal Court.[52]

The Supreme Court soon found themselves facing a knotty if not unparalleled set of questions. New York City wanted to build their dam on the East (Pepacton) Branch of the Delaware, wholly within the boundaries of New York State—the very same river John Burroughs explored in the late 1870s. Did New York have a legal right to claim the water? Would New Jersey be materially injured by a reduced Delaware flow? Would the decrease in volume injure the highly lucrative recreational qualities of the river? Would less water increase the dangers of pollution? Pennsylvania, representing the interests of Philadelphia, entered the case as an intervenor. The Commonwealth was in the process of building its own dam to intercept water entering the Upper Delaware, in 1924 granting permission to the Pennsylvania Power and Light Company to impound the waters of Lackawaxen Creek on the border of Wayne and Pike Counties. Ousting roughly one hundred landowners from the vicinity of Wilsonville at the flat rate of twenty dollars an acre, the Company employed 2,700 laborers to raze most of the buildings and construct a dam to provide flood control and cheap hydroelectric power. The resulting Lake Wallenpaupack, thirteen miles long (the third-largest lake in Pennsylvania), took seven months to fill in 1926. New Jersey had no issue with this project. Pennsylvania Power and Light just wanted the flow to turn giant turbines—no one intended to drink the water.

A similar but more complicated hydroelectric project took shape across the river at much the same time. Orange and Rockland Utilities, one of several small power companies to appear in upstate New York in the early twentieth century, began building dams on the Mongaup River in 1923. There were five by the time they finished in 1937, creating three power stations and five small lakes: Cliff Lake, Swinging Bridge Reservoir, Toronto Reservoir, Mongaup Falls Reservoir, and the Rio Reservoir, the largest inundating just nine hundred acres. Working with the succession of power companies operating the site, New York's Department of Conservation has since established a Wildlife Management Area encompassing nearly twelve thousand acres. The State owns a little more than half; conservation easements make up the rest. Again, no one downstream much objected to this "wise use"; the water would reach Delaware Bay eventually. The issue was the water to be rerouted to New York, disappearing forever from the system.

Borrowing a page from Western battles over the Colorado River, the Court appointed a "special master" to consider and arbitrate the dispute among the States. In 1931, the Justices approved the plan the master negotiated. New York would get their water, though not as much as they asked. Timed releases from the reservoir would ensure steady volumes downstream.

And New York would build a sewage plant at Port Jervis, cleansing the water before the stream entered New Jersey.[53]

The decision came as the Great Depression tightened grip on the nation's purse strings. Despite the ever-increasing dangers of shortage, New York was unable to begin construction on the Pepacton Branch until after World War II. The project unfolded to much the same pattern as the east side of the Catskills—the eminent domain condemnations, the drowning of four small towns, the massive inconvenience visited on the remaining residents, the restrictive regulations, the local resentment. The rural microcosm Burroughs captured so delightedly in his "Pepacton" essay was gone, replaced by an artificial lake with a surrounding buffer of planted forests, overlooked by high, reforested hills. The Pepacton became the largest of the City's reservoirs. As one disgusted resident expressed the anger, "Distant villages and valleys are ravaged by the blades of bulldozers so that careless and wasteful New Yorkers can let their leaky taps run." The reservoir filled in 1956. A tunnel beneath the mountains connected the artificial lake to a Roundout River Reservoir further south, completed in 1951.

Following another negotiated settlement with New Jersey, New York City began construction on one last reservoir, this time damming the West Branch of the Delaware, drowning the village of Cannonsville, engendering bitterness still felt. Completed in 1964, the Cannonsville Reservoir, the largest of all, lies outside the Catskill Park, in a more populated region dotted with the farms John Burroughs loved. In fact, dairy farms accounted for a full twenty percent of land use, inevitably meaning a large degree of runoff pollution, no matter how many regulations the City imposed. Waste water treatment plants quickly became a necessity, and still the water quality suffers from large algae blooms, the product of far too much nutrient in the reservoir. Not every mountain stream runs clear and sparkling toward nature's destiny. Not in modern times, anyway.[54]

Both the Ashokan and the Pepacton Reservoirs lie within the boundaries of the Catskill State Park, an entity with its own set of restrictions and regulations, created in the name of resource conservation, functioning as a preserve of at least somewhat wild nature, where visitors can breathe a little of the atmosphere so inspiring to Cooper, Cole, Bryant. Local residents tend to believe that the park was created to protect the reservoirs, which is technically untrue (the reservoirs were not yet planned); though in a larger sense the sentiment is transcendently correct. The state justified creation of the parks as a means to protect the watersheds. But the parks quickly assumed a larger significance, becoming in the public eye havens of wilderness, refuges for the spirit. The Catskill Park is a compromised wilderness, a crazy quilt of nature reconstructed, returned to the wild, made artificial and utilitarian all at once. Preservation and conservation co-exist uneasily in the Catskills. John Muir would be appalled; John Burroughs bemused. Burroughs was always more taken with nature compromised—the farm house in the wood, the woodcutter's path into the mountain. But most of all, the spirit of Gifford Pinchot is alive and well in the Catskill Mountains. Dams impounding water in the midst of a park designated "forever wild." Natural resources, scientifically managed (sort of). Just as the author of conservation prescribed—and achieved—out west for Yosemite. Though Gifford Pinchot had no direct influence in the making of the modern Catskill Park, his hand, his vision predominates. The greatest good for the greatest number. Defining the concept of "good" remains the problem.[55]

EIGHT

A Forest for
the Modern World

Whatever philosopher first asserted that history repeats itself needed turning out of high school history class. The world is far too complicated for that. Tracking the history of something so plain and obvious as a woodland evinces the pattern of unceasing change. An individual cannot hike the same forest twice, no more than step into the same river. Despite all the "laws of history" pontificated down through the long years, there is just one that matters: change is constant, never ending. Deciding whether a forest even exists outside the human mind just adds to the complication.

More often than not, change is subtle yet perceptible, once you know how to look. Every season brings a challenge; each and every tree responds to the limits of the species. Animal life, from the smallest micro-organism to the largest bears, helps or hurts depending on behavior, population dynamics and opportunity. Shifting weather and climate patterns alter the water table; windstorms open the canopy, beckoning perhaps different species. Fire or the lack of fire will affect the tenor of the reshaping. A forest may appear more or less the same year after year, but even a protected wood, left emphatically to nature's devices, alters continually.

Sometimes the change is drastic, a disturbance of surpassing impact—a glacier, a hurricane, a clear-cut such as took place in the Upper Delaware in the nineteenth century. The old forest is vanished forever. If conditions permit, renewed woodland will establish in the open spaces, but never the same forest. For two reasons. The first lies in the very nature of the unaided reforestation process. The general conditions may seem much the same—the climate, the topography, the soil—but the environment will be subject to the contingent but random actions of myriad plant and animal species. No two patterns of reforestation will be precisely the same. The second reason is the unalterable effect of human decision-making, past and present. For better and for worse, people are intertwined in the very environment of the

Earth, discouraging or removing plants and animals, nourishing others. Nature can only work with the materials at hand. People unavoidably influence the menu.

In the early decades of the twentieth century, Frederick Clements strenuously maintained that nature behaved as a kind of super-organism, a community of plants and animals specifically and precisely adapted to a given environment. Left alone, an altered vegetation community would restore itself, succeeding through a series of definable stages until climax arrived, a replica of the original vegetation flourishing in place. Clements did allow that "even the most stable association is never in complete equilibrium, nor is it free from disturbed areas in which secondary succession is evident." But in his vision, a disturbance was no more than a temporary bump on the path to a predictable equilibrium—in the Upper Delaware, the restoration of the white pine-hemlock-hardwood community, with greater numbers of hardwoods the farther south the forest extended. Clements could not possibly have been more mistaken, again for two reasons. Nature itself does not adhere to the precise patterns he envisioned; the only real constant is variation. More importantly, Clements steadfastly refused to acknowledge the presence of the human factor in the environment; people, he argued, could only screw up the otherwise inevitable pattern of natural succession. But people are everywhere, making decisions—often contradictory decisions—regarding the future of a forest's components, weakening, sometimes strengthening, always disturbing whatever ecosystem may exist. Nowhere is this more true than the Upper Delaware Valley, where an absolute cacophony of voices attempt to guide a forest's future.[1]

Environmental protection is not for those in search of a simple life. A mere roll call of the agencies involved in the valley in the twenty-first century is a time-consuming, taxing proposition.

Probably the entity to first recall is New York State's Catskill Forest and Park, established in 1885, the pioneer effort to afford protection to small portions of the watershed. Hypothetically created to protect some of the forests between the Hudson River and the Delaware, the designation came far too late; the legislation safeguarded woodlands that no longer existed. The real task of the park was to secure what was left of the landscape, try to encourage the restoration of some sort of second (or third) growth woodland. The Park's original boundaries included just the uppermost eastern streams feeding the Delaware watershed; most of the river system remained unshielded. This changed a bit in 1957, when the State Legislature enlarged the Park's western boundaries to include more of Delaware and Sullivan Counties. The new boundary extended some form of environmental protection down the Delaware's East Branch past the Pepacton Reservoir, leaving much of the West Branch to the tender mercies of New York City's Water Board.[2]

Extending the Park boundaries begged the problem of delineating how best to actually preserve the forests inside the park boundaries, much less encourage their growth. In this imperfect world, it is the nature of park administration to be pulled in competing directions: the desire to build and sustain the wilderness setting on the one hand, the urge to provide proper recreation opportunities for an increasing numbers of visitors on the other. The fact that fifty-nine percent of the lands within the park boundaries remain private property was (and is) a challenging complication. Part of the problem is making the discussion something other than a bureaucratic outline; the rest is not making the list too much a travelogue.

Examining the problem carefully in 1975, a Temporary Commission to Study the Catskills recommended authorities adopt a land classification system to mitigate the conflicting goals. All the properties managed by the Park should be evaluated and classified, designated according to best use. Stringent regulation for more fragile wilderness areas; more open policies for lands tough enough to stand a steady stream of hikers, bicyclists, hunters, photographers, historians, whatever. It took ten years, but the Park did follow the suggestion, organizing their lands into five categories: wilderness, wild forest, primitive bicycle corridor, intensive use, and administrative. In so far as encouraging the forest recovery is concerned, the first two categories are the important ones.[3]

The wilderness areas, rigorously protected, lie generally among the Catskill Mountain Peaks; none are designated along the East Branch or major Delaware tributaries. What do exist are six Wild Forest Areas, defined (as only an advanced bureaucracy can explain) as

> Forest Preserve land whose character as a natural plant and animal community receives the same degree of protection under Article XIV of the Constitution as in areas classified as wilderness, but which differs from wilderness in that generally: The physical characteristics of wild forest areas are capable of withstanding higher levels of recreational use; Wild forest areas convey less of a sense of remoteness and provide fewer outstanding opportunities for solitude for visitors, and therefore; Wild forest Areas are managed to provide opportunities for a greater variety of recreational activities and a higher intensity of recreational use.

A spectacular sentence, most specific and inherently vague at once, suggesting just how complicated a stab at defining environmental preservation can be.[4]

Located in the northern reaches of the Delaware watershed, the six Wild Forest Areas managed by the Park are places to hike, fish, watch birds, located in the high hills overlooking the Pepacton (East Branch) Valley. These are hills lined with trees, encouraged in large part by the efforts of the Civilian Conservation Corps back in the 1930s. A small portion of the Upper Delaware drainage, secured by the Catskill Forest mandate, is returned to woodland.[5]

Extensive farm abandonment throughout New York in the twentieth century created more opportunities for forest repair. Rambling the woods near old country roads, hikers today will often encounter old stone walls among young trees, mute testimony to the farm boundaries of a century past. Nature has taken possession; wind and animals have reclaimed the land for forest. Failure to pay property taxes made these farms the property of county governments. Given the opportunity, the counties in turn gladly turned such lands over to the State. Woven into a series of small parks and designated areas dotting less populous regions, New York has created a web of small preservation units, each with specific purpose.

There are State Forests. Though much of the land lining the Upper Delaware remains in private hands, at least eleven State Forests secure small woodlands along reaches of the river and the Branches. Tomanex State Park, along the East Branch in the Town of Hancock, encompasses nine thousand acres, one of the largest. Steam Mill, on the West Branch overlooking the Cannonsville Reservoir, amounts to fifty-six hundred acres. The rest are smaller. Each of these State Forests tries to appeal to a different kind of enthusiast. If one is great for fishing, another beckons the bird watcher, a third the long-range hiker. Different emphases limit the attraction to the visitors, reducing use, preserving something of the wilds.[6]

Still different designations dot the map. In the Upper Delaware, one "Multiple Use Site" exists, a thousand acres set aside at Hickock Brook in Sullivan County. As the name suggests, Multiple Use means open to a considerable variety of recreation enthusiasts. Not the place to go for a quiet contemplation of nature's beauty. More preferable might be the small designated "Forest Preserves" established on remote hilltops, afforded the same protections as the Catskill Park. More accessible are "Wildlife Management Areas." There is Bear Spring Mountain in Delaware County for one, and the twelve thousand acres set aside in Sullivan County's Mongaup Valley, where bald eagles nest and beavers build dams. (As good a place as any to gauge whether the beaver are thinking things out.)[7]

If you are trying to keep track, that makes a total of five different but interconnected designations aimed at natural preservation (and outdoor recreation) administered by the State of New York. We are barely begun.

Pennsylvania has a system, too, although the Commonwealth was a little more tardy in their efforts to mend the devastation wrought by the tanners and the lumbermen. Doctor Joseph Trimble Rothrock, a physician with an accompanying degree in botany, was the voice behind the State's conservation efforts, using his position as head of the Pennsylvania Forestry Association to advocate forest protections. Appointed the State's first Commissioner of Forestry in 1896, Rothrock began purchasing cutover properties in 1897 with the intention of establishing a park system. Subsequent administrations followed his lead, not least one Gifford Pinchot, governor of Pennsylvania from

1922 through 1927. Maurice K. Goddard, first director of the Pennsylvania Department of Environmental Resources, organized in 1971, had earlier set a goal of establishing parks within twenty-five miles of every citizen. Glancing at a map, the system seems to come mighty close.[8]

No state parks occur in Pennsylvania on the scale of the Catskills or the Adirondacks. The Federal Government has established two very large preserves, the Allegheny National Forest in western Pennsylvania, and the Erie National Wildlife Preserve, farther west still. The State has made due with a considerable number of much smaller preserves, amounting to an impressive 283,000 acres. A small few of these reserves are located along the Upper Delaware, scene of so much "improvement" in the nineteenth century. As in New York, preservation areas in Wayne and Pike County are small, and administered under a variety of labels according to purpose.

Of the twenty State Forests in Pennsylvania, just one, the Delaware State Forest (83,519 acres) may be found on the Upper Delaware, in Pike County, not far from the defined end of the valley. Not far away is the Buckhorn Natural Area, 559 acres devoted to preservation of a high mountain swamp and an abandoned bluestone quarry. Far more prevalent are the State Game Lands strung along the river—six of them, all designated by stark numbers rather than names. The stated purpose of the reserves is just as unvarnished: these are "public hunting grounds." A portion of State Game Land 209 is further reserved and given a name, the Stairway Lake Wild Area, intended to preserve the "wild character" of a small part of the forest in Wayne County. "Managed by nature," is the articulated intention for this bit.[9]

That's four kinds of reserves operated by the State of Pennsylvania, all administered by the Pennsylvania Department of Conservation. The stated purpose is to "promote wildlife reproduction and survival." The hunting lobby proved very influential in shaping environmental protection for the Commonwealth. Not that this was this unusual. Aldo Leopold, regarded as one of the most articulate voices in support of environmental conservation, constructed his "land ethic" philosophy out of a desire to secure wild lands for continued hunting and fishing.[10]

Apart from the two states, another more or less "local" agency not to be forgotten is New York City's Water Board, master of the reservoirs damming both Branches of the Delaware above Hancock, New York—not least because so much of the river's quality derives from those reservoirs. The City's presence in rural areas a hundred miles removed from Manhattan has proven less than smooth. Apart from engendering massive local resentment stemming from drowned villages and ousted farm families at the start, subsequent management of the impounded water was short-sighted and environmentally irresponsible. Focused on the health of the reservoirs, the purity of the water contained, the obligation to maintain enough of a flow downstream to satisfy the lower states, city officials released waters from the dams at sporadic intervals, entirely overlooking any and all ecological consequences. The negligence very nearly ruined the angling on one of the finest fly-fishing streams in the Northeast. Released waters flowed downstream from the bottoms of the reservoirs, icy cold. The abrupt drop in water temperature—as much as twenty degrees—was more than several fish species could withstand; bass especially suffered. Accompanying silt clogged streams, destroying trout nesting places. People suffered as well. Dense fogs blighted summer days. No one could swim in water that cold. Supplying drinking water to New York City, the Water Board was in the process of ruining one of the very few reasons outsiders ever visited the Upper Delaware.[11]

Frustration and anger grew steadily over a quarter-century. Ecological consciousness permeated society by the 1970s—Earth Day and all that; concerned local citizenry allied with an increasingly anxious State government to force the City to pay attention. In 1976, the New York Legislature passed the State Environmental Quality Review Act, a law which, among other things, required the City to take responsibility for the upstate environments they so dramatically influenced. A first step was a more conscientious approach to the water releases—better timed and more often, stabilizing water temperatures. The bass were gone for good, but the trout fishery recovered. Fly fishers came back.[12]

That was a beginning. Friction not much abated, the City continued to view locals as threats to their water supply; the locals saw the City as greedy usurpers, grasping for complete control of the countryside. With the State government no longer so sympathetic to the City's concerns, Metropolitan and local governments hammered out a Watershed Memorandum of Agreement in 1995, establishing the foundation for a more cooperative partnership. Delaware County residents agreed to take a more active role in discouraging water pollution, farm runoff especially; New York City promised to pay the full costs of any pollution mitigation projects. Most importantly, the City agreed to discontinue exercise of the right of eminent domain to obtain property surrounding the reservoirs. Any future purchases would come only if the owner freely agreed to sell; the City would have to pay full market value. Local residents had control over their own real estate once more. By this time, New York City owned fifty-eight thousand acres of land surrounding five reservoirs; much of it in the Delaware watershed. Looking to the future of the river environment, both New York City and the citizens of Delaware County would bear considerable responsibility.[13]

Yet another voice maintains a tiny presence on the West Branch. The Nature Conservancy, the private organization devoted to environmental protection through purchase of sensitive landscapes, manages a single small tract in the Upper Delaware: the West Branch Preserve, four hundred forty-six acres on a ridge located between Hamden and Walton. Originally a farm abandoned as long ago as 1830, the property shelters exceedingly rare first growth stands of hemlock, white pine, red maple, and black cherry. A physician donated the land in 1973; the Conservancy looks after two hiking trails running through the forest. A severe windstorm in 2003 uprooted several old trees—not even protected old growth will last forever.[14]

The dams at Cannonsville and Pepacton were not the only ones impounding water in the Upper Delaware system. The Pennsylvania Power and Light Company dam on the Lackawaxen River has been turning hydroelectric turbines to light Pennsylvania since 1926. On the other side of the Delaware, the concerted effort over ten years on the Mongaup River wrought no fewer than five reservoirs and three hydroelectric stations, properties of one of the apparently innumerable small power companies since consolidated across southern New York. Two stations operate still. Eagle Creek Renewable Energy purchased the complex from a power conglomerate called NY-Gen, LLC in 2012, enlarging a renewable energy system spread across seven states and parts of Canada. New York's Department of Conservation maintains the Mongaup Valley Wildlife Management Area in cooperation with the power company, a series of artificial lakes made home to the beaver and the eagles. A trade-off appropriate to modern times.[15]

Living in an ever more electrified world, not all the approaches will be so benign. In 2007, a proposal floated to run a power transmission line the length of the corridor, severely compromising whatever of nature time has restored. Though the plan was nixed, even the suggestion illustrates the forces in wait, fully prepared to jeopardize the rural character of the countryside to make the Upper Delaware speak money once again. Energy demands are endless. The valley lies astride the Marcellus Shale, site of long coveted natural gas reserves eyed by frackers with greedy eyes. Corporate reach is constant; environmental preservation can never sleep.[16]

Always the watershed seemed to need more dams. Yet another government entity went to work in the late 1950s, about the time the Cannonsville Reservoir neared completion. The United States Army Corps of Engineers, an outfit with what might be described as a different perspective on the issue of environmental responsibility, decided that the Lackawaxen River, despite the huge Lake Wallenpaupak reservoir, was a flooding danger. The consequence was two more dams. Dyberry Creek, emptying into the Lackawaxen above Wallenpaupack, saw construction of the General Edwin Jadwin Dam, built in 1959. The associated lake bed is generally dry, a standing bet against potential flooding. The second act, completed in 1960, created the two-hundred-ninety acre Prompton Lake Reservoir; Pennsylvania established a State Park to go along.[17]

All told, these various smaller dams add two private power companies and a massive Federal agency to the growing list of players conditioning the health of the Upper Delaware. All must release waters from time to time; the waters will necessarily be cold. Careful monitoring, largely unconsidered when the dams first appeared, is critical to the valley's ecological health. A great many voices must concern themselves in much more than their own parochial concerns to maintain a river's "natural" rhythms. The more people intervene in their own self-serving ways, the more delicate the system becomes.

The Delaware is a large and long-flowing river, important to a lot of folks in a great many fashions. Continued squabbles over Delaware waters— which states had rights to what percentage of the supply, who was responsible for cleanup of the unholy pollution problems besetting the lower stretches of the river—gave rise to another, altogether new form of management. Weary of the ongoing struggles, the Federal Government in 1961 brokered the for-mation of the Delaware River Basin Commission, intended to foster reason-able cooperation among the four States bordering the river. Congress and the legislatures of the four states—New York, Pennsylvania, New Jersey, and Delaware—adopted agreeing legislation to create the unique interstate reg-ulatory body. The commission has a membership of five: the four state gov-ernors, together with the Division Engineer, North Atlantic Division, U.S. Army Corps of Engineers, who represents the Federal Government. Each member has one vote. Now the states could argue face to face, with a military general to referee. Majority rule decides most issues, although a declaration of drought or any apportionment of cash requires unanimity.[18]

This is a commission with a lot to do. The Delaware is the longest river in the Northeast; water has become an increasingly precious commodity as populations grow and waste problems multiply. The Basin Commission was forced to confront very serious issues from the outset; ungoverned manufac-turing pollution during World War II left the waters around Philadelphia "an open sewer," while a severe drought threatened water supplies in 1965. The Commission instituted several programs, beginning with a series of regula-tions establishing the most stringent water quality standards in the country. Results proved encouraging; shad returned in large numbers to the Upper Delaware from the sea for the first time in decades, able to breathe in the cleaner water downstream. The Commission now boasts that the Delaware is the cleanest river in the Northeast. (New York City's almost pathological determination to keep the Branches clean has much to do with that accom-plishment.) Of course, there may not be that much of a contest for cleanest river, given the chief competitor is the Hudson.[19]

The work marches on. The Basin Commission supports programs to track the water quality, encourage water conservation, allocate the supply, supervise regulatory permits, plan out management of the watershed, manage drought emergencies (not much call for drought management just lately), and reduce loss from flooding. At the bottom of the list, but no less important for that, come recreational considerations. The Delaware River Basin Commission has attended carefully to recreational responsibilities, among other matters playing a large role in crafting legislation making the Upper Delaware into a park of sorts.[20]

Riding the wave inspired by Rachel Carson and the "Age of Ecology," the United States Congress in 1968 passed the Wild and Scenic Rivers Act, declaring a policy "that certain selected rivers of the Nation, which with their immediate environments, possess outstandingly remarkable scenic, recreational, geologic, fish and wildlife, historic, cultural, or other similar values, shall be preserved in free-flowing condition, and that they and their immediate environments shall be protected for the benefit and enjoyment of present and future generations."[21]

The first rivers to be protected under the act were out west, where the Army Corps of Engineers was damming every stream they could find, hoping to make the deserts bloom. The most eastern of the original scenic rivers flowed through Wisconsin. Gradually Congress added more streams, including rivers in Maine. In 1978, Congress brought the concept to the more industrial Northeast, declaring a few streams wild and scenic enough to merit what protection the Act of 1968 could offer. The Federal Bureau of Outdoor Recreation (one more bureaucracy) spent seven years assessing conditions on the Upper Delaware, confirming finally that protection might not be a bad idea. Passed on November 10, Section 704 of Public Law 95–625 declared the "Upper Delaware River, New York and Pennsylvania" a Wild and Scenic River, to be placed under the supervision of the National Park Service.[22]

The people drafting this legislation recognized a minefield when they saw one. An early provision required the Secretary of the Interior "to provide for the participation in the development of … guidelines by all levels of State, county, and local government, and concerned private individuals and organizations, and also shall seek the advice of the Upper Delaware Citizens Advisory Council…." That Advisory Council, defined by the Act, was to include two representatives each from Orange, Sullivan, and Delaware Counties in New York, three members each from Wayne and Pike Counties, Pennsylvania, two members each appointed by the Governors of each state, and one beleaguered member chosen by Interior. At least one of the appointees from each of the five counties was supposed to actually reside in close proximity to the river.[23]

The Wild and Scenic River concept was a different kind of ballgame for the National Park Service. Born in 1916, the Service had spent much of its existence administering … well, parks—carefully delineated, generally large chunks of real estate reserved as property of the United States, places where the rangers pretty much controlled decision-making. These Scenic Rivers were a more nebulous proposition. The river corridors were well enough defined—54,981 acres in the case of the Upper Delaware—but the preponderance of the property would remain in private hands. The Act specified that the Secretary of the Interior was to acquire no more than four hundred-fifty acres for any purpose, unless something most highly unusual developed. The Park rangers would be supervising the land use of private citizens. And businesses. And States. Small wonder that large among the Park's management goals was the desire to "anticipate, avoid, and resolve potential conflicts."[24]

People actually living along the river greeted the designation with mixed emotions at best. While the population of the counties bordering the Upper Delaware has grown considerably since 1900, the numbers of people living in the towns nearest the river have remained remarkably stable. On the New York side, the population in 1875 stood at 23,253; in 2010 at 22,935, a decline of about one percent. In Pennsylvania, the number has climbed from 15,474 in 1880 to 17,978 in 2010, a rise of about nine percent. Much of the increase was in Pike County, at the southern end of the valley. Overall, this was a small, relatively rural population nested in the midst of one of the most crowded regions in the United States. Proud of their separation from Big Cities and Big Government, Federal authority was the last thing many wanted to experience. But even in this remote stretch of real estate, conditions were inevitably changing. One large difference was the growing number of seasonal homes—goodly numbers of folks were coming up for the summer to escape big city heat—from New York especially. Old and new, a lot of people living close to the river were getting fed up with raucous commotion on the water.

The Age of Ecology brought people outdoors throughout the Northeast. Recreation boomed. Camping, hiking, boating, swimming, getting back to the garden. The Upper Delaware—shallow, rocky, sporting a few intense whitewater riffs—became increasingly popular with canoe enthusiasts, along with the more traditional fishers and hunters. The forest industries long gone, tourism had become the essential cog attracting outside money to the valley. But hooliganism was on the rise, litter pollution an increasing problem. Maybe the National Park Service could do something to bring the burgeoning crowds under control.[25]

Shaping an approach to the peculiar difficulties inherent in the Wild and Scenic River definition, Park Service officials faced an old problem: the conflicting goals inherent to the heart of environmental preservation philosophy. Frederick Law Olmsted had set forth the basic ideals at Yosemite back in 1865; legislation creating the Wild and Scenic concept enshrined his definition. The rivers were to be protected for "the benefit and enjoyment of present and future generations." Present and future. There is the rub, in a nutshell. How does the Park Service ensure that folks coming now can enjoy the place to the fullest, while striving to make sure that the same wild qualities will still be there for the indefinite future? The National Park Service is in the unenviable position of playing policeman, preservation scientist and cultural guardian at once.[26]

Working with the Citizens Advisory Council, Park Service officials struggled to develop a series of management goals reflecting their broad range of responsibilities. The path was far from smooth; efforts to construct a viable management plan twice met outraged resistance from local citizenry, leading to formation of a Conference of Upper Delaware Townships in 1981. Coalesced from an array of concerned individuals and groups, the Conference gradually morphed into the Upper Delaware Council, a body still functioning, keeping a weather eye on developments. Consulting closely with the Conference membership, the Park Service in 1986—a full eight years after the initial park designation—managed to articulate a set of management goals everyone could live with. Periodically re-examined through the years, the goals articulated in 2014 largely reflect the initial determinations made back in 1979. The first and most obvious is to protect the river and the "landscape-scale ecological connectivity." A river is wild and scenic largely from context—the surroundings are fundamentally important. (When the Citizen's Advisory Council first met in 1979, one member advocated chopping down all the trees next to the roads on both sides of the river. If the region was supposed to be wild and scenic, motorists should be able to see the scenery, she contended. Rather missed the point.)[27]

Further goals articulated the desire to maintain the resources—and the values to be found in the valley—in good condition, using the "best available science." The cultural heritage remains another concern, which means attending to historic and archaeological preservation even as the Parks Service shapes facilities to accommodate the considerable numbers of hikers, canoeists, hunters, and fishers attracted to the valley. (Investigation of the cultural heritage began in 1979, when a horde of young archaeologists and one slightly grubby historian descended on the valley.)

That said, much of the management goals reflect the essential reality of Upper Delaware governance. The ongoing need for Federal, State, and local cooperation remains a fundamental concern. A "regional collaboration" is to be hoped for. "Working partnerships."[28] Let us say that the Upper Delaware runs vexed to the sea. There are a great many fingers in this particular pie. By my count, two agencies of the national government, an interstate commission, four separate state bureaucracies, five county governments, several town and village governments, two municipal utilities, one private environmental organization, and many private citizens all have a voice in preserving and enhancing the environment. (There may be more. If there are, I really don't want to know.) While very few would want to return the valley to the conditions so stark in the 1870s, the fact remains that all these forces must inevitably pull in conflicting directions.

In the end, no one has control over the future of the natural environment. Least of all the trees. Human beings are not merely present; we possess a defining if contradictory power to determine the future shape of the Upper Delaware forests. That alone is enough to guarantee that the forests existing at the beginning of the nineteenth century will never come back, whatever succession ecology might suggest. There is just one world, and people are in it and of it. Every management decision conditions the future of the forest environment.

Moving past the inescapable fact of human presence, an array of further elements guarantee that the forest of today and tomorrow will bear a character different from the woodlands of the past. There is more to the forest equation than the human governance. Environmental forces continue at work, altering conditions, spurring alteration, discouraging or even destroying the chances for a few species, enhancing others. Even in the small spaces not directly influenced by human activity, change is occurring. The climate, for starters. The coarse-grained disturbance wrought by the settlers, the tanners, the lumbermen in the nineteenth century took place during a period of global cooling, now called the "Little Ice Age." Beginning as long ago as 1350, winters across the world went longer and colder. Glaciers advanced, the polar ice caps grew, vegetation zones shifted in response. More northerly conifers migrated southward; southerly species retreated. Such were the conditions shaping the forests when the first settlers began chopping away in the Upper Delaware. The comparatively cold conditions persisted through to pretty much the end of the valley's "improvement"; the climate began to warm, returning to conditions resembling the optimum of the first millennium, around 1870. Now, of course, climate change is moving in the opposite direction, whether politicians want to accept the fact or not. Simple everyday facts convey that the world is warming; who or what is at fault does not matter so much. (The government has quietly changed the planting instructions on seed packets, reflecting the earlier beginning of the growing season, the shifting vegetation zones in most locales.) As the climate warms, the trees naturally respond, cold weather species retreating northward, southerly trees taking their places. One more effect of the warming is greater weather instability—more frequent and violent windstorms, more torrential rains. Sharp, rapid, natural forms of forest disturbance will have greater effect, contributing to more abrupt alterations in forest composition. Windstorms in the Catskills blew down significant numbers of trees in 1950, and again in 1954. Major hurricanes have become more frequent. Irene in 2011 and Sandy in 2012 are the most recent examples, bringing high winds and torrential rains to the Northeastern interior.[29]

As the climate has changed, so too has the composition of the atmosphere—one more consequence of concentrated human activity. Acid precipitation was all the buzz in the 1980s, the focus of the moment for the environmentally concerned. The Reagan administration actually attempted to ban importation of Canadian films detailing the acid rain problem, declaring them foreign propaganda. But Congress did act after a fashion, passing a Clean Air Act in 1990 to limit emissions of sulfur dioxides into the air. Environmentalists largely moved on, focusing on rain forests, climate change, nuclear radiation—all issues ominous enough. But acid precipitation continues to fall in the Northeast, especially heavy in wintertime. The acid negatively affects a tree's resistance to frost, increasing the chances of winter kill. The precipitation leaches nutrients from the soil while concentrating toxic elements, poison to the trees. Planes, trains, automobiles, power plants, factories—air pollution may be abated in some degree, but far from vanished. As long as the acid falls, no forest is remote enough to escape the effects.[30]

A different matter, and far more enigmatic, is fire. Fire has long been an elemental component in the shaping of forest ecosystems—eons before people entered the Upper Delaware region at all, lightning-ignited fires were burning large spaces in the woods, opening the canopy, provided bursts of rich nutrient to forest soils. Native Americans sustained and abetted this effect, purposely setting fires to burn off the understory, create a more park-like forest attractive to deer. European settlement saw to considerable burning of the trees they chopped down, but did their best to discourage forest fires. Mustn't burn down the neighborhood. Wholesale industrial barking of the hemlocks literally sparked a devastating return of broadcast fires in the 1880s, as Charles Carpenter so vividly described in his report on Catskill conditions. More fragile parts of the forest were left sterile. Since, fire has been absent, almost completely. In such a populous environment, fire suppression is a given. Forecasters in New York and Pennsylvania issue danger warnings whenever conditions warrant; fire is to be discouraged at all costs. Whatever forests take shape from here on, fire will have little influence, so long as people remain.[31]

So what kind of forest is the National Park Service in the business of protecting and encouraging in the twenty-first century? (A survey published by the State of New York in 1980 determined 530,000 acres in Delaware and Sullivan Counties could be considered "Sawtimber"—48.7 percent of the total forest acreage.) Curious themselves, the Park Service undertook an inventory of the vegetation lining the Upper Delaware Valley in 2006–'07, mapping and classifying the fifty-five-thousand acres of mostly forest area under their jurisdiction. The final report, an exhaustive examination of the valley's forest communities, appeared in 2008. Not surprisingly, the researchers found an ecosystem in transition, in many ways still recovering from the long and thorough disturbance of the nineteenth century. Most notably, they identified not one or two, but a host of forest varieties struggling together—a young woodland with an unclear identity.[32]

To map the vegetation patterns, botanists divided the corridor into a series of polygons encompassing fifteen-acre areas—3,729 in all. Aerial photography supplied six hundred forty-eight pictures capturing the length of the valley; the analysts combined a third of these into a composite mosaic, providing them a complete image of the study area for close examination. Teams subsequently sampled a representative series of the defined plots, gathering field results to compare with the data drawn from the aerial survey. What they discovered were a considerable array of vegetation communities— fifty different types, reflecting varying degrees of somewhat mature forest, interspersed with lands in early stages of succession—the very image of patch dynamics at work. Deciduous forest accounted for the most polygons—959, just over one-fourth; followed by Mixed Evergreen-Deciduous—894, twenty-four percent. Clearly the forest canopy of the Upper Delaware is vastly different from the woodland standing in 1800, or rapidly disappearing by 1875.[33]

Though succession remains a term in general use among ecologists, several have now chosen to redefine the changes in vegetation cover as a series of developmental patterns, each with its own characteristics. After a prolonged disturbance, an initial recovery would likely exhibit some pattern of stand re-initiation, with herbs and shrubs dominating the disturbed site for up to ten years. Tree seedlings would establish themselves slowly, eventually becoming dominant. Then comes a stem exclusion stage, when the canopy closes, shutting off light and limiting rainfall reaching the ground. Herbs and grasses largely disappear; new trees find no opening to take root. As time passes, the trees (for reasons not understood) lose dominance, creating opportunities for understory re-initiation. The herbs and grasses grow once more, and a few new trees may even take root. Finally comes an old growth stage, where the pioneer trees slowly die off, to be replaced by more shade-tolerant species growing in the opened gaps. None of these stages is inevitable or predictable—disturbances large and small can and will upset the pattern at any time. The result is the patchwork mosaic such as appears in the Upper Delaware. Forest conservation is a concerted effort to save something that must inevitably change.[34]

Farm abandonment still figures. Not much, just 417 acres, but enough to suggest the likely appearance of much of the region soon after large-scale abandonment began back in the 1860s. The botanists discerned three distinct patterns; "Old Field," characterized by nonnative grasses and herbs; "Northeastern Successional Shrubland," found on high, gentle slopes, identified by the large numbers of Allegheny blackberry shrubs; and "Little Bluestem Old Field," full of little bluestem and goldenrod. Barring disturbance, the vegetation in these fields will provide the cover and nutrients for trees to eventually take root.

If farmlands are being abandoned still, lands in the early stages of forest succession—young, short-lived, opportunistic species—should be expected. The analysts found 3,287 acres of such successional forest, identifying three different types. There was the "Northeastern Modified," stands of "weedy species" such as black locust and bitternut hickory, found on low, flat terraces close to the river; the "Northeastern Oak–Red Maple," coming to life on old fields, full of young white pines in the company of the oaks and maples; and the "Red Maple–Sweet Birch Hardwood," young maples and birches growing on east-facing midslopes. Composition will change with time, the so- called weedy species giving way to more dominant trees.

Oaks there are in plenty. Squirrels and blue jays have been industrious in the decades since 1880, transporting acorns to likely spots. Oak dominant forests account for more of the vegetation cover than any other classification—more than sixteen thousand acres, almost thirty percent. Again, the analysts identified three different types: the "Northeastern Dry Oak-Hickory Forest" found on dry slopes, a nearly closed canopy consisting of four or five oak species; the "Lower New England Slope Chestnut Oak Forest," lots of chestnut oaks and associated trees residing on higher ridges and knobs; and the "Dry, Rich Oak-Hickory Forest," many hickories, several kinds of oaks, and almost no conifers collecting on higher slopes.

The study found three categories of northern hardwood forest covering 7,908 acres (14.4 percent of the study area). Hemlocks, once upon a time the dominant species throughout the Upper Delaware, appear at last in these woods. The "Hemlock-Northern Hardwood Forest," the dominant cover throughout much of the first-growth forest of the early 1800s, survives, mainly on "rocky, moist, north-facing slopes at low to mid-elevations." Hemlocks for the moment dominate these forest communities, generally accompanied by sugar maples and basswoods. The "Central Appalachian Northern Hardwood Forest," found on gentle east-facing slopes, comprises stands of red and sugar maple, sweet birch, and American beech, with maybe a few white pines peeking above the canopy. The "Semi-Rich Northern Hardwood Forest" includes a large variety of hardwoods—birches, white ash, maples, basswoods, along with the occasional white pine.

No single forest type dominates the corridor; describing the vegetation pattern as a mosaic makes very sound sense. Even the most oft-identified forest type, the "Hemlock-Beech-Oak Forest," takes up only 10,836 acres, slightly less than one-fifth of the total vegetation cover. The study explains that "this association occurs on dry, nutrient-poor, well-drained soils over acidic bedrock," a description of soil conditions throughout much of the Upper Delaware if ever there was one. (Probably an analyst studying the corridor not long after the glaciation would have said much the same thing.) Occupying this unpromising environment is a community dominated by hemlocks, with a fair number of beech trees, some birches, five species of dry oak, some red maples, and white pines. Something perhaps approaching what the forest was like so long ago.[35]

The vegetation analysis makes the almost obligatory reference to the march of invasive species—the nonnative variety, that is. (Semantically speaking, just about all the species are invaders of a sort; there were very few trees at all in 1886.) Two nonnative invaders have made enough of an impact to raise concerns. Japanese knotweed is an herb, a very aggressive herb that tends to crowd out the native vegetation, growing in dense stands reaching ten feet tall, looking a little like bamboo. And, an exotic strain of reed canary grass, introduced into America to blend with native species, has gone rogue, invading natural habitats in dense colonies, growing seven feet tall. Each has dug in along the riparian zones lining the river, taking over wetland areas, displacing native herbs and grasses. Effective means of control remain very much a question. The knotweed may have some effect on future lowland forest growth, the dense colonies leaving little room for native tree species to take root.[36]

Beyond the basic achievement of tallying the numbers and relative percentages of the large variety of vegetation associations currently found in the Upper Delaware, the 2008 study underscores one indisputable fact. The forest cover has come back to the river, enough to make the corridor bear the appearance of wild and scenic, but this is a new and different forest. No single classification comes close to defining the canopy; strikingly different cover types occupy considerable stretches, dependent largely on very local conditions. If anything, this is a forest with far more hardwoods, oaks, especially, than the pioneers encountered (and cleared away) two centuries ago. In some part, this has got to be a product of the climatic warming trends of the past century and a half—the hardwoods advance, the conifers hold on in the cooler, moister areas, but mostly retreat northward. Too, the current composition is a consequence of the peculiar opportunities taking shape at the close of the nineteenth century. Ravaged forests, laden with the rotting remains of pillaged hemlocks, so prone to fires, abandoned slopes that should never have been farmed—in such conditions, the agents of hardwood spread found opportunity. Caching squirrels. Flying blue jays.

There is the also the action of simple chance. Not random chance—not just anything is going to grow in the particular environment of the Upper Delaware—but contingent chance. In keeping with their unique biologies, the best-suited kinds of trees compete for space, each employing their own specific strategies. By whatever agency—wind patterns, bird and animal activities—seeds are cast. So much matters then. The soil, the slope, the rainfall, the water table, the available sunlight, the shelter provided by the understory, the local animal population and behavior. All variables in the equation of survival. Chance disposes the outcome. A new forest takes shape. And continues to take shape, on into an uncertain future. Every forest species will compete for space in accordance with the limits of a specific biology, conditioned by the patterns of disturbance to come. The system will remain open; no definitive climax will arrive. Ever.[37]

Certainly the animal kingdom will have a crucial role in whatever forests are to come. Animals other than people. One of the more noted effects of the nineteenth-century deforestation was the accompanying disappearance of mammal and bird species. An important few have returned, while others critical to the ecosystem at work in 1700 have not. A mammal inventory sponsored by the National Park Service between 2006 and 2010 reports that beaver are indeed back—"probably common and widespread." White-tailed deer too—"widespread and abundant." Abundant indeed.[38]

To a limited extent, the beaver are able to take up the ecological role missing since the extirpation of the seventeenth century, building their dams, regulating water flow, raising the water table, opening the forest canopy, providing wetland habitats for a wide variety of plant, fish, amphibian, reptile, mammal, and bird species. The limit is the ability of people to tolerate their constructions—a nice pond in the forest is one thing, a flooded back yard another. Tolerance is often very low; control officers in both New York and Pennsylvania receive regular calls to rid an area of "nuisance beavers." Wayne County, Pennsylvania, fronting on the Upper Delaware, is one of the State's least populous, but leads all the rest in beaver complaints.[39]

The white-tailed deer are a trickier proposition. Efforts to restore deer populations have proven successful—wildly so; a cynic might complain we are up to our clavicles in deer. This is a good thing and a bad thing. Deer hunting is an important aspect of rural economies; hunters bring welcome money (and welcome dinners to poor families). The more deer the better, theoretically. But deer populations possess no mechanism to control their own numbers. Encouraged to multiply unchecked, deer soon overpopulate, straining food supplies, negatively affecting forest growth by too extensive foraging on seedlings and young shoots. Long years of too many deer result in a middle-aged collection of trees, with no younger trees to succeed them. Often, over-extensive deer browsing has resulted in the flourishing of beech at the expense of other hardwoods or hemlock.[40]

An integral part of the problem is the lack of predators. In 1600, when deer roamed the Upper Delaware, hunted very lightly by the Indians, wolves and panthers kept the numbers down. But the carnivores disappeared at much the same time as the deer early in the nineteenth century, and they have not been invited back. A few wolves may have infiltrated the Adirondacks from Canada, but New York's Department of Environmental Conservation has firmly stated they will make no effort to assist any return. Farther south, in the Catskills or the Upper Delaware, wolves are beyond imagining. The largest predators at work in the region are coyotes, smaller dogs that entered New York State in the 1940s, largely because the wolves were not there to stop them. The Park Service mammal inventory found coyotes throughout the Upper Delaware, but they are not going to be much help controlling the deer. As much as hunters would like to see the coyotes removed as unwanted competitors, the coyotes are far more likely to bring down a rabbit or a squirrel than anything as big as a deer.[41]

That leaves the hunters. The agencies in New York and Pennsylvania maintain careful track of deer hunting, adjusting the length of the seasons, the numbers of permits each year, trying hard to maintain a balance between the estimated deer population, the expectations of hunters, and the health of the environment. In Wayne County, Pennsylvania, the deer count has risen steadily over the past nine years, reaching as high as 83,000, while forest health has just as steadily declined, to fifty-five percent defined as "adequate." Pike County has proven more stable—maybe thirty thousand deer, with sixty-one percent of the forest in adequate health. In New York, Delaware and Sullivan have experienced some wild swings in deer numbers. Sullivan County runs low (according to the hunters, anyway), while Delaware was extremely high until the winter of 2014–2015, when bitterly cold and snowy weather left a population of just twenty to twenty-five deer per square mile. Managing the deer is an elaborate game of chess with nature, much conditioned by public perception. Probably the hottest discussions New York's Conservation officials have to face are about damage inflicted by too many deer. Or the economic pain resulting from too few. Whichever, forest health is very much contingent on human decision-making. Manipulating the deer population is manipulating the condition of the woods.[42]

The greater threat derives from the work of much smaller critters. At a minimum, five species of beetles, seven varieties of moths, and six different fungi menace Upper Delaware trees. As might be expected, several have come from very far away, the consequence of human commerce, intentional or accidental. Plucked from their native environments, the natural enemies that typically controlled their numbers still live far away, making conditions ripe for uncontrolled epidemics. A recitation of the dangers they pose makes for sobering reading.

North American trees have long endured the presence of several native insect pests. Five species of native moths make themselves at home in the Upper Delaware. There is the hemlock looper, whose larvae feed on the leaves of various oaks and white spruces, but much prefer hemlock needles. Spruce budworms nest in balsam firs, their larvae spreading out to chew on neighboring conifers. Eastern tent caterpillars prefer black and choke cherry trees, consuming the tender leaves in spring. Saddled prominent moth larvae go for sugar maples, beech, and yellow birch. Forest tent caterpillars are also big fans of sugar maples. Populations of these native moths rise and fall; natural defenses generally keep the numbers in check. The last serious outbreak of forest tent caterpillars in New York occurred in 2002.

A native American beetle, the hemlock borer, a shiny metallic fellow, can also cause serious problems, opening wounds in hemlocks deep enough for disease to gain hold. Another native beetle approaches, worrisome enough for Pennsylvania Department of Conservation to issue warnings. The walnut twig beetle is a tolerable if annoying nuisance in its own habits. Targeting black walnut trees, the beetle bores tunnels into the branches to lay eggs, opening the tree to disease. In 2010, the beetle began carrying passengers. As near as entomologists can figure, walnut twig beetles in New Mexico began hosting a fungus inflicting a dreaded tree sickness known as Thousand Canker Disease. Spreading eastward, the fungus, courtesy of the beetles, has now reached the Philadelphia area, where officials are working desperately to maintain a quarantine. Black walnut trees, exhibiting little in the way of defense, have withered quickly.[43]

These are the more troublesome homegrown threats. Recent invaders from abroad—beetles, fungi, a couple of truly ominous moths—make the lot seem tame.

Three invasive beetles have made their presence known in the Upper Delaware, unwanted imports from Asia, probably arriving imbedded in wooden packing crates bound for American addresses. The common pine shoot beetle first appeared in Ohio in 1992, spreading rapidly in all directions to make meals of conifers, pines especially. Asian long-horned beetles showed in Brooklyn in 1996 and immediately began working northward, tunneling into maples, girdling and eventually killing the trees.

More dreaded is the emerald ash borer, a beetle that has not yet reached the valley, though they are rapidly killing ash trees at no great distance away. Thought to have found their way into the United States sometime in the 1990s, ash borers established themselves as a dire threat when an outbreak exploded in Michigan in 2002. Strenuous quarantine efforts have slowed the spread a bit. Ash borers are ravenous and thorough, rapidly wiping out whatever stands of ash they find. Ashes are not abundant in the Upper Delaware. The vegetation survey found a few white ashes associated with successional forests, a few more in the stands identified as "Semi-Rich Northern Hardwood." A little to the east, at the edge of the Catskills, ash trees were the foundation of a small but culturally significant industry begun in the nineteenth century. The day may come when America sees the last of ash baseball bats.[44]

Lots and lots of native fungi can and do infect American trees, inflicting small losses. But trees have their defenses, evolved immunities born of millennia of co-existence. Not so with at least five relative newcomers, fungi for which the trees have little resistance. Beech bark disease, entering North America from Europe at Nova Scotia in 1890, has spread southward slowly, reaching the Catskills in 1970. Spread by mechanisms as annoyingly diverse as wind, rain, the feet of birds and animals, or automobile tires, the fungi breed a scale disease severely weakening the beech host. White pine blister rust reached the Pacific Northwest from Eurasia around 1900, spreading to become a major concern throughout North America by the 1930s.

Beech bark disease and pine blister rust are benign compared to what followed after. Chestnut blight invaded New York City in 1904, shipped accidentally from Japan. The blight is little more than a nuisance in Asia, where chestnuts can tolerate the disease, but American chestnuts, a separate but closely related species, could offer no defense. All too quickly, the chestnuts disappeared from Northeastern forests, often replaced by oaks. The resultant devastation altered the very character of the woodland; native chestnuts were once a principal component. (Chestnut boards were much favored for railroad ties in New England.) Young trees may still be found, sometimes sprouted from the stump of a predecessor; the blight does not take hold until the chestnut reaches mature age. But large chestnuts no longer grace the forest canopies. Efforts are underway to graft Asian chestnuts onto American shoots, hopefully bestowing a more effective genetic resistance.[45]

Not long after the chestnut blight, Dutch elm disease struck, also in New York. This was a disaster of another sort, an Andrew Jackson Downing nightmare. Responding to Downing's insistence that Americans beautify their streets, elms had become the tree of choice in countless cities and villages throughout the Northeast, gracefully overhanging quiet lanes, lending much to an atmosphere of quiet peace. Dutch elm disease put close to that. Originating in China, the fungus spread to Europe in the distant past. In 1928, a nursery in New York City inadvertently imported infected logs from Holland. The smallest foothold was all the fungus required; the disease spread rapidly, attacking the vascular system of the elms, killing a host tree in one to five years. Elms across the country withered and died. By the 1950s, a healthy elm was a truly rare sight, the ghostly remnant of a bygone time.[46]

The march goes on. Conservation botanists now find themselves struggling to contain the Sirex wood wasp, an insect common to Eurasia that found its way into the Great Lakes region in 2006. Relatively harmless themselves, the wasps are the vector for another fungus, this one targeting pines.

Left for last, but surely not least, consider the ongoing career of two invasive insects, each infamous in its own special way. The gypsy moth, common to Eurasia, came to America in 1869, purposely imported to Massachusetts by a scientist dreaming of improving silkworm stocks. Needless to say, the moth escaped, and began a slow and steady progress southward and westward, courtesy of just about anything that moves. The sticky egg masses cling to birds, animals, clothing, automobiles, baby carriages, whatever. They can also ride the wind. Once attached to a tree in springtime—preferably an oak or hickory, sometimes an aspen—the moth larvae begin dining on tender young leaves. The tree can survive such an attack, growing new leaves, but is severely weakened, opened to a host of other infections. The forest suffers. Most years, the problem is not serious, but severe outbreaks at odd times occur as the gypsy moth population occasionally explodes. Gypsy moth outbreaks visited New York in 1981, in 1992, and again in 1996–97. Each provoked considerable controversy; the advocates of chemical insecticides are not good at listening. After World War II and before Rachel Carson, the recommended response to gypsy moth infestation was widespread aerial spraying of insecticides such as DDT. This had limited effect on the moths, but did much to eliminate bald eagles and several other bird species from Northeastern forests. Bald eagles, reintroduced into upstate New York in 1976, have done well in forested streams such as the Upper Delaware no longer laden with chemicals. Introduced insect enemies, species of beetles especially, have proven far more successful in reducing gypsy moth numbers. Anticipated outbreaks in the twenty-first century have not come to much.[47]

That leaves one highly forbidding insect to regard. The hemlock wooly adelgid poses the greatest danger to the Upper Delaware hemlocks since the halcyon days of the tanning industry. Adelgids are native to Japan. They apparently reached the American West coast as early as 1924, but did little noticeable damage. Eastern exposure initiated in 1951, when a Virginia family imported an ornamental tree unknowingly laden with adelgids. The aphid-like insects were in southern Pennsylvania by 1967, and slowly advancing northward. Long Island first reported the insect in 1985. Eight years later, wooly adelgids were in the southern portions of Sullivan and Pike Counties, reaching into Wayne and Delaware Counties by 2002. Adelgids are now thoroughly at home in the Upper Delaware, where the only thing slowing their rapid destruction of the hemlocks are cold, hard winters. That respite is wholly temporary.[48]

Adelgids can reproduce asexually, and cycle through two generations each year. (A third, winged brood appears in native Japan, though not in the United States.) Attached to the underside of hemlock needles the egg sacks look to be bits of cotton. Each adelgid can produce one hundred to three hundred eggs; spread is rapid. Once established, an infestation of adelgids literally sucks the life out of a hemlock, inserting long tubes into small twigs to draw sugars from the tree. The exact cause of the hemlock's eventual death remains something of a mystery, but the end comes within five years. The adelgids are prolific and numerous, able to completely eliminate entire stands in short order. Dying hemlocks disintegrate standing, losing first needles, then larger and larger branches, eventually collapsing. The trees have no defense; the biologists have few answers either. Chemical insecticides have been the first line of attack (God help the rest of the ecosystem); really effective biological controls have yet to emerge. The hemlocks are falling fast. "This is most definitely a tragedy," forest scientist David Foster writes. "We will lose hemlock. We will lose our flagship old-growth and primaeval forest in the Northeast. We'll lose distinctive variation in our landscape. And we will lose the history and experiences embodied in these woods."[49]

Oddly enough, though the character of the Upper Delaware forest will dramatically change—biologically and historically—if the hemlocks completely disappear, the effect will not be entirely negative. Hemlocks most often dominate the canopy, overshadowing much of the surrounding forest, creating a cooler, damper world. Should the hemlocks wither, the forest will open up, promoting greater biodiversity. A distant echo of events as long ago as 5000 BP seems to resonate. Hemlocks disappeared for seven hundred years back then, only to eventually re-establish and grow dominant. Paleobiologists have long debated the cause; the current infestation evokes suspicion. Tiny insects do not leave much in the way of fossil evidence.[50]

The drumroll of invasive pests besetting the Upper Delaware woodlands points a grim but obvious conclusion. History will not repeat itself. Nothing even faintly resembling the fairytale "primaeval forest" will ever come back. Inadvertent or not, the human mercantile web has visited nearly complete mortality on the chestnuts and the elms, is too damned close to the same for the ashes and hemlocks. More trees suffer—pines, spruce, beech, oaks, hickories, sugar maples. Any relief from the onslaught will derive from the research of forest scientists. We are embarked on a road of no return; the forests we have chosen to preserve will survive with human effort.

A century and a quarter since the last industrial tanner stripped the last bark from nearly the last defenseless hemlock, trees have reclaimed much of the land, relining the Upper Delaware. This is a modern woodland, a product of modern times, a reminder that there is, finally, just one world. Human beings have sewn that world together into an inextricable whole; a forest along a river in New York and Pennsylvania is linked unavoidably to species migrated from Europe and Asia. For better and for worse, the forest exists as it does because of human decisions, human activities. People are the ultimate force in nature, constructing a world of our visions, desires, needs.

Consider the web of protective agencies at work in the Upper Delaware, all seeking more or less the same outcome—a wild and scenic river, a reserve to be spared from too much disturbance. Two sets of State agencies (with competing bureaucracies in each), a large metropolitan government, an interstate commission, and two very powerful Federal bureaucracies, each seek to manage some portion of this small slice of the natural world. All for nature's own good. Add to that the multitude of local governments, the private industries, the private citizens who actually own and control much of the land; the sum comes to a very large number of competing, often contradictory voices. The goal may be to sustain and nurture nature's way, but the path is narrow, carefully bounded and confined. Beaver regulating the water table? Only until they become a nuisance. Wolves limiting the deer population, keeping the forest healthy? You've got to be kidding. Fires opening spaces in the forest, clearing away the underbrush? Not in the twenty-first century. The modern world demands a different kind of ecosystem, one where beaver stay in their places, wolves have no place, fire has no role.

Down to the very plants and animals, human beings make the decisions on what belongs. Beaver are nice, until they get to be a nuisance. Deer? How many? How many is too many? Are they chomping on trees we want to grow healthy? There is a solution for that. Wolves? That makes ecological sense, but no thank you. No cougars either, please. Wish we could get rid of the coyotes. They threaten all those wonderful deer over-browsing the young tree shoots.

Even the tiny, unwanted creatures are the gifts of humankind, products of a world drawn into one vast web of commerce. Chestnut blight. Dutch elm disease. Gypsy moths. Wooly adelgids. All came from far across the oceans, brought to America in the course of everyday routine. The decision to combat them—obvious enough—is one more conscious decision to shape a world to our desires—what we want, what we do not. Japanese knotweed is another case, an invasive plant pushing out native species humans have decided to prefer. Plant invasion has been going on for millennia—many of the plants we regard as native originated in faraway places. Having disturbed the natural world beyond endurance, we aim now to protect and restore what has escaped our harvest. Conditionally. Just certain species need apply.

Perhaps forests really are nothing more than a product of the human mind. For the past eleven thousand years, the woodlands have been shaped in ever increasing part by human activity. We contemplate what we ourselves have created. We embrace a woodland born of our own human history, a product of our disturbances, our attempts to restore what we so ruthlessly destroyed. Now we have no choice but to keep a finger on the pulse of nature, decide what is good, what is healthy. What is not. For the forest, and most of all, for ourselves.

And yet…. Looking upward from the river, up into the hills covered in a canopy of green, we look at something beyond the reach of ourselves, something stirring to the heart. All the dividing, the studying, the classifying, the analyzing adds nothing to that essential contemplation. In a modern world, we look to a modern forest to provide a sense of a more peaceful, more bucolic, more natural past. We see what we desire. Daniel Skinner looked up into the same hills two hundred fifty years ago, and saw money waiting. We look to see a world we sense may be slowly fading. But for now, the forest exists once more, a beckoning vision of peace in a maddening world.

Whether the forest exists or not.

Chapter Notes

Introduction

1. Robert C. McGregor, *History and Archaeology 4.3 Part B: Contact and Euro-American (Historical Synthesis)* in Albert A. Dekin, Principal Investigator, *Cultural Resource Survey: Upper Delaware National Scenic and Recreational River, Pennsylvania and New York* (Philadelphia: National Park Service, 1982), pp. 27–30; Charles T. Curtis, *Rafting on the Delaware* (Ithaca: William Heidt, Jr., 1957); Barbara F. Sivertsen and Barbara L. Covey, eds., *The Legend of Cushetunk: The Nathan Skinner Manuscript and the Early History of Cochecton* (Westminster, MD: Heritage Books, 2011); Mark Stell, *Protestantism, Capitalism, and Nature in America* (Albuquerque: University of New Mexico Press, 1997), pp. 55–76.

2. Thomas M. Bonnicksen, *America's Ancient Forests: From the Ice Age to the Age of Discovery* (New York: John Wiley and Sons, 2000), p. 15; John J. Berger, *Forests Forever: Their Ecology, Restoration, and Protection* (Chicago: Center for American Places, 2008), pp.11–12; Frank Benjamin Golley, *A History of the Ecosystem Concept in Ecology* (New Haven: Yale University Press, 1993), p. 190; E. C. Pielou, *The World of Northern Evergreens*, 2nd ed. (Ithaca: Comstock Publishing Associates, 2011), p.67.

3. Peter J. Bowler, *The Environmental Sciences* (New York: W.W. Norton and Company, 1992), pp. 428–517; Gerard Helferich, *Humboldt's Cosmos: Alexander Von Humboldt and the Latin American Journey That Changed the Way We See the World* (New York; Gotham Books, 2004); Golley, *History of the Ecosystem Concept*, 2, 27; Robert Kuhn McGregor, *A Wider View of the Universe: Henry Thoreau's Study of Nature* (Champaign: University of Illinois Press, 1997), pp. 175–98.

4. Donald Worster, *Nature's Economy: A History of Ecological Ideas* (Cambridge: Cambridge University Press, 1994).

5. Sharon E. Kingsland, *The Evolution of American Ecology, 1890-2000* (Baltimore: Johns Hopkins University Press, 2005), pp. 3–19, 96–128, 179.

6. Stephen A. Forbes, "The Lake as a Microcosm," *Bulletin of the Illinois State Natural History Survey* 15 (1925): 537–50 (reprint of 1887 paper published in *Bulletin of the Peoria Scientific Association* (1887).

7. Croker Ra, *Stephen Forbes and the Rise of American Ecology* (Washington DC: Smithsonian, 2001).

8. Kingsland, *Evolution of American Ecology*, 4, 94, 103.

9. *Ibid.*, 145–46; Henry Chandler Cowles, "The Ecological Relations of the Vegetation on the Sand Dunes of Lake Michigan," *The Botanical Gazette* 27 (February, 1899): 95–117, 167–202, 281–308, 361–91; Charles C. Addams, *An Ecological Survey of Isle Royale, Lake Superior* (Lansing, MI: Wynkoop Hallenbeck Crawford Company, State Printers, 1909).

10. Frederic E. Clements, *Plant Succession: An Analysis of the Development of Vegetation* (Washington, D.C.: Carnegie Institution of Washington, 1916).

11. Kingsland, *Evolution of American Ecology*, 141–46; Golley, *Ecosystem Concept in Ecology*, 23–24.

12. *Ibid.*, Frederic E. Clements, "Nature and Structure of the Climax," *The Journal of Ecology* 24 (1936): 252–84

13. David R. Foster, ed., *Hemlock: A Forest Giant on the Edge* (New Haven: Yale University Press, 2014), pp. 32, 68; Pielou, *World of Northern Evergreens*, 141; Golley, *Ecosystem Concept in Ecology*, 3.

14. *Ibid.*, 57; Kingsland, *Evolution of Amer-*

ican Ecology, 157–61; Golley, *Ecosystem Concept in Ecology*, 187; Henry Allan Gleason, "The Individualistic Concept of the Plant Association," *Bulletin of the Torrey Botanical Club* 53 (1926): 7–26; Foster, ed., *Hemlock*, 57–58.

15. Kingsland, *Evolution of American Ecology*, 184–85; Golley, *Ecosystem Concept in Ecology*, 8–16, 33–41.

16. Arthur G. Tansley, "The Use and Abuse of Vegetational Concepts and Terms," *Ecology* 16 (July, 1935): 284–307.

17. Kingsland, *Evolution of American Ecology*, 184–85; Golley, *Ecosystem Concept in Ecology*, 8–16, 33–41.

18. Kingsland, *Evolution of American Ecology*, 188; Golley, *Ecosystem Concept in Ecology*, 44, 48–51; Raymond L. Lindeman, "The Trophic-Dynamic Aspect of Ecology," *Ecology* 23: (October, 1942): 399–418.

19. *Ibid.*

20. Kingsland, *Evolution of American Ecology*, 191–99; Golley, *Ecosystem Concept in Ecology*, 1, 62, 81.

21. Donald Worster, "Ecology of Order and Chaos," *Environmental History Review* 14 (Spring/Summer 1990): 4–16; Golley, *Ecosystem Concept in Ecology*, 2–3.

22. Kingsland, *Evolution of American Ecology*, 3–6, 179–85; Golley, *Ecosystem Concept in Ecology*, 2–3, 73–74.

23. Kingsland, *Evolution of American Ecology*, 6, 200; Golley, *Ecosystem Concept in Ecology*, 3, 180–84; Rachel Carson, *Silent Spring* (New York: Houghton Mifflin, 1962).

24. Tom Fenchel, "Comment on Carney's Article by T. Fenchel," *Functional Ecology* 3 (1989): 641; Golley, *Ecosystem Concept in Ecology*, 189–90.

25. Kingsland, *Evolution of American Ecology*, 215; Golley, *Ecosystem Concept in Ecology*, 2–4, 189.

26. Kingsland, *Evolution of American Ecology*, 191, 231.

27. Golley, *Ecosystem Concept in Ecology*, 145–50.

28. *Ibid.*, 148–49.

29. Kingsland, *Evolution of American Ecology*, 226; Golley, *Ecosystem Concept in Ecology*, 22–23; Bonnicksen, *America's Ancient Forests*, 219; S.T.A. Pickett and P.S. White, *The Ecology of Natural Disturbance and Patch Dynamics* (Orlando: Academic Press, 1985), pp. xiii, 5–12.

30. John L. Harper, "The Contributions of Terrestrial Plant Studies to the Development of the Theory of Ecology," *The Changing Scenes in the Natural Sciences, 1776–1976*, ed.

C.E. Goulden (Philadelphia: Academy of the Natural Sciences, 1977), pp. 139–57.

31. Pickett and White, *Ecology of Natural Disturbance and Patch Dynamics*, 5–12; E.C. Pielou, *After the Ice Age: The Return of Life to Glaciated North America* (Chicago: University of Chicago Press, 1991), p. 101; Worster, "Ecology of Order and Chaos," 4–16.

32. Pickett and White, *Ecology of Natural Disturbance and Patch Dynamics*, 7, 384, 441.

33. Worster, "Ecology of Order and Chaos," 4–16; William Drury and Ian Nesbit, "Succession" *Journal of the Arnold Arboretum* 54 (July, 1973): 331–68; Margaret Bryan Davis, "Quaternary History and the Stability of Forest Communities," *Forest Succession: Concepts and Applications*, ed. Darrell C. West, Herman H. Shugart, and Daniel B. Botkin (New York: Springer-Verlag, 1981), pp. 132–53.

34. Foster, ed., *Hemlock*, 68; Pielou, *World of Northern Evergreens*, 141

35. Robert Kuhn McGregor, "Deriving a Biocentric History: Evidence from the Journal of Henry David Thoreau," *Environmental Review* 12 (Summer, 1988): 117–26.

36. McGregor, *History and Archaeology 4.3 Part B: Contact and Euro-American*; Robert Charles McGregor, "Radical Environmental Change: Deforestation in the Upper Delaware River Valley, 1800–1875," Ph.D. dissertation, State University of New York at Binghamton, 1984; James R. Runkle, "Disturbance Regimes in Temperate Forests," Pickett and White, eds., *Ecology of Natural Disturbance and Patch Dynamics*, 17–34.

Chapter One

1. Pielou, *The World of Northern Evergreens*, 67; Pielou, *After the Ice*, 5–15; Y. W. Isachsen, E. Landing, J.M. Lauber, L.V. Rickard, W.B. Rogers, eds. *Geology of New York: A Simplified Account*, 2nd ed. (Albany: New York State Museum Educational Leaflet 28, 2000), pp. 161–165; Robert Titus, *The Catskills in the Ice Age*, revised ed. (Fleischmanns, NY: Purple Mountain Press, 2003), pp. 18–20.

2. Titus, *Catskills in the Ice Age*, 18–20; Donald W. Fisher, *The Rise and Fall of the Taconic Mountains: A Geological History of Eastern New York* (Hensonville, NY: Black Dome Press, 2006), p. 127; Bonnicksen, *America's Ancient Forests*, 3–4; Donald H. Caldwell and Ernest H. Muller, "New York Glacial Geology, U.S.A.," *Quaternary Glaciations, Extent and Chronology, Part II: North America*, ed.

J. Ehlers and P.L. Gibbard (Amsterdam: Elsevier, 2004), pp. 201–07.

3. Ian M. Lange, *Ice Age Mammals of North America* (Missoula, MT: Mountain Press Publishing, 2002), p. 37; Bonnicksen, *America's Ancient Forests*, 3–7; Titus, *Catskills in the Ice Age*, 47, 52–53; Isachsen et al., *Geology of New York*, p. 127; Titus, *Catskills in the Ice Age*, 115–18; Fisher, *Taconic* Mountains, 127; Richard J. Dent, "The Upper Delaware Valley: Recent Past and Present Biophysical Conditions"; "Amerinds and the Environment: Myth, Reality, and the Upper Delaware Valley"; Charles W. McNett, Jr., "The Shawnee Minisink Site: An Overview," Charles W. McNett, Jr., ed., *Shawnee Minisink: A Stratified Paleoindian-Archaic Site in the Upper Delaware Valley of Pennsylvania* (Orlando: Academic Press, 1985), pp. 35–54, 121–42; 321–26.

4. Titus, *Catskills in the Ice Age*, 47, 52–53; Isachsen et al., *Geology of New York*, 159.

5. Titus, *Catskills in the Ice Age*, 47, 52–53; Isachsen et al., *Geology of New York*, 159.

6. Titus, *Catskills in the Ice Age*, 47, 52–53; Isachsen et al., *Geology of New York*, 48; Isachsen et al., *Geology of New York*, 167; Fisher, *Taconic Mountains*, 127.

7. Titus, *Catskills in the Ice Age*, 115, 117–18; Pielou, *After the Ice*, 89; Michael Kudish, *The Catskill Forest: A History* (Fleischmanns, NY: Purple Mountain Press, 2000), pp. 1–11.

8. Pielou, *After the Ice*, 25; Kudish, *Catskill Forest*, 2–3; Bonnicksen, *America's Ancient Forests*, 17; Berger, *Forests Forever*, 20; Peter J. Marchand, *Autumn: A Season of Change* (Hanover: University Press of New England, 2000), pp. 128–132.

9. Kudish, *Catskill Forest*, 2–3.

10. Titus, *Catskills in the Ice Age*, 120.

11. Bonnicksen, *America's Ancient Forests*, 18; Pielou, *World of Northern Evergreens*, 78.

12. Adrian Lister and Paul Bahn, *Mammoths: Giants of the Ice Age*, Revised ed. (Berkeley: University of California Press, 2007), pp. 88–90, 103, 142.

13. Peter J. Marchand, *Life in the Cold: An Introduction to Winter Ecology*, 2nd ed. (Hanover, NH: University Press of New England, 1991), p71–87; Marchand, *Autumn*, 11–14; Pielou, *World of Northern Evergreens*, 6; Donald H. DeHayes, Paul G. Shaberg, and G. Richard Strimbeck, "Red Spruce (*Picea* Rubens Sarg.) Cold Hardiness and Freezing Injury Susceptibility," *Conifer Cold Hardiness*, ed. F. J. Bigras and Stephen J. Columbo (Dordrecht, The Netherlands: Kluwer Academic Publishers, 2001), pp. 495–529.

14. Kudish, *Catskill Forest*, 9–18; Dent,

"Amerinds and the Environment," McNett, *Shawnee Minisink*, 129–30.

15. Fisher, *Taconic Mountains*, 128; Marchand, *Autumn*, 72; Pielou, *World of Northern Evergreens*, 115–17; Lange, *Ice Age Mammals*, 94–96, 139–147; Brian Fagan, ed. *The Complete Ice Age: How Climate Change Shaped the World* (London: Thames and Hudson, 2009), p. 174.

16. Titus, *Catskills in the Ice Age*, 120; Lange, *Ice Age Mammals*, 176–78; Judith Drumm, *Mammoths and Mastodons: Ice Age Elephants of New York* (Albany: State Museum and Science Service, 1963), pp. 11–12; William A. Ritchie, *The Archaeology of New York State*, Revised ed. (Harrison, NY: Harbor Hill Books, 1980), p. 10; Dent, "Amerinds and the Environment," McNett, *Shawnee Minisink*, 129–30.

17. Marchand, *Autumn*, 11–22; Marchand, *Life in the Cold*, 71–87; Pielou, *World of Northern Evergreens*, 4; Kudish, *Catskill Forest*, 14.

18. Pielou, *World of Northern Evergreens*, 64, 125–27; Bonnicksen, *America's Ancient Forests*, 34–38; Foster, ed., *Hemlock*, 105; Pielou, *After the Ice Age*, 215–17.

19. Kudish, *Catskill Forest*, 14; Pielou, *World of Northern Evergreens*, 64; Bonnicksen, *America's Ancient Forests*, 34–38.

20. Pielou, *After the Ice Age*, 180.

21. Davis, "Quaternary History," *Forest Succession*, 132–53.

22. Fisher, *Taconic Mountains*, 128; Lange, *Ice Age Mammals*, 45.

23. Titus, *Catskills in the Ice Age*, 120; Drumm, *Mammoths and Mastodons*, 5–20; David R. Foster, ed., *Hemlock: A Forest Giant on the Edge* (New Haven: Yale University Press), p. 219; J. Alan Holman, *Ancient Life of the Great Lakes Basin: Precambrian to Pleistocene* (Ann Arbor: University of Michigan Press, 1995), pp. 179–94; Pielou, *After the Ice Age*, 63; Lange, *Ice Age Mammals*, 167; Lister and Bahn, *Mammoths*, 19–21; Fagan, *Complete Ice Age*, 184.

24. Lange, *Ice Age Mammals*, 120; Holman, *Ancient Life of the Great Lakes Basin*, 189; Sid Perkins, "Earth: Ancient Beavers Did Not Eat Trees: Now-Extinct Giant Creatures Had Hippopotamus-Like Diet," *Science News* 176, v. 11 (Nov., 2009): 10.

25. Lange, *Ice Age Mammals*, 100; Holman, *Ancient Life of the Great Lakes Basin*, 186.

26. Lange, *Ice Age Mammals*, 61–63; Drumm, *Mammoths and Mastodons*, 13–20; Kudish, *Catskill Forest*, 14, 33; Pielou, *After the Ice Age*, 91–93; Davis, "Quaternary His-

tory," *Forest Succession*, 146; Douglas Frink and Allen Hathaway, "Behavioral Continuity on a Changing Landscape," David L. Cremeens and John P. Hart, eds., *Geoarchaeology of Landscapes in the Glaciated Northeast* (Albany: New York State Museum, Bulletin 497, 2003), p. 105.

27. Robert S. Feranec and Andrew Kozlowski, "New AMS Radiocarbon Dates from Late Pleistocene Mastodons and Mammoths in New York State, USA," *Radiocarbon* 54, no. 2 (2012): 275–79.

28. Perkins, "Giant Beaver," *Science News*; Holman, *Ancient Life of the Great Lakes Basin*, 186–89, 219; Lange, *Ice Age Mammals*, 94–96; Lister and Bahn, *Mammoths*, 148–58; Paul S. Martin and R. G. Klein, *Quaternary Extinctions: A Prehistoric Revolution* (Tuscon: University of Arizona Press, 1984); Thomas Dillehay, *Settlement of the Americas: A New Prehistory* (New York: Basic Books, 2001).

29. Kudish, *Catskill Forest*, 16–17, 31; Pielou, *After the Ice Age*, 92; Davis, "Quaternary History," *Forest Succession*, 152.

30. Foster, *Hemlock*, 55; Pielou, *After the Ice Age*, 30, 91–93, 142, 230; Bonnicksen, *America's Ancient Forests*, 20, 32, 40.

31. Foster, *Hemlock*, 55, 111; Pielou, *After the Ice Age*, 30, 91–93, 142, 230; Bonnicksen, *America's Ancient Forests*, 20, 32, 40, Kudish, *Catskill Forest*, 16–17, 33;

32. Foster, *Hemlock*, 111; Pielou, *After the Ice Age*, 270–71; Bonnicksen, *America's Ancient Forests*, 50; Philip A. Meyers, "Evidence of Mid-Holocene Climate Instability from Variations in Carbon Burial in Seneca Lake, New York" *Journal of Paleoclimatology* 28 (2002): 237–44.

33. Foster, *Hemlock*, 2–4, 20, 86, 94.

34. Pielou, *After the Ice Age*, 291–99.

35. Foster, *Hemlock*, 20, 58, 105–09, 134, 147–50, 167–68; Kudish, *Catskill Forest*, 5, 33; Bonnicksen, *America's Ancient Forests*, 44.

36. Kudish, *Catskill Forest*, 16–17, 34; Bonnicksen, *America's Ancient Forests*, 59.

Chapter Two

1. Charles L. Redman, *Human Impact on Ancient Environments* (Tuscon: University of Arizona Press, 1999).

2. Brian M. Fagan, *Ancient North America: The Archaeology of a Continent*, 2nd ed. (New York: Thames and Hudson, 1995), pp. 79–80; Robert E. Funk, *Archaeological Investigations in the Upper Susquehanna Valley, New York State* (Buffalo, NY: Partners Press,

1993), p. 51; David J. Meltzer, *The Great Paleolithic War: How Science Forged an Understanding of America's Ice Age Past* (Chicago: University of Chicago Press, 2015).

3. James B. Petersen, "Forward: West Athens Hill, the Paleo-Indian Period, and Robert E. Funk in Northeastern Perspective," Robert E. Funk, *An Ice Age Quarry-Workshop: The West Athens Hill Site Revisited* (Albany: The University of New, New York State Museum Bulletin 504, 2004), pp. xiii–xiv; Vernon Leslie, *Faces in Clay: The Archaeology and Early History of the Red Man in the Upper Delaware Valley* (Middletown, NY: T. Emmett, Publisher, 1973), p. 2; Esther K. Braun and David P. Braun, *The First Peoples of the Northeast* (Lincoln, MA: Moccasin Hill Press, 1994), p. 18.

4. Lister and Bahn, *Mammoths*, 35; Hìtakonanu'laxk, *The Grandfathers Speak: Native American Folk Tales of the Lenapé People* (New York: Interlink Books, 2012), pp. 107–08.

5. Peterson, "Forward: West Athens Hill," *Ice Age Quarry*, pp. xiv, xxxi; Fagan, *Ancient North America*, 117; Leslie, *Faces in Clay*, 4; Braun and Braun, *First Peoples of the Northeast*, 18; William A. Ritchie, *The Archaeology of New York State* Revised Edition (Harrison NY: Harbor Hill Books, 1980), pp. 1–11; Herbert Clemens Kraft, "The Plenge Site: A Paleo-Indian Occupation Site in New Jersey," *Archaeology of Eastern North America* 1 (1): 56–117; Sydne B. Marshall, "Aboriginal Settlement in New Jersey During the Paleo-Indian Cultural Period Ca. 10,000 B.C—6,000 B.C." www.Nj.Gov/Dep/Hpo/1identity.

6. Peterson, "Forward: West Athens Hill," *Ice Age Quarry*, p. xxviii; McNett, *Shawnee Minisink*, 3–4; June Evans, "Paleo-Indian to Early Archaic Transition at the Shawnee Minisink Site," *Shawnee Minisink*, pp. 223–25.

7. William Andrefsky, "History and Archaeology Part A: Prehistory in the Upper Delaware Valley," Dekin, *Cultural Resource Survey: Upper Delaware*, pp 3–9; Fagan, *Ancient North America*, 111–17; Kingsland, *Evolution of American Ecology*, 169; Bonnicksen, *America's Ancient Forests*, 44, 59; Pielou, *World of Northern Evergreens*, 125–27; Evans, "Paleo-Indian to Early Archaic Transition," *Shawnee Minisink*, 223–55; Richard J. Dent, "Amerinds and the Environment: Myth, Reality, and the Upper Delaware Valley," *Shawnee Minisink*, 158; McNett, "The Shawnee Minisink: An Overview," *Shawnee Minisink*, 321–322.

8. Hìtakonanu'laxk, *The Grandfathers Speak*, 76–77.

9. Leslie, *Faces in Clay*, 4; Peterson, "Forward: West Athens Hill," *Ice Age Quarry*, p. xix.

10. Evans, "Paleo-Indian to Early Archaic Transition," *Shawnee Minisink*, 223–55.

11. Andrefsky, "History and Archaeology Part A," 3-10-3-12; Braun and Braun, *First Peoples of the Northeast*, 29–39; Leslie, *Faces in Clay*, 6; McNett, "The Shawnee Minisink: An Overview," *Shawnee Minisink*, 321–322; Funk, *Archaeological Investigations in the Upper Susquehanna*, 70–71.

12. Marchand, *Autumn*, 106; Ritchie, *Archaeology of New York State*, 42, 59.

13. Kudish, *Catskill Forest*, 34; Bonnicksen, *America's Ancient Forests*, 261; Funk, *Archaeological Investigations in the Upper Susquehanna*, 46–48.

14. Funk, *Archaeological Investigations in the Upper Susquehanna*, 46–48.

15. Andrefsky, "History and Archaeology Part A," 3-12-3-13; Ritchie, *Archaeology of New York State*, 31–59; Section of Archaeology at the State Museum of Pennsylvania, "This Week in Pennylvania Archaeology," www.Twipa.Blogspot.Com., 2015.

16. Leslie, *Faces in Clay*, 32; Foster, ed., *Hemlock*, 119; Braun and Braun, *First Peoples of the Northeast*, 46–49; Fagan, *Ancient North America*, 379–86; Jay F. Custer, *Prehistoric Cultures of Eastern Pennsylvania* (Harrisburg: Commonwealth of Pennsylvania, Pennsylvania Historical and Museum Commission, 1996), pp. 163–216.

17. *Ibid.*

18. Andrefsky, "History and Archaeology Part A," 3-14-3-17; Leslie, *Faces in Clay*, 8–18; 213–16; Custer, *Prehistoric Cultures*, 214–16 quotation 216.

19. Pielou, *After the Ice Age*, 291–99; Bonnicksen, *America's Ancient Forests*, 51.

20. Andrefsky, "History and Archaeology Part A," 3-17-3-20; Leslie, *Faces in Clay*, 8–25; Ritchie, *Archaeology of New York State*, 150–54; McNett, *Shawnee Minisink*, 324.

21. Andrefsky, "History and Archaeology Part A," 3-21-3-23; Leslie, *Faces in Clay*, 53–59; Ritchie, *Archaeology of New York State*, 179; Braun and Braun, *First Peoples of the Northeast*, 60–71.

22. Braun and Braun, *First Peoples of the Northeast*, 60–71; Richard Dent and Barbara E. Kauffman, "Aboriginal Subsistence and Site Ecology as Interpreted from Microfloral and Faunal Remains," *Shawnee Minisink*, 55–78; Gayle J. Fritz, "Levels of Native Biodiversity in Eastern North America," Paul e. Minnis and Wayne J. Elisens, *Biodiversity &*

Native America (Norman: University of Oklahoma Press, 2000), pp. 232–33.

23. Andrefsky, "History and Archaeology Part A," 3-21-3-23; Leslie, *Faces in Clay*, 68–76; Ritchie, *Archaeology of New York State*, 201–05.

24. *Ibid.*

25. Bonnicksen, *America's Ancient Forests*, 93.

26. Bruce D. Smith, *The Emergence of Agriculture* (New York: Scientific American Library, 1988), pp. 183–205.

27. *Ibid.*, 150–160 ; Fritz, "Levels of Native Diversity," 223–47.

28. Fritz, "Levels of Native Diversity," 223–47.

29. *Ibid.*

30. Kudish, *Catskill Forest*, 47; Ritchie, *Archaeology of New York State*, 208–11.

31. Fritz, "Levels of Native Diversity," 223–47; Braun and Braun, *First Peoples of the Northeast*, 72.

32. Andrefsky, "History and Archaeology Part A," 3-21-3-23; Leslie, *Faces in Clay*, 70–76.

33. Fagan, *Ancient North America*, 453–62; Hìtakonanu'laxk, *The Grandfathers Speak*, 45–52.

34. Fagan, *Ancient North America*, 453–62.

35. Hìtakonanu'laxk, *The Grandfathers Speak*, 57–59.

36. *Ibid.*, 1–2; Fagan, *Ancient North America*, 453–62.

37. Braun and Braun, *First Peoples of the Northeast*, 72–84; Leslie, *Faces in Clay*, 84–100; Fagan, *Ancient North America*, 461–62; Ritchie, *Archaeology of New York State*, 274–300.

38. Fagan, *Ancient North America*, 461–62; Ritchie, *Archaeology of New York State*, 274–300.

39. *Ibid.*

40. Andrefsky, "History and Archaeology Part A," 3-26-3-30; Leslie, *Faces in Clay*, 102–130; W.W. Munsell, ed., *The History of Delaware County* (New York: W.W. Munsell and Company, 1880), pp. 43–45; Richard Smith, *A Tour of Four Great Rivers: The Hudson, Mohawk, Susquehanna and Delaware in 1769*, ed. Francis Whiting Halsey (New York: Charles Scribner's Sons, 1906), p. 70.

41. Andrefsky, "History and Archaeology Part A," 3-26-3-30; Leslie, *Faces in Clay*, 130; David Murray, ed., *Centennial History of Delaware County, New York: 1797–1897* (Delhi NY: William Clark, Publisher, 1897); Section of Archaeology, "This Week in Pennylvania Archaeology," www.Twipa.Blogspot.com.

42. Fritz, "Levels of Native Diversity," 223–47.

43. Hitakonanu'laxk, *The Grandfathers Speak*, 35, 67–69.

Chapter Three

1. Berger, *Forests Forever*, 19.

2. Dietland Muller-Schwarze and Lixing Sun, *The Beaver: Natural History of a Wetlands Engineer* (Ithaca: Cornell University Press, 2003), pp. 10–12.

3. *Ibid.*, 30, 88–98; Alice Outwater, *Water: A Natural History* (New York: Basic Books, 1996), pp. 3–33.

4. Muller-Schwarze and Sun, *The Beaver*, 66–70; Pielou, *World of Northern Evergreens*, 82.

5. Muller-Schwarze and Sun, *The Beaver*, 55–60; Earl L. Hilfiker, *Beavers: Water, Wildlife and History* (Interlaken, NY: Windswept Press, 1990), pp. 109–40.

6. Muller-Schwarze and Sun, *The Beaver*, 32, 124–31, 166; Paul Strong, *Beavers: Where Waters Run* (Minoqua, WI: Northword Press, Inc., 1997), pp. 65–71.

7. Joseph A. Chapman and George A. Feldhamer, eds. *Wild Mammals of North America: Biology, Management, Economics* (Baltimore: The Johns Hopkins University Press, 1982), pp. 83–121, 146–66, 460–90, 711–27; 878–901; Maurice Hornocker and Sharon Negri, eds., *Cougar: Ecology and Conservation* (Chicago: University of Chicago Press, 2010).

8. Wallace, *Teedyuscung*, 15.

9. Douglas Hunter, *Half Moon: Henry Hudson and the Voyage That Redrew the Map of the New World* (New York: Bloomsbury Press, 2009).

10. R.H. Tawney, *Religion and the Rise of Capitalism* (London: Penguin Books, 1977); Alfred A. Crosby, *Ecological Imperialism: The Biological Expansion of Europe, 900–1900*, 2nd ed. (Cambridge: Cambridge University Press, 2004).

11. Crosby, *Ecological Imperialism*; Peter C. Mancall, *Hakluyt's Promise: An Elizabethan's Obsession for an English America* (New Haven: Yale University Press, 2007).

12. Francis Bacon, *Novum Organum*, ed. Thmas Fowler (Oxford: Clarendon Press, 1878); Carolyn Merchant, *Reinventing Eden: The Fate of Nature in Western Culture* (New York: Routledge, 2004); Frederick Turner, *Beyond Geography: The Western Spirit Against the Wilderness*, 2nd Ed. (New Brunswick, NJ: Rutgers University Press, 1992).

13. Oliver A. Rink, *Holland on the Hudson: An Economic and Social History of Dutch New York* (Ithaca: Cornell University Press, 1986); Janny Venema, *Beverwijck: A Dutch Village on the American Frontier, 1652–1664* (Albany: State University of New York Press, 2003); Wallace, *Teedyuscung*, 2–4.

14. Wallace, *Teedyuscung*, 10; Leslie, *Faces in Clay*, 200.

15. Amy C. Schutt, *Peoples of the River Valleys: The Odyssey of the Delaware Indians* (Philadelphia: University of Pennsylvania Press, 2007), pp. 7–30.

16. *Ibid.*; Hitakonanu'laxk, *Grandfathers Speak*, 123–27.

17. Schutt, *Peoples of the River Valleys*, 40–42; Alfred A. Crosby, *The Columbian Exchange: Biological and Cultural Consequences of 1492*, 30th Anniv. ed. (Westport, CT: Praegar, 2003); Leslie, *Faces in Clay*, 255.

18. Leslie, *Faces in Clay*, 189–207; Wallace, *Teedyuscung*, 11, 150, 216.

19. Wallace, *Teedyuscung*, 233; Muller-Schwarze and Sun, *The Beaver*, 138, quotation 136; Leslie, *Faces in Clay*, 208.

20. Muller-Schwarze and Sun, *The Beaver*, 139, 173; Hilfiker, *Beavers*, 51–90; Lewis Henry Morgan, *The American Beaver: A Classic of Natural History and Ecology* (New York: Dover Publications, 1986), pp. 218–47; Calvin Martin, *Keepers of the Game: Indian-Animal Relationships and the Fur Trade* (Oakland: University of California Press, 1982); Sylvia Van Kirk, *Many Tender Ties: Women in Fur-Trade Society, 1670–1870* (Norman: University of Oklahoma Press, 1983).

21. Muller-Schwarze and Sun, *The Beaver*, 139–143; Hilfiker, *Beavers*, 73–77;

22. Andrefsky, "History and Archaeology Part A," 3–31–3–35; Leslie, *Faces in Clay*, 208–09; McGregor, *History and Archaeology 4.3 Part B: Contact and Euro-American*, 4–5.

23. Schutt, *Peoples of the River Valleys*, 32; Hitakonanu'laxk, *Grandfathers Speak*, 19; William Cronon, *Changes in the Land*, rev. ed. (New York: Hill and Wang, 2003).

24. Rink, *Holland on the Hudson*, 214–63.

25. Ronald W. Howard, "The English Province [1664–1776]," *The Empire State: A History of New York*, Milton M. Klein, ed. (Ithaca: Cornell University Press, 2001), pp. 113–29; David Lovejoy, *The Glorious Revolution in America* (Middletown, CT: Wesleyan University Press, 1987).

26. Philip J. Schwarz, *The Jarring Interests: New York's Boundary Makers* (Albany: State University of New York Press, 1979); Leslie, *Faces in Clay*, 218.

27. Schwarz, *Jarring Interests*, 81–82; H. Fletcher Davidson, *Delaware County: Fur Trading to Farming* (Delhi, NY: R.B. Decker Advertising, 1976), pp. 11–20.

28. Barbara F. Sivertsen and Barbara L. Covey, eds., *The Legend of Cushetunk: The Nathan Skinner Manuscript and the Early History of Cochecton* (Westminster, MD: Heritage Books, 2011), pp. 5, 48; Smith, *Tour of Four Great Rivers*, lxvii; Schwarz, *Jarring Interests*, 87.

29. Davidson, *Delaware County*, 11–20.

30. John Moretta, *William Penn and the Quaker Legacy* (New York: Pearson, 2006).

31. Schutt, *Peoples of the River Valleys*, 87–88; Leslie, *Faces in Clay*, 265–88; Wallace, *Teedyuscung*, 26–30.

32. Schutt, *Peoples of the River Valleys*, 119–29; Leslie, *Faces in Clay*, 289–91; Wallace, *Teedyuscung*, 195–96; George J. Fluhr, *A Generation of Suffering on the Upper Delaware Frontier, 1742–1782* (Shohola, PA: Reprinted from the *News Eagle*, Hawley, PA, 1976).

33. Wallace, *Teedyuscung*, 39.

34. Douglas R. McManis, *Colonial New England: A Historical Geography* (Oxford: Oxford University Press, 1976).

35. Edmund S. Morgan and Helen M. Morgan, *The Stamp Act Crisis* (New York: Collier MacMillian Publishers, 1962), p. 290.

36. Julian Boyd, ed., *The Susquehanna Company Papers, Volume I: 1750–55* (Ithaca: Cornell University Press, 1962), 196; Wallace, *Teedyuscung*, 50, 154; quotation from *Pennsylvania Colonial Records* (Harrisburg: Theo Fenn and Company, 1831) 8: 565.

37. Wallace, *Teedyuscung*, 61; Sivertson and Covey, *Legend of Cushetunk*, 31–34.

38. Wallace, *Teedyuscung*, 227; Hìtakonanu'laxk, *Grandfathers Speak*, 23.

39. Wallace, *Teedyuscung*, 224; Sivertson and Covey, *Legend of Cushetunk*, 1–3, 35–43; *Pennsylvania Colonial Records* 8: lxxix; James W. Burbank, *Cushetunk: A Brief History of the Early Settlers Who Called Themselves the Delaware Company* (Callicoon, NY: Sullivan County Democrat, 1952).

40. Sivertson and Covey, *Legend of Cushetunk*, 4–5; *Pennsylvania Colonial Records* 8: lxxxvii, 308–14.

41. Wallace, *Teedyuscung*, 258–64; Sivertson and Covey, *Legend of Cushetunk*, 5–8.

42. Fluhr, *A Generation of Suffering*, 16.

43. Smith, *Tour of Four Great Rivers*, lxxi.

44. *Ibid.*, 71–76; Schutt, *Peoples of the River Valleys*, 16–18; Bonnicksen, *America's Ancient Forests*, 204.

45. Smith, *Tour of Four Great Rivers*, lxxii, 71–76.

46. Fluhr, *A Generation of Suffering* ; Sivertson and Covey, *Legend of Cushetunk*, 27.

47. McGregor, *History and Archaeology 4.3 Part B: Contact and Euro-American*, 18–24; B.F. Fackenthal, Jr., "Improving Navigation on the Delaware River, with Some Account of Its Ferries, Bridges, Canals, and Floods," *Papers, Bucks County (PA) Historical Society*, 6:103–230.

48. Sivertson and Covey, *Legend of Cushetunk*, 12–13; Leslie Wood, *Rafting on the Delaware River* (Livingston Manor, NY: Livingston Manor Times, 1934).

Chapter Four

1. Frederick Jackson Turner, *The Significance of the Frontier in American History* (Madison: State Historical Society of Wisconsin, 1894).

2. Murray, ed. *Centennial History of Delaware County*.

3. New York State, Bureau of the Census, *Census of the State of New York, for 1855* (Albany: Department of State, Printed by Carroll and Cook, 1855).

4. Lucy E. Braun, *Deciduous Forests of Eastern North America* (Philadelphia: The Blakiston Company, 1950), p. 12; A. F. Hough, "A Climax Forest on East Tionesta Creek in Northwestern Pennsylvania," *Ecology* 17 (Spring, 1936): 9–28; H. J. Lutz and A. L. McComb, "Origin of White Pine in Virgin Forest Stands of Northwestern Pennsylvania as Indicated by Stem and Basal Branch Features," *Ecology* 16 (Winter, 1936): 252–56; Alfred Mathews, *History of Wayne, Pike, and Monroe Counties, Pennsylvania* (Philadelphia: R.T. Peck and Company, 1886), p. 327.

5. New York State, Bureau of the Census, *Census of the State of New York for 1821, 1825, 1836, 1845*. Unless otherwise noted, all statistics in the chapter regarding population, improved acreage, numbers of sawmills, tanneries, and asheries derive from these sources.

6. Brooke Hindle, ed., *America's Wooden Age: Aspects of Its Early Technology* (Tarrytown, NY: Sleepy Hollow Press, 1975); *Material Culture of the Wooden Age* (Tarrytown, NY: Sleepy Hollow Press, 1981).

7. Louis C. Hunter, *Water-Power in the Age of the Steam Engine* (Charlottesville: University of Virginia Press, 1979), pp. 54–60; Oliver Evans, *The Young Millwright and*

Miller's Guide (Philadelphia: Lea and Blanchard, 1850), pp. 340–48.

8. Hunter, *Water-Power*, 293–98.

9. McGregor, "Radical Environmental Change," 77–80. The production figures derived from the manuscript schedules of the United States Census of Industry, 1880.

10. *Ibid.*, 66–80.

11. Thomas R. Cox, Robert S. Maxwell, Phillip Drennon Thomas, and Joseph J. Malone, *This Well-Wooded Land: Americans and Their Forests from Colonial Times to the Present* (Lincoln: University of Nebraska Press, 1985), pp. 9–11.

12. Stephen M. Silverman and Raphael D. Silver, *The Catskills: Its History and How It Changed America* (New York: Alfred A. Knopf, 2015), pp. 137–49; Cynthia A. Kierner, "Landlord and Tenant in Revolutionary New York: The Case of Livingston Manor," *New York History* 70 (April, 1989): 133–152.

13. Cox, Maxwell, Thomas, and Malone, *This Well-Wooded Land*, 3–12; Michael Williams, *Americans & Their Forests: A Historical Geography* (Cambridge: Cambridge University Press, 1992), pp. 112–18.

14. *Ibid.*; Foster, ed., *Hemlock*, 138–43.

15. Ulysses Prentiss Hedrick, *A History of Agriculture in the State of New York* (New York: Hill and Wang, 1933), pp. 1–9.

16. Henry J. Kauffman, *The American Farmhouse* (New York: Bonanza Books, 1975); Eric Sloane, *An Age of Barns* (New York: Funk and Wagnalls, 1963); *Transactions of the New York State Agricultural Society*, Vol. 2 (Albany: E. Mack, Printer to the Senate, 1843), pp. 121–35; McGregor, "Radical Environmental Change," 111–12.

17. United States Department of State, *Sixth Census of the United States, 1840* (Washington, D.C.: Bureau of the Census, 1841); R. V. Reynolds and Albert H. Pierson, *Fuel Wood Used in the United States, 1630–1930* (Washington, D.C.: United States Department of Agriculture, Circular No. 641, February, 1942); Henry S. Graves, *The Use of Wood for Fuel* (Washington: United States Department of Agriculture, Bulletin No. 753, March 10, 1919).

18. Charles T. Curtis, *Stories of the Raftsmen* (Callicoon, NY: Sullivan County Democrat, 1922); Thaddeus S. Kenderdine, "Lumbering Days on the Delaware," *Papers, Bucks County (PA) Historical Society* 4 (1917): 239–52; Joshua Pine III, "A Rafting Story of the Delaware River," *Papers, Bucks County (PA) Historical Society* 6 (1932): 467–524; Harry B. and Grace M. Weiss, *Rafting on the Delaware*

(Trenton: New Jersey Agricultural Society, 1967); Mathews, *Wayne Pike, and Monroe Counties*, 327–29; McGregor, *Upper Delaware Cultural Resource Survey*, 3–67 to 3–77.

19. Works Progress Administration, "Rafting," 3 vols., unpublished, on file, Minnisink Valley Historical Society, Port Jervis, NY.

20. McGregor, "Radical Environmental Change," 66–70, 89, 166–70; United States Department of State, *Eighth Census of the United States, 1850* (Washington, D.C.: Bureau of the Census, 1851); *Tenth Census of the United States, 1870* (Washington, D.C.: Bureau of the Census, 1871).

21. Pine, "Rafting Story of the Delaware," 467–69.

22. Silverman and Silver, *The Catskills*, 112–114.

23. William F. Fox, *History of the Lumber Industry in the State of New York* (Harrison, NY: Harbor Hill Books, 1976), pp. 61–62; Hunter, *Water-Power*, 25–28; Jared Van Wagenen, Jr., *The Golden Age of Homespun* (Ithaca: Cornell University Press, 1953), pp. 183–91; Foster, ed., *Hemlock*, 220–22; Silverman and Silver, *The Catskills*, 116.

24. Kudish, *Catskill Forest*, 58–59.

25. James E. Quinlan, *History of Sullivan County* (Liberty, NY: G.M. Beebe and W.T. Morgans, 1873); Munsell, *History of Delaware County*.

26. Joseph M. Petulla, *American Environmental History* (San Francisco: Boyd and Fraser Publishing Company, 1977), pp. 42–43; Hedrick, *History of Agriculture in New York*, 110.

27. William L. Webb, Donald F. Behrend, and Boonrang Saisorn,"Effect of Logging on Songbird Populations in a Northern Hardwood Forest," *Wildlife Monographs*, supplement to *The Journal of Wildlife Management* 41, No. 3 (July, 1977): 6–35.

28. Murray, ed., *Centennial History of Delaware County*; Marchand, *North Woods*, 27–31; Silverman and Silver, *The Catskills*, 116; Marchand, *North Woods*, 27–31; Elizabeth Stephens Lotterer, *Stockport on the Delaware* (Hancock, NY: Hancock Herald, 1964); Peter Matthiessen, *Wildlife in America*, rev. ed. (New York: Viking, 1987), pp. 56–58, 83–85, 119–21, 158–61. The phrase is stolen from Aldo Leopold's *A Sand County Almanac*. Leopold remarked that farmers were endeavoring to make Illinois safe for soybeans.

29. Titus, *Catskills in the Ice Age*, 79; McGregor, "Radical Environmental Change," 90–92.

30. McGregor, "Radical Environmental

Change," 90–92; McGregor, *Upper Delaware Cultural Resource Survey*, 3–14 to 3–17.

31. Joseph A. Durrenberger, *Turnpikes: A History of the Toll Road Movement in the Middle Atlantic States and Maryland* (Cos Cob, CT: J.E. Edwards, 1968), pp. 144–58.

32. A.W. Kuchler, *Potential Natural Vegetation of the Conterminous United States* (New York: American Geographical Society, Special Publication No. 36, 1964); Ann Sutton and Myron Sutton, *The Audubon Society Nature Guides: Eastern Forests* (New York: Alfred A. Knopf, 1990); Kudish, *Catskill Forest*, 31–36; United States, Census of Agriculture, Schedules, 1850.

33. Quinlan, *History of Sullivan County*, 373.

34. Noble E. Whitford, *History of the Canal System of the State of New York* (Albany: Brandon Printing Company, 1905), pp. 729–44; Diane L. Jacox, *Delaware and Hudson, Past and Present* (Philadelphia: National Parks Service, Division of History, 1979).

35. "Stourbridge Lion Historical Marker," www.ExplorePahistory.com; Jim Shaughnessy, *Delaware and Hudson* (Berkeley CA: Howell-North Books, 1967).

36. Charles T. Curtis, *Stories of the Raftsmen*, 7; Manville B. Wakefield, *Coal Boats to Tidewater* (Steingart Associates, 1965).

37. Working on the cultural resource management survey of the Upper Delaware undertaken by the Public Archaeology Facility (SUNY-Binghamton) for the National Park Service, a colleague observed that the original plan was to have the canal tunneled under the river. I suspect this was not true.

38. Robert M. Vogel, *Roebling's Delaware & Hudson Canal Aqueducts* (Washington, D.C.: Smithsonian Institution Press, Smithsonian Studies in History and Technology, No. 10, 1971).

39. Delaware and Hudson Canal Company, *Annual Report of the Board of Managers of the Delaware and Hudson Canal Company to the Stockholders* (Harrisburg, PA: 1825 to 1900).

40. John Lord, "Personal Notebooks, 1838–46," Unpublished MS. On file at the Minisink Valley Historical Society, Port Jervis, New York.

41. E. M. Ruttenber and L. H. Clark, *History of Orange County, New York* (Philadelphia: Everts and Peck, 1881), pp. 118–21, 710–12.

42. Cox, Maxwell, Thomas, and Malone, *This Well-Wooded Land*, 13–32, 36–37; Williams, *Americans & Their Forests*, 136,
178–82; Carol Sheriff, *The Artificial River: The Erie Canal and the Paradox of Progress, 1817–1862* (New York: Hill and Wang, 1996).

43. Pickett and White, eds., *Ecology of Natural Disturbance*, 7, 384; Canham and Marks, "Response of Woody Plants to Disturbance," *Ecology of Natural Disturbance*, Pickett and White, eds., 197–216.

44. Cox, Maxwell, Thomas, and Malone, *This Well-Wooded Land*, 51–110; Williams, *Americans & Their Forests*, 146–89.

Chapter Five

1. Eric Homberger, *The Historical Atlas of New York City: A Visual Celebration of Nearly 400 Years of New York City's History* (New York: Henry Holt, 1994), pp. 70–89; Kenneth T. Jackson, "Asher B. Durand's New York," *Kindred Spirits: Asher B. Durand and the American Landscape*, Linda S. Ferber, ed. (Brooklyn: D. Giles Limited, 2007), 38.

2. Phillip Lopate, "The Days of the Patriarchs: Washington Irving's a *History of New York*, *Dutch New York: The Roots of Hudson Valley Culture*," Roger Panetta, ed. (New York: Fordham University Press, 2009), pp. 191–222; Washington Irving, a *History of New York* (New York: Penguin Books, 2008) [Originally published in 1809].

3. Lopate, "Days of the Patriarchs," 191–222; Washington Irving, *The Legend of Sleepy Hollow and Other Stories or the Sketch Book of Geoffrey Crayon, Gent.* (New York: Penguin Books, 2001) [originally published in 1819]; Raymond Beecher, *Kaaterskill Clove: Where Nature Met Art* (Hensonville, NY: Black Dome Press, 2004), p. 20; Silverman and Silver, *The Catskills*, 37–41.

4. Irving, "The Legend of Sleepy Hollow," *Legend of Sleepy Hollow*, 294, "Rip Van Winkle," 35.

5. Irving, "Rip Van Winkle," *Legend of Sleepy Hollow*, 30.

6. Alan Taylor, *William Cooper's Town: Power and Persuasion on the Frontier of the Early American Republic* (New York: Random House: 1995); Wayne Franklin, *James Fenimore Cooper: The Early Years* (New Haven: Yale University Press, 2007); Silverman and Silver, *The Catskills*, 41–47.

7. James Fenimore Cooper, *The Pioneers* (New York: Penguin Books, 2006) [originally published in 1823]; quotations on pp. 8, 28, 98, 239.

8. Franklin, *James Fenimore Cooper*, 457, 471–78; James Fenimore Cooper, *The Last of*

the Mohicans (New York: Barnes and Noble Classics, 2003) [originally published in 1826], p. 22.

9. Franklin, *James Fenimore Cooper*, 367–68, 519; John Durand, *The Life and Times of Asher B. Durand* (Hensonville, NY: Black Dome Press, 2006) [originally published in 1894], p. 80, 96; Barbara Babcock Millhouse, *American Wilderness: The Story of the Hudson River School of Painting* (Hensonville, NY: Black Dome Press, 2007), pp. 17–18, 31–32; Gilbert H. Muller, *William Cullen Bryant: Author of America* (Albany: State University of New York Press, 2008), 84, 238.

10. Franklin, *James Fenimore Cooper*; Cooper, *The Pioneers*, 110.

11. Cooper, *Last of the Mohicans*, 21; Muller, *William Cullen Bryant*, 1–27.

12. Quoted in Muller, *William Cullen Bryant*, 23.

13. *Ibid.*, 37–103.

14. *Ibid.*, 104, 119, 181.

15. Franklin, *James Fenimore Cooper*, 397–98; Silverman and Silver, *The Catskills*, 42; Judith Hansen O'Toole, *Different Views in Hudson River School Painting* (New York: Columbia University Press, 2005), p. 12.

16. Millhouse, *American Wilderness*, 2–7; Earl A. Powell, *Thomas Cole* (New York: Harry N. Abrams, 1990), pp. 18–20.

17. Barbara Novak, *Nature and Culture: American Landscape and Painting, 1825–1875* (Oxford: Oxford University Press, 2007), p. 16.

18. Millhouse, *American Wilderness*, 7–12; Powell, *Thomas Cole*, 19; Linda S. Ferber, *The Hudson River School: Nature and the American Vision* (New York: New York Historical Society, 2009), p. 199.

19. Millhouse, *American Wilderness*, 20.

20. Titus, *Catskills in the Ice Age*, 25, 68.

21. Evelyn D. Trebilcock and Valerie A. Balint, *Glories of the Hudson: Frederic Edwin Church's Views from Olana* (Ithaca: Cornell University Press, 2009), p. 19; Powell, *Thomas Cole*, 12–23, quotation, 73;

22. Powell, *Thomas Cole*, 9–10; Muller, *William Cullen Bryant*, 53; Millhouse, *American Wilderness*, 20; David Schuyler, "The Mid-Hudson Valley as Iconic Landscape: Tourism. Economic Development, and the Beginnings of a Preservationist Impulse," *Within the Landscape: Essays on Nineteenth-Century American Art and Culture*, ed. Phillip Earenfight and Nancy Siegel (University Park: Pennsylvania State University Press, 2005), pp. 11–42.

23. Ferber, *Hudson River School*, 68; Trebilcock and Balint, *Glories of the Hudson*, 32;

24. Millhouse, *American Wilderness*, 14–16; Muller, *William Cullen Bryant*, 57; Ferber, *Hudson River School*, 168, 199.

25. Millhouse, *American Wilderness*, 25–30, 55; Ferber, *Hudson River School*, 82; Powell, *Thomas Cole*, 46–49, quotation, 97.

26. Powell, *Thomas Cole*, 62–70, 108–09; Millhouse, *American Wilderness*, 55, 62–71; quotation, 66.

27. Millhouse, *American Wilderness*, 46; O'Toole, *Different Views*, 124; Schuyler, "Mid-Hudson Valley as Iconic Landscape," *Within the Landscape*, Earenfight and Siegel, eds., 33.

28. Durand, *Life and Times of Durand*, 67.

29. Silverman and Silver, *The Catskills*, 63.

30. Ferber, *Hudson River School*, 82; Franklin, *James Fenimore Cooper*, 376; Beecher, *Kaatersville Clove*, 99; Schuyler, "Mid-Hudson Valley as Iconic Landscape," *Within the Landscape*, Earenfight and Siegel. eds., 12.

31. Silverman and Silver, *The Catskills*, 101–10; Trebilcock and Balint, *Glories of the Hudson*, 30–31.

32. *Ibid.*, 79; Ferber, *Hudson River School*, 44–46; Muller, *William Cullen Bryant*, 124; Barbara Dayer Gallati, "A Year of Toilsome Exile': Asher B. Durand's European Sojourn," Ferber, ed., *Kindred Spirits*, 56; Linda S. Ferber, "Asher B. Durand, American Landscape Painter," Ferber, ed., *Kindred Spirits*, 130; David S. Reynolds, *Walt Whitman's America: A Cultural Biography* (New York: Alfred A. Knopf, 1995), p. 286. The young journalist was Whitman.

33. Millhouse, *American Wilderness*, 69.

34. *Ibid.*; Trebilcock and Balint, *Glories of the Hudson*, 20; O'Toole, *Different Views*, 15.

35. Durand, *Life and Times of Durand*, 25–26, 132, quotation, 131; Jackson, "Durand's New York," Ferber, ed., *Kindred Spirits*, 31; Gallati, "Asher B. Durand's Early Career: A Portrait of the Artist as an Ambitious Man," Ferber, ed., *Kindred Spirits*, 54; Ferber, "Asher B. Durand," Ferber, ed., *Kindred Spirits*, 159.

36. Jackson, "Durand's New York," Galati, "Durand's Early Career," Ferber, ed., *Kindred Spirits*, 35–69; Durand, *Life and Times of Durand*, 177.

37. Millhouse, *American Wilderness*, 71–72; Ferber, "Asher B. Durand," Ferber, ed., *Kindred Spirits*, 162; Muller, *William Cullen Bryant*, 206.

38. Millhouse, *American Wilderness*, 67; Ferber, "Asher B. Durand," Ferber, ed., *Kindred Spirits*, 130; Durand, *Life and Times of Durand*, 81, 188.

39. Millhouse, *American Wilderness*, 86; Gallati, "Year of Toilsome Exile," Ferber, ed., *Kindred Spirits*, 82; Ferber, "Asher B. Durand," Ferber, ed., *Kindred Spirits*, 153, 171; Durand, *Life and Times of Durand*, 193.

40. Cooper, *Last of the Mohicans*, 118; Muller, *William Cullen Bryant*, 56; O'Toole, *Different Views*, 12–18; Ferber, *Hudson River School*, 68; Judith K. Major, *To Live in the New World: A.J. Downing and American Landscape Gardening* (Cambridge: The MIT Press, 1997), p. 136; Powell, *Thomas Cole*, 11,39.

41. Helferich, *Humboldt's Cosmos*; Millhouse, *American Wilderness*, 89–95; Kevin J. Avery, *Treasures from Olana: Landscapes by Frederic Edwin Church* (Ithaca: Cornell University Press, 2005), p. 39.

42. Millhouse, *American Wilderness*, 63, 89, 95; Trebilcock and Balint, *Glories of the Hudson*, 47; Avery, *Treasures from Olana*.

43. Muller, *William Cullen Bryant*, 151.

44. Harold McCracken, *George Catlin and the Old Frontier* (New York: The Dial Press, 1959), pp. 13–20.

45. *Ibid.* 29–182.

46. *Ibid.*, 183–209; Muller, *William Cullen Bryant*, 90–91; Gallati, "Year of Toilsome Exile," Ferber, ed., *Kindred Spirits*, 88.

47. George Catlin, *North American Indians* (New York: Penguin Classics, 2004) [originally published 1841]; O'Toole, *Different Views*, 13–14.

48. Schuyler, "Mid-Hudson Valley as Iconic Landscape," *Within the Landscape*, eds. Earenfight and Siegel, 23.

49. Major, *To Live in the New World*, 2–6.

50. *Ibid.*, 7–56, 69–87.

51. *Ibid.*, 91–101.

52. *Ibid.*, 129–49.

53. Muller, *William Cullen Bryant*, 181.

54. Millhouse, *American Wilderness*, 85; McGregor, *Wider View of the Universe*, 35–36.

55. Robert C. Williams, *Horace Greeley: Champion of American Freedom* (New York: New York University Press, 2006), pp. 76–86; John Matteson, *The Lives of Margaret Fuller: A Biography* (New York: W.W. Norton and Company, 2012), pp. 249–92.

56. Walter Harding, *The Days of Henry Thoreau: A Biography* (New York: Dover Publications, Inc., 1965), pp. 147–53; Raymond R. Borst, *The Thoreau Log: A Documentary Life of Henry David Thoreau 1817–1862* (New York: G.K. Hall and Company, 1992), pp. 86–103, 121–35; Williams, *Horace Greeley*, 84–86; McGregor, *Wider View of the Universe*, 59–86.

57. McGregor, *Wider View of the Universe*, 87–120.

58. Harding, *Days of Henry Thoreau*, 373; Borst, *Thoreau Log*, 411.

59. Reynolds, *Walt Whitman's America*, 1–114; Walt Whitman, *Leaves of Grass: First and "Death-Bed" Editions* (New York: Barnes and Noble Classics, 2004) [First edition originally published 1855].

60. *Ibid.*, 114, 319, 519, 589.

61. *Ibid.* 244–46; 296.

62. Whitman, *Leaves of Grass*, 1st ed., 40.

63. Justin Martin, *Genius of Place: The Life of Frederick Law Olmsted, Abolitionist, Conservationist, and Designer of Central Park* (Cambridge, MA: DaCapo Press, 2011), pp 50–51.

64. *Ibid.*, 53–66.

65. *Ibid.*, 67–129.

66. Franklin, *James Fenimore Cooper*, xxi; Herman Melville, *Pierre, or the Ambiguities* (New York, Penguin Books, 1996) [originally published 1852]; Thomas Bender, *Toward an Urban Vision: Ideas and Institutions in Nineteenth-Century America* (Lexington: The University Press of Kentucky, 1975), pp.159–88; Bender provides the Melville quotation, 161.

67. Muller, *William Cullen Bryant*, 184, 222; Martin, *Genius of Place*, 127; Ferber, "Asher B. Durand," Ferber, ed., *Kindred Spirits*, 154; Bender, *Toward an Urban Vision*, 159–88.

68. Bender, *Toward an Urban Vision*, 159–88; Martin, *Genius of Place*, 125–27.

69. Bender, *Toward an Urban Vision*, 159–88; Martin, *Genius of Place*, 137–57.

70. Charles Darwin, *On the Origin of Species* (London: John Murray, 1859); Phillip Appleman, ed., *Darwin: A Norton Critical Edition* (New York: W.W. Norton and Company, 1979); Avery, *Treasures from Olana*, 16–20.

71. Harding, *Days of Henry Thoreau*, 439–40; Williams, *Horace Greeley*, 85–86; McGregor, *Wider View of the Universe*, 188–204.

72. Henry David Thoreau, "On the Succession of Forest Trees," *The Natural History Essays* (Salt Lake City: Peregrine Smith, 1980), pp. 72–92.

73. Bradley P. Dean, "Henry D. Thoreau and Horace Greeley Exchange Letters on the Spontaneous Generation of Plants," *New England Quarterly* 66 (December, 1993): 630–38; McGregor, *Wider View of the Universe*, 189–91.

74. McGregor, *Wider View of the Universe*, 175–98; Worster, *Nature's Economy*.

Chapter Six

1. Herbert H. Harwood, Jr., *Impossible Challenge: B&O* (Baltimore: Barnard, Roberts and Company, 1979).

2. Albert J. Churella, *The Pennsylvania Railroad, Volume 1: Building an Empire, 1846–1917* (Philadelphia: University of Pennsylvania Press, 2012).

3. Alvin F. Harlow, *The Road of the Century: The Story of the New York Central* (New York: Century Age Press, 1947); Timothy Starr, *Railroad Wars of New York State* (Charleston: The History Press, 2012), pp. 80–81.

4. Edward Hungerford, *Men of Erie: A Story of Human Effort* (New York: Random House, 1946), pp. 80–85.

5. Quinlan, *History of Sullivan County*, 663–74.

6. *Ibid.*; Hungerford, *Men of Erie*, 80; Harper and Brothers, *New York and Erie Rail-Road Guide Book* (New York: Harper and Brothers, 1851), p. 65.

7. Quinlan, *History of Sullivan County*, 652; Wakefield, *Coal Boats to Tidewater*, 106–07; Hungerford, *Men of Erie*, 80–81.

8. Charles Maples to Uriah Gregory, 17 March, 1848, "Uriah Gregory Papers," Broome County Historical Society, Roberson Center, Binghamton, New York.

9. Robert E. Woodruff, *Erie Railroad—Its Beginnings!* (New York: Newcomen Society of England, 1851).

10. Hungerford, *Men of Erie*, 111–14; Harper and Brothers, *New York and Erie Rail-Road Guide*, 59–101; George J. Fluhr, *Pike County: Highlights of History in Northeastern Pennsylvania* (Shohola, PA: George J. Fluhr, 1975), p. 9; Lotterer, *Stockport on the Delaware*, 20.

11. New York State, *Census, 1845 and 1855.*

12. Whitford, *History of the Canal System of New York*, 748–50.

13. Ruttenber and Clark, *History of Orange County*, 710–12.

14. Quinlan, *History of Sullivan County*, 649–50.

15. Arthur N. Meyers, *Douglass: The Delaware Valley City, 1867–78* (Narrowsburg, NY: Delaware Valley Press, 1969).

16. Durrenberger, *Turnpikes*, 144–52.

17. N. L. Jones to Uriah Gregory, 15 February, 1853, "Uriah Gregory Papers."

18. Durrenberger, *Turnpikes*, 150–52; Munsell, *History of Delaware County*, 266–68; Mathews, *Wayne, Pike, and Monroe Counties*, 260.

19. Durrenberger, *Turnpikes*, 150–52.

20. *Ibid.*; Quinlan, *History of Sullivan County*, 607.

21. "The Lumber Trade: History of the Business in New York and Pennsylvania," *New York Times* (May 11, 1872); J.H. French, *Gazetteer of the State of New York* (Syracuse: Pearsall Smith, 1860), p. 257.

22. New York State, *Census, 1845 and 1855.*

23. McGregor, "Radical Environmental Change," 129–31.

24. Alfred J. Van Tassel, *Mechanization in the Lumber Industry* (Philadelphia: Works Progress Administration National Research Project Report #M-5, 1940), p. 8.

25. Edward H. Knight, *Knight's American Mechanical Dictionary*, 3 vols. (Boston: Houghton, Mifflin, 1876).

26. Nelson Courtlandt Brown, *The Small Sawmill in New York* (Syracuse: Syracuse University, Bulletin of the New York State College of Forestry, Technical Publication #50, October, 1937), p. 17.

27. *Knight's American Mechanical Dictionary*; *Port Jervis Evening Gazette*, 18 March, 1884; "The Lumber Trade," *New York Times*, May 11, 1872; Mathews, *Wayne, Pike, and Monroe Counties*, 50.

28. The discussion of waterwheel technology derives from two basic sources, each complimenting the other. They are: Hunter, *Water-Power*, and Arthur T. Safford and Edward P. Hamilton, "The American Mixed-Flow Turbine and Its Setting," *Transactions of the American Society of Civil Engineers* 85, Paper 1503 (1922): 1237–1356. See also Edward W. Constant, "Scientific Theory and Technological Testability: Science, Dynamometers and Water Turbines in the 19th Century," *International Quarterly of the Society for the History of Technology and Culture* 24 (April, 1983): 183–98.

29. Information regarding individual wheel manufactures is derived from a list entitled "United States Government Patents for Waterwheel Technologies Issued During the Nineteenth Century," on file at the Hanford Mills Museum, East Meredith, New York. Source unknown.

30. Edwin T. Layton, "From Rule of Thumb to Scientific Engineering: James B. Francis and the Invention of the Francis Turbine," *NLA Monograph Series* (Stony Brook, NY: Research Foundation of the State University of New York, 1992); "The Gibbs Turbine Water Wheel," pamphlet on file at the Hanford Mills Museum, East Meredith, New York, dated 1882.

31. J. Wallace Hoff, *Two Hundred Miles on*

the Delaware River (Trenton, NJ: The Brandt Press, 1893), p. 34.

32. United States Census, "Products of Industry," manuscript schedules, 1880.

33. McGregor, "Radical Environmental Change," 129–43.

34. Hunter, *Water Power*, 514–28; James Stryker, "Steam Boiler Explosions," *Stryker's American Register and Magazine* 2 (March, 1849): 100–01; Robert H. Thurston, *The Growth of the Steam Engine* (New York: D. Appleton and Company, 1878); Mathews, *Wayne, Pike, and Monroe Counties*, 53.

35. For an explication of the progress arguments, see Lewis Mumford, *Technics and Civilization* (New York: Harcourt, Brace and Company, 1934).

36. United States, *Census of Manufactures*, 1880; Mathews, *Wayne, Pike, and Monroe Counties*, 50.

37. Hamilton Child, *Gazetteer and Business Directory of Sullivan County, New York, for 1872–73* (Syracuse: Hamilton Child, 1872), pp. 108–09; French, *Gazetteer of New York*, 257.

38. Hunter, *Water Power*, 25–28; William F. Fox, *History of the Lumber Industry in New York*, 61–62; Van Wagenen, Jr., *Golden Age of Homespun*, 183–91.

39. Silverman and Silver, *The Catskills*, 112–23.

40. Quinlan, *History of Sullivan County*, 448.

41. *Ibid.*, 209; Foster, *Hemlock*, 220–22;

42. Child, *Gazetteer of Sullivan County*, 108–09.

43. Quinlan, *History of Sullivan County*, 209; Mathews, *Wayne, Pike, and Monroe Counties*, 326.

44. Silverman and Silver, *The Catskills*, 116–18.

45. John Burroughs, "The Heart of the Southern Catskills," *In the Catskills: Selections from the Writings*, reprint edition, ed. Clifton Johnson (LaVergne, TN: Bibliobazaar, 2009), p. 112.

46. Charles Carpenter, *Second Annual Report of the State of New York, for the Year 1886* (Albany: The Argus Company, printers, 1887), reprinted in Norman J. Van Valkenburgh and Christopher W. Olney, *The Catskill Park: Inside the Blue Line* (Henson ville, NY: Blackdome Press, 2004), pp. 163–64; Kudish, *Catskill Forest*, 75–77.

47. United States, *Census of Agriculture*, 1880; McGregor, "Radical Environmental Change," 160.

48. McGregor, "Radical Environmental Change," 157–60; "The Lumber Trade," *New York Times*, May 11, 1872; Carpenter, *Second Annual Report*, 164;, Wayne, Pike, and Monroe Counties, 328.

49. Arthur N. Meyers, "A Brief History of Acidalia (City of Acid)," *The Echo* 2, No. 4 (Spring 1982); 4–5; Guy Wormuth, *My Memories of Acid Factories* (Hancock, NY: 1977), pp. 1–32; Barry Foster, "Makin' Acid," *Upper Delaware Magazine* 2 (Spring, 1979): 14; Kudish, *Catskill Forest*, 64; Mathews, *Wayne, Pike, and Monroe Counties*, 328.

50. Wormuth, *Memories of Acid Factories*, 1–32; Foster, "Makin' Acid," 14; Kudish, *Catskill Forest*, 71; Carpenter, *Second Annual Report*, 165.

51. McGregor, *Cultural Resource Survey: Upper Delaware National Scenic and Recreational River, Pennsylvania and New York, Part B*, 65–67.

52. McGregor, "Radical Environmental Change," 164–180; Kudish, *Catskill Forest*, 56; French, *Gazetteer*, 261, 647.

53. Murray, ed., *Delaware County*, 364.

54. "Few and Far Between: Recollections of an Old Delaware River Lumberman," *Port Jervis Evening Gazette* (April 30, 1888), collected by historians working for the Works Progress Administration, on file, Minisink Valley Historical Society, Port Jervis, New York.

55. Murray, ed., *Delaware County*, 6.

56. Harper and Brothers, *New York and Erie Rail-Road Guide*, 66–96.

57. *Ibid.*, 79.

58. Mathews, *Wayne, Pike, and Monroe Counties*, 328; Quinlan, *History of Sullivan County*, 508; Joseph Purcell, "That Dam Project at Narrowsburg," *Headwaters* 1 (1977): 1.

59. Runkle, "Disturbance Regimes in Temperate Forests," *Ecology of Natural Disturbance*, ed. Pickett and White, 17–23; Peter M. Vitousek, "Community Turnover and Ecosystem Dynamics," *Ecology of Natural Disturbance*, 325–33; Charles D. Canham and P. L. Marks, "The Response of Woody Plants to Disturbance: Patterns of Establishment and Growth," *Ecology of Natural Disturbance*, ed. Pickett and White, 197–216; Foster, ed., *Hemlock*, 167–68.

60. Carpenter, *Second Annual Report*, 164.

61. Marchand, *North Woods*, 16–23.

Chapter Seven

1. Frank Graham, Jr., *The Adirondack Park: A Political History* (Syracuse: Syracuse

University Press, 1984), p. 75; Berger, *Forests Forever*, 35–38.

2. Graham, *Adirondack Park*, 66; Ferber, ed. *Kindred Spirits*, 195; Ferber, *Hudson River School*, 13.

3. Darwin, *On the Origin of Species*; Ronald L. Numbers, *Darwinism Comes to America* (Cambridge, MA: Harvard University Press, 1998); Richard Hostadter, *Social Darwinism in American Thought*, reprint ed. (Boston: Beacon Press, 1992).

4. Jane Curtis, Will Curtis and Frank Lieberman, *The World of George Perkins Marsh* (Woodstock, VT: Countryman Press, 1982); Kingsland, *Evolution of American Ecology*, 7–15; Graham, *Adirondack Park*, 67; George Perkins Marsh, *Man and Nature: Or, Physical Geography as Modified by Human Action* (New York: Scribner's, 1864).

5. Marsh, *Man and Nature*.

6. Graham, *Adirondack Park*, 67.

7. *Ibid.*, 105, 119–20, 126.

8. Roderick Frazier Nash, *Wilderness and the American Mind*, 5th ed. (New Haven, CT: Yale University Press, 2014), pp. 96–121.

9. *Ibid.*, 106–07, 114; Martin, *Genius of Place*, 266–67.

10. Nash, *Wilderness and the American Mind*, 108–81; Stephen Fox, *The American Conservation Movement: John Muir and His Legacy* (Madison: University of Wisconsin Press, 1985).

11. Edward Kanze, *The World of John Burroughs: The Life and Work of One of America's Greatest Naturalists* (San Francisco: Sierra Club Books, 1996), pp. 12–42; Silverman and Silver, *The Catskills*, 156–77.

12. Kanze, *World of John Burroughs*, 42–52; Silverman and Silver, *The Catskills*, 166; John Burroughs, *Wake-Robin* (Boston: Hurd and Houghton, 1871).

13. Kanze, *World of John Burroughs*, 53–60; Silverman and Silver, *The Catskills*, 169; Stradling, *Making Mountains*, 112–15.

14. Kanze, *World of John Burroughs*, 54–57 (Henry James quotation, 57); John Burroughs, *Winter Sunshine* (Boston: Hurd and Houghton, 1875).

15. John Burroughs, "Pepacton: A Summer Voyage," *Pepacton* (Boston: Houghton, Mifflin and Company, 1881), pp 7–42; Silverman and Silver, *The Catskills*, 168–77; Kudish, *Catskill Forest*, 51; Titus, *Catskills in the Ice Age*, 79–80, 84, 97.

16. John Burroughs, *Signs and Seasons* (Boston: Houghton, Mifflin and Company, 1886); John Burroughs, "In the Hemlocks," "The Heart of the Southern Catskills," "A Bed

of Boughs," *In the Catskills*, 83, 115, 155–56. "In the Hemlocks" originally appeared in *Wake Robin*, "The Heart of the Southern Catskills in *Riverby* (1904), and "A Bed of Boughs" in *Locusts and Wild Honey* (1879).

17. John Burroughs, "Phases of Farm Life," *In the Catskills*, 42–59. The essay originally appeared in *Signs and Seasons* (1886); Silverman and Silver, *The Catskills*, 161.

18. Ralph H. Lutts, *The Nature Fakers: Wildlife, Science, and Sentiment* (Golden, CO: Fulcrum Publishing, 1990), pp. 143–45, 164–75; Henry David Thoreau, *Walden* (Princeton: Princeton University Press, 1989), pp. 211–13 (originally published in 1854).

19. Kanze, *World of John Burroughs*, 90; Lutts, *Nature Fakers*, 1–138; John Burroughs, "Real and Sham Natural History," *Atlantic Monthly* 91 (March, 1903): 298; Bernd Heinrich, *The Mind of the Raven: Investigations and Adventures with Wolf-Birds* (New York: Harper Collins, 1999); Muller-Schwarze and Lixing Sun, *The Beaver*, 54–61.

20. Kanze, *World of John Burroughs*, ; 77–79, 90; Nash, *Wilderness and the American Mind*, 122–40.

21. Char Miller, *Gifford Pinchot and the Making of Modern Environmentalism* (Washington, D.C.: Island Press, 2001), pp. 1–12; Robert H. Wiebe, *The Search for Order: 1977–1920* (New York: Hill and Wang, 1966).

22. Miller, *Gifford Pinchot*, 21–55. (Having long relied on Nash's *Wilderness and the American Mind* and Fox's *American Conservation Movement*, which largely portray Pinchot as the villain of the piece, I sought out Miller's biography to gain a more sympathetic insight. Oddly enough, this book, balanced as it is, convinced me that Nash and Fox are generally correct.)

23. *Ibid.*, 66–90.

24. *Ibid.*, 101–15; Martin, *Genius of Place*, 360–95; Graham, *Adirondack Park*, 133–36.

25. Miller, *Gifford Pinchot*, 120–38; Nash, *Wilderness and the American Mind*, 161–81.

26. Miller, *Gifford Pinchot*, 131–55.

27. Gifford Pinchot, *A Primer of Forestry*, 2 vols. (Washington, D.C.: U.S. Department of Agriculture, Division of Forestry, Government Printing Office, 1900).

28. *Ibid.*, 2: 24.

29. Miller, *Gifford Pinchot*, 80.

30. Graham, *Adirondack Park*, 75.

31. *Ibid.*, 74–75.

32. *Ibid.*, 70–73; Paul Schaefer, ed. *Adirondack Explorations: Nature Writings of Verplanck Colvin* (Syracuse: Syracuse University Press, 1997).

33. Graham, *Adirondack Park*, 79.

34. *Ibid.*, 76.

35. *Ibid.*, 87–93; David Soll, *Empire of Water: An Environmental and Political History of the New York City Water Supply* (Ithaca: Cornell University Press, 2013), pp. 1–36.

36. Graham, *Adirondack Park*, 87–90; Pielou, *World of Northern Evergreens*, 136; Burroughs, "Pepacton," 23; Silverman and Silver, *The Catskills*, 180.

37. Graham, *Adirondack Park*, 100–05; Soll, *Empire of Water*, 18–19.

38. Graham, *Adirondack Park*, 86–87; Martin, *Genius of Place*, 347–51; David Stradling, *The Nature of New York: An Environmental History of the Empire State* (Ithaca: Cornell University Press, 2010), pp. 95–96.

39. Graham, *Adirondack Park*, 105–06; Stradling, *Nature of New York*, 101–03.

40. Stradling, *Making Mountains*, 120–24; Silverman and Silver, *The Catskills*, 402; *A Plea for the Adirondack and Catskill Parks. an Argument for the Resumption by the State of New York, of the Policy of Acquiring Lands for the Public Benefit Within the Limits of the Forest Preserve* (New York: Association for the protection of the Adirondacks, 1902), pp. 24–29; State of New York, *Catskill Park State Land Master Plan* (Albany: www.Dec.Ny.Gov/Docs/Lands_Forests_Pdf/Cplsmp.Pdf, August, 2008), pp. 1–3.

41. Graham, *Adirondack Park*, 107–10.

42. *Ibid.*, 126–28; New York, *Catskill Park Master Plan*, 78.

43. *Plea for the Adirondack and Catskill Parks*, 29.

44. Stradling, *Making Mountains*, 120–23; Stradling, *Nature of New York*, 102–05; Graham, *Adirondack Park*, 122–24; Soll, *Empire of Water*, 66; New York, *Catskill Park Master Plan*, 1–3.

45. Muller-Schwarze and Lixing Sun, *The Beaver*, 156–57; Cooper, *Last of the Mohicans*, 341.

46. Graham, *Adirondack Park*, 148; Kanze, *World of John Burroughs*, 96–97; Stradling, *Making Mountains*, 125; Elbert Hubbard, *Old John Burroughs* (East Aurora, NY: The Roycroft Shop, 1901).

47. Stradling, *Nature of New York*, 160–65; "Civilian Conservation Corps Legacy," *CCC Camps* (Edinburg, VA: www.Ccclegacy.Org/CCC_Camps_New_York.Html, 2015).

48. Soll, *Empire of Water*, 12, 105.

49. *Ibid.*, 18–21.

50. *Ibid.*, 14–26.

51. *Ibid.*, 37–51; Stradling, *Making Mountains*, 152–71.

52. Soll, *Empire of Water*, 79–86; Silverman and Silver, *The Catskills*, 195; John Burroughs, "Speckled Trout," *In the Catskills*, 133 (originally published in *Locusts and Wild Honey* (1879).

53. Soll, *Empire of Water*, 79–86.

54. *Ibid.*, 87–100, 137–38; Stradling, *Making Mountains*, 171–72.

55. Soll, *Empire of Water*, 1–10; Miller, *Gifford Pinchot*, 80–149; Stradling, *Making Mountains*, 114–15.

Chapter Eight

1. Clements, *Plant Succession*, 4; S.T.A. Pickett and P.S. White, "Patch Dynamics: A Synthesis," Pickett and White, *Natural Disturbance and Patch Dynamics*, 371–72.

2. *Catskill Park State Land Master Plan.*

3. *Ibid.*, 1–3.

4. *Ibid.*, 38.

5. National Geographic, *New York Recreation Atlas* (Washington, D.C.: National Geographic, 2013); National Geographic, *Pennsylvania Recreation Atlas* (Washington, D.C.: National Geographic, 2013).

6. www.nysparks.com.

7. www.dec.ny.gov/lands.

8. www.Denr.State.Pa.Us/State parks.

9. *Pike Outdoors: A Public Land Guide for Sportsmen and Outdoor Enthusiasts* (Pittsburgh: Pennsylvania Environmental Council, 2012).

10. www.Dcnr.State.Pa.Us; Aldo Leopold, *For the Health of the Land: Previously Unpublished Essays and Other Writings*, ed. J. Baird Callicott (Washington, D.C.: Island Press, 2001).

11. Soll, *Empire of Water*, 107–08, 139.

12. *Ibid.*, 143–46.

13. *Ibid.*, 6–10; 170–74.

14. Kudish, *Catskill Forest*, 144;

15. www.eaglecreekre.com/facilities/northeast-region/mongaup-river-ny

16. John Church, Shannon M. Williams, and Howard P. Whidden, *Targeted Mammal Inventory for the Upper Delaware Scenic & Recreational River* (Philadelphia: National Park Service Natural Resource Technical Report NPS/NER/ERMN/NRTR, 2011/154), p. 103.

17. www.waterdata.usgs.gov/pa/nwis.

18. Delaware River Basin Commission, *Water Resources: Delaware River Basin Commission's Management of Certain Water Activities* (Washington, D.C.: United States Government Printing Office, 2013).

19. www. nj.gov/drbc/about/accomplishments.

20. DRBC, *Water Resources.*

21. An Act to Provide for a National Wild and Scenic Rivers System, and for Other Purposes, 85th Congress, 2nd Sess., 82 stat, 906.

22. www. upperdelawarecouncil.org/history; National Parks and Recreation Act of 1978, 95th Congress, 2d sess., Public Law 95–625, November 10, 1978, 92 Stat., 3467, 3523–3527.

23. *Ibid.*, 92. Stat. 3526–27.

24. *Ibid.*, 92. Stat. 3525; www.nps.gov; Upper Delaware Scenic and Recreational River: Purpose and Management Goals.

25. McGregor, *Cultural Resource Survey, Upper Delaware, Part B,* 88.

26. Martin, *Genius of Place,* 266–68; Alson Chase, *Playing God in Yellowstone: The Destruction of America's First National Park* (New York: Harvest Books, 1987).

27. www. upperdelawarecouncil.org/history; Citizen's Advisory Council, Upper Delaware Scenic and Recreational River, 1978 (unpublished transcript); www.upperdelaware council.org.

28. www. nps.gov; Upper Delaware Scenic and Recreational River: Purpose and Management Goals.

29. Pielou, *After the Ice,* 308–09; Brian Fagan, *After the Ice: How Climate Made History 1300 to 1850* (New York: Basic Books, 2000); Richard B. Primack, *Walden Warming: Climate Change Comes to Thoreau's Woods* (Chicago: University of Chicago Press, 2014), pp. 148–49; Kudish, *Catskill Forest,* 11.

30. Kudish, *Catskill Forest,* 81.

31. Pielou, *World of Northern Evergreens,* 64, 125–27; Bonnicksen, *America's Ancient Forests,* 34–38; Carpenter, "Report to the State Forest Commission."

32. Thomas J. Considine, Jr., and Thomas S. Frieswyk, *Forest Statistics for New York, 1980* (Albany: New York State Department of Environmental Conservation, 1982); Stephanie J. Perles, Gregory S. Podniesinski, Mary Ann Furedi, Bradley A. Eichelberger, Aissa Feldman, Greg Edinger, Elizabeth Eastman, and Lesley A. Sneddon, *Vegetation Classification and Mapping at Upper Delaware Scenic and Recreational River* (Philadelphia: National Park Service Technical Report NPS/NER/ERMN/NRTR, 2008/133).

33. *Ibid.*, 11–36.

34. Douglas G. Sprugel, "Natural Disturbance and Ecosystem Energetics," *Ecology of Natural Disturbance and Patch Dynamics,* ed. Pickett and White, 335–52; Pickett and White, "Patch Dynamics: A Synthesis," *Ecology of Natural Disturbance and Patch Dynamics,* 371–84.

35. *Ibid.*, 84–319.

36. *Ibid.*, 51.

37. Julie Sloan Denslow, "Disturbance-Mediated Coexistence of Species," *Ecology of Natural Disturbance and Patch Dynamics,* ed. Pickett and White, 307–24.

38. Church, Williams, and Whidden, *Mammal Inventory.*

39. Muller-Schwarze and Sun, *The Beaver,* 161–65; www.apps.dcnr.state.pa.us.

40. Chapman and Feldhamer, eds., *Wild Mammals of North America,* 878–901; Matthiessen, *Wildlife in America,* 197–98; Runkle, "Disturbance Regimes in Temperate Forests," Pickett and White, *Natural Disturbance and Patch Dynamics,* 17–33; Kudish, *Catskill Forest,* 81.

41. Chapman and Feldhamer, eds., *Wild Mammals of North America,* 447–59; www.dec.ny.gov/animals.

42. www.Dec.Ny.Gov/Animals; www. dcnr.state.pa.us/forestry.

43. *Ibid.*; Pielou, *World of Northern Evergreens,* 99–107; Kudish, *Catskill Forest,* 79–80; ww.apps.dcnr.state.pa.us.

44. Kudish, *Catskill Forest,* 64; Marchand, *North Woods,* 75.

45. *Ibid.*, 34–35, 79–80; www.esf.edu/chestnut.

46. Kudish, *Catskill Forest,* 80.

47. www.Dec.Ny.Gov/Animals; Rachel Carson, *Silent Spring* (Boston: Houghton Mifflin, 1962).

48. Foster, ed., *Hemlock,* 4, 227–29.

49. *Ibid.*, 227–28; www.dec.ny.gov/animals.

50. Foster, ed., *Hemlock,* 227–29.

Bibliography

Journal Articles

Burroughs, John. "Real and Sham Natural History." *Atlantic Monthly* 91 (March, 1903): 298.

Cowles, Henry Chandler. "The Ecological Relations of the Vegetation on the Sand Dunes of Lake Michigan." *The Botanical Gazette* 27 (February, 1899): 95–117, 167–202, 281–308, 361–91.

Clements, Frederic E. "Nature and Structure of the Climax." *The Journal of Ecology* 24 (1936): 252–84.

Constant, Edward W. "Scientific Theory and Technological Testability: Science, Dynamometers and Water Turbines in the 19th Century." *International Quarterly of the Society for the History of Technology and Culture* 24 (April, 1983): 183–98.

Davis, Margaret Bryan. "Quaternary History and the Stability of Forest Communities." *Forest Succession: Concepts and Applications*. Eds. Darrell C. West, Herman H. Shugart, and Daniel B. Botkin. New York: Springer-Verlag, 1981: pp. 132–53.

Dean, Bradley P. "Henry D. Thoreau and Horace Greeley Exchange Letters on the Spontaneous Generation of Plants." *New England Quarterly* 66 (December, 1993): 630–38.

Drury, William, and Ian Nesbit. "Succession." *Journal of the Arnold Arboretum* 54 (July, 1973): 331–68.

Fackenthal, B.F. Jr. "Improving Navigation on the Delaware River, with Some Account of its Ferries, Bridges, Canals, and Floods." *Papers, Bucks County (PA) Historical Society*, 6:103–230.

Fenchel, Tom. "Comment on Carney's Article by T. Fenchel." *Functional Ecology* 3 (1989): 641.

Feranec, Robert S., and Andrew Kozlowski. "New AMS Radiocarbon Dates from Late Pleistocene Mastodons and Mammoths in New York State, USA." *Radiocarbon* 54, no. 2 (2012): 275–79.

"Few and Far Between: Recollections of an Old Delaware River Lumberman." *Port Jervis Evening Gazette* (April 30, 1888).

Forbes, Stephen A. "The Lake as a Microcosm." *Bulletin of the Illinois State Natural History Survey* 15 (1925): 537–50.

Foster, Barry. "Makin' Acid." *Upper Delaware Magazine* 2 (Spring, 1979).

Gleason, Henry Allan. "The Individualistic Concept of the Plant Association." *Bulletin of the Torrey Botanical Club* 53 (1926): 7–26.

Harper, John L. "The Contributions of Terrestrial Plant Studies to the Development of the Theory of Ecology." *The Changing Scenes in the Natural Sciences, 1776–1976*. Ed. C.E. Goulden. Philadelphia: Academy of the Natural Sciences, 1977, pp. 139–57.

Hough, A. F. "A Climax Forest on East Tionesta Creek in Northwestern Pennsylvania." *Ecology* 17 (Spring, 1936): 9–28.

Kenderdine, Thaddeus S. "Lumbering Days on the Delaware." *Papers, Bucks County (PA) Historical Society* 4 (1917): 239–52.

Kierner, Cynthia A. "Landlord and Tenant in Revolutionary New York: The Case of Livingston Manor." *New York History* 70 (April, 1989): 133–152.

Kraft, Herbert Clemens. "The Plenge Site: A Paleo-Indian Occupation Site in New Jersey." *Archaeology of Eastern North America* 1 (1973): 56–117.

Layton, Edwin T. "From Rule of Thumb to Scientific Engineering: James B. Francis and the Invention of the Francis Turbine." *NLA Monograph Series*. Stony Brook, NY: Research Foundation of the State University of New York, 1992.

Likens, Gene E., F. Herbert Bormann, Noye M. Johnson, D.W. Fisher, and Robert S. Pierce, "Effects of Forest Cutting and Herbicide Treatment on Nutrient Budgets in the Hubbard Brook Watershed-Ecosystem." *Ecological Monographs* 40 (Winter, 1970): 23–47.

Lindeman, Raymond L. "The Trophic-Dynamic Aspect of Ecology." *Ecology* 23: (October, 1942): 399–418.

Lutz, H.J., and A.L. McComb. "Origin of White Pine in Virgin Forest Stands of Northwestern Pennsylvania as Indicated by Stem and Basal Branch Features." *Ecology* 16 (Winter, 1936): 252–56.

"The Lumber Trade: History of the Business in New York and Pennsylvania." *New York Times* (May 11, 1872).

Marshall, Sydney B. "Aboriginal Settlement in New Jersey During the Paleo-Indian Cultural Period ca. 10,000 B.C–6,000 B.C." www.nj. *gov/ dep/hpo/1identity*. no date.

McGregor, Robert Kuhn. "Deriving a Biocentric History: Evidence from the Journal of Henry David Thoreau." *Environmental Review* 12 (Summer, 1988): 117–26.

Meyers, Arthur N. "A Brief History of Acidalia (City of Acid)." *The Echo* 2, No. 4 (Spring 1982); 4–5.

Meyers, Philip A. "Evidence of mid–Holocene climate instability from variations in carbon burial in Seneca Lake, New York." *Journal of Paleoclimatology* 28 (2002): 237–44.

Perkins, Sid. "Earth: Ancient Beavers Did Not Eat Trees: Now-extinct giant creatures had hippopotamus-like diet." *Science News* 176, v. 11 (Nov., 2009): 10.

Pine, Joshua III. "A Rafting Story of the Delaware River." *Papers, Bucks County (PA) Historical Society* 6 (1932): 467–524.

Purcell, Joseph. "That Dam Project at Narrowsburg." *Headwaters* 1 (1977): 1.

Safford, Arthur T., and Edward P. Hamilton. "The American Mixed-Flow Turbine and Its Setting," *Transactions of the American Society of Civil Engineers* 85, Paper 1503 (1922).

Stryker, James. "Steam Boiler Explosions." *Stryker's American Register and Magazine* 2 (March, 1849): 100–01.

Tansley, Arthur G. "The Use and Abuse of Vegetational Concepts and Terms." *Ecology* 16 (July, 1935): 284–307.

Webb, William L., Donald F. Behrend, and Boonrang Saisorn. "Effect of Logging on Songbird Populations in a Northern Hardwood Forest." *Wildlife Monographs*, supplement to *The Journal of Wildlife Management* 41, No. 3 (July, 1977): 6–35.

Worster, Donald. "Ecology of Order and Chaos." *Environmental History Review* 14 (Spring/Summer 1990): 4–16.

Government Documents

Considine, Thomas J., Jr., and Thomas S. Frieswyk. *Forest Statistics for New York, 1980*. Albany: New York State Department of Environmental Conservation, 1982.

New York State, Bureau of the Census. *Census of the State of New York, for 1821, 1825, 1835, 1845*. Albany: Department of State, printed by Carroll and Cook, 1821, 1825, 1835, 1845.

New York State. *Transactions of the New York State Agricultural Society*, Vol. 2. Albany: E. Mack, Printer to the Senate, 1843.

Pennsylvania, *Colonial Records of Pennsylvania*, Vol. VIII. Harrisburg: Theo Fenn and Company, 1852.

United States Congress. An Act to Provide for a National Wild and Scenic Rivers System, and for Other Purposes. 85th Congress, 2nd Sess. 82 stat, 906.

_____. National Parks and Recreation Act of 1978. 95th Congress, 2d sess. Public Law 95–625. November 10, 1978. 92 Stat. 3467, 3523–3527.

United States Department of State. *Sixth Census of the United States, 1840*. Washington, D.C.: Bureau of the Census, 1841.

_____. *Eighth Census of the United States, 1850*. Washington, D.C.: Bureau of the Census, 1851.

_____. *Tenth Census of the United States, 1870*. Washington, D.C.: Bureau of the Census, 1871.

Reference Guides

National Geographic. *New York Recreation Atlas*. Washington, D.C.: National Geographic, 2013.
_____. *Pennsylvania Recreation Atlas*. Washington, D.C.: National Geographic, 2013.
Nelson, Gil, Christopher J. Earle, and Richard Spellenberg. *Trees of Eastern North America*. Princeton: Princeton University Press, 2014.
Sutton, Ann and Myron Sutton. *The Audubon Society Nature Guides: Eastern Forests*. New York: Alfred A. Knopf, 1990.
Tekiela, Stan. *Trees of New York: Field Guide*. Cambridge, MN: Adventure Publications, 2006.

Books

Addams, Charles C. *An Ecological Survey of Isle Royale, Lake Superior*. Lansing, MI: Wynkoop Hallenbeck Crawford Company, State Printers, 1909.
Andrefsky, William, et al. *History and Archaeology 4.3 Part B: Contact and Euro-American (Historical Synthesis)*. Albert A. Dekin, Principal Investigator. *Upper Delaware National Scenic and Recreational River, Pennsylvania and New York*. Philadelphia: National Park Service, 1983.
Appleman, Phillip, ed. *Darwin: A Norton Critical Edition*. New York: W.W. Norton and Company, 1979.
Association for the protection of the Adirondacks. *A Plea for the Adirondack and Catskill Parks. An argument for the resumption by the state of New York, of the policy of acquiring lands for the public benefit within the limits of the forest preserve*. New York: Association for the protection of the Adirondacks, 1902.
Avery, Kevin J. *Treasures from Olana: Landscapes by Frederic Edwin Church*. Ithaca: Cornell University Press, 2005.
Bacon, Francis. *Novum Organum* Thomas Fowler, ed. Oxford: Clarendon Press, 1878.
Beecher, Raymond. *Kaaterskill Clove: Where Nature Met Art*. Hensonville, NY: Black Dome Press, 2004.
Bender, Thomas. *Toward An Urban Vision: Ideas and Institutions in Nineteenth-Century America*. Lexington: The University Press of Kentucky, 1975.
Benjamin, Vernon. *The History of the Hudson River Valley: from Wilderness to the Civil War*. New York: The Overlook Press, 2014.
Berger, John J. *Forests Forever: Their Ecology, Restoration, and Protection*. Chicago: Center for American Places at Columbia College, 2018.
Bigras, F.J., and Stephen J. Columbo, eds. *Conifer Cold Hardiness*. Dordrecht, The Netherlands: Kluwer Academic Publishers, 2001.
Bonnicksen, Thomas M. *America's Ancient Forests: From the Ice Age to the Age of Discovery*. New York: John Wiley and Sons, 2000.
Borst, Raymond R. *The Thoreau Log: A Documentary Life of Henry David Thoreau 1817–1862*. New York: G. K. Hall and Company, 1992.
Bowler, Peter J. *The Environmental Sciences*. New York: W. W. Norton and Company, 1992.
Boyd, Julian, ed. *The Susquehanna Company Papers, Volume I: 1750–55*. Ithaca: Cornell University Press, 1962.
Braun, Esther K., and David P. Braun. *The First Peoples of the Northeast*. Lincoln, MA: Moccasin Hill Press, 1994.
Braun, Lucy E. *Deciduous Forests of Eastern North America*. Philadelphia: The Blakiston Company, 1950.
Brown, Nelson Courtlandt. *The Small Sawmill in New York*. Syracuse: Syracuse University, Bulletin of the New York State College of Forestry, Technical Publication #50, October, 1937.
Burbank, James W. *Cushetunk: A Brief History of the Early Settlers Who Called Themselves the Delaware Company*. Callicoon, NY: Sullivan County Democrat, 1952.
Burroughs, John. *In the Catskills: Selections from the Writings*, reprint edition, ed. Clifton Johnson. LaVergne, TN: Bibliobazaar, 2009.
_____. *Pepacton*. Boston: Houghton, Mifflin and Company, 1881.
_____. *Signs and Seasons.*(Boston: Houghton, Mifflin and Company, 1886.
_____. *Winter Sunshine*. Boston: Hurd and Houghton, 1875.

Carpenter, Charles. *Second Annual Report of the State of New York, for the Year 1886*. Albany: The Argus Company, printers, 1887.

Carson, Rachel. *Silent Spring*. Boston: Houghton Mifflin, 1962.

Catlin, George. *North American Indians*. New York: Penguin Classics, 2004.

Chapman, Joseph A., and George A. Feldhamer, eds. *Wild Mammals of North America: Biology, Management, Economics*. Baltimore: The Johns Hopkins University Press, 1982.

Chase, Alston. *Playing God in Yellowstone: The Destruction of America's First National Park*. New York: Harvest Books, 1987.

Child, Hamilton. *Gazetteer and Business Directory of Sullivan County, New York, for 1872–73*. Syracuse: Hamilton Child, 1872.

Church, John, Shannon M. Williams, and Howard P. Whidden. *Targeted Mammal Inventory for the Upper Delaware Scenic & Recreational River*. Philadelphia: National Park Service Natural Resource Technical Report NPS/NER/ERMN/NRTR, 2011/154.

Churella, Albert J. *The Pennsylvania Railroad, Volume 1: Building an Empire, 1846–1917*. Philadelphia: University of Pennsylvania Press, 2012.

Clements, Frederic E. *Plant Succession: An Analysis of the Development of Vegetation*. Washington, D.C.: Carnegie Institution of Washington, 1916.

Cooper, James Fenimore. *The Last of the Mohicans*. New York: Barnes and Noble Classics, 2003.

_____. *The Pioneers*. New York: Penguin Books, 2006.

Cox, Thomas R., Robert S. Maxwell, Phillip Drennon Thomas, and Joseph J. Malone. *This Well-Wooded Land: Americans and Their Forests from Colonial Times to the Present*. Lincoln: University of Nebraska Press, 1985.

Cremeens, David L., and John P. Hart, eds. *Geoarchaeology of Landscapes in the Glaciated Northeast*. Albany: New York State Museum, Bulletin 497, 2003.

Crosby, Alfred A. *The Columbian Exchange: Biological and Cultural Consequences of 1492*, 30th Anniversary ed. Westport, CT: Praeger, 2003.

_____. *Ecological Imperialism: The Biological Expansion of Europe, 900–1900*, 2nd ed. Cambridge: Cambridge University Press, 2004.

Curtiss, Charles T. *Rafting on the Delaware*. Ithaca: William Heidt, Jr., 1957.

_____. *Stories of the Raftsmen*. Callicoon, NY: Sullivan County Democrat, 1922.

Curtis, Jane, Will Curtis, and Frank Lieberman. *The World of George Perkins Marsh*. Woodstock, VT: Countryman Press, 1982.

Custer, Jay F. *Prehistoric Cultures of Eastern Pennsylvania*. Harrisburg: Commonwealth of Pennsylvania, Pennsylvania Historical and Museum Commission, 1996.

Darwin, Charles. *On the Origin of Species*. London: John Murray, 1859.

Davidson, H. Fletcher. *Delaware County: Fur Trading to Farming*. Delhi, NY: R.B. Decker Advertising, 1976.

Dekin, Albert A. *Cultural Resource Survey: Upper Delaware National Scenic and Recreational River, Pennsylvania and New York*. Philadelphia: National Park Service, 1983.

Delaware and Hudson Canal Company. *Annual Report of the Board of Managers of the Delaware and Hudson Canal Company to the Stockholders*. Harrisburg, PA: 1825 to 1900.

Delaware River Basin Commission. *Water Resources: Delaware River Basin Commission's Management of Certain Water Activities*. Washington, D.C.: United States Government Printing Office, 2013.

Dillehay, Thomas. *Settlement of the Americas: A New Prehistory*. New York: Basic Books, 2001.

Drumm, Judith. *Mammoths and Mastodons: Ice Age Elephants of New York*. Albany: State Museum and Science Service, 1963.

Durand, John. *The Life and Times of Asher B. Durand*. Hensonville, NY: Black Dome Press, 2006.

Durrenberger, Joseph A. *Turnpikes: A History of the Toll Road Movement in the Middle Atlantic States and Maryland*. Cos Cob, CT: J.E. Edwards, 1968.

Earenfight, Phillip, and Nancy Siegel, eds. *Within the Landscape: Essays on Nineteenth-Century American Art and Culture*. University Park: Pennsylvania State University Press, 2005.

Ehlers, J., and P.L. Gibbard, eds. *Quaternary Glaciations, Extent and Chronology, Part II: North America*. Amsterdam: Elsevier, 2004.

Evans, Oliver. *The Young Millwright and Miller's Guide*. Philadelphia: Lea and Blanchard, 1850.

Fagan, Brian. *After the Ice: How Climate Made History 1300 to 1850*. New York: Basic Books, 2000.

_____. *Ancient North America: The Archaeology of a Continent*, 2nd ed. New York: Thames and Hudson, 1995.

_____. *The Complete Ice Age: How Climate Change Shaped the World*. London: Thames and Hudson, 2009.

Ferber, Linda S. *The Hudson River School: Nature and the American Vision*. New York: New York Historical Society, 2009.

_____, ed. *Kindred Spirits: Asher B. Durand and the American Landscape*. Brooklyn: D. Giles Limited, 2007.

Fisher, Donald W. *The Rise and Fall of the Taconic Mountains: A Geological History of Eastern New York*. Hensonville, NY: Black Dome Press, 2006.

Fluhr, George J. *A Generation of Suffering on the Upper Delaware Frontier, 1742–1782*. Shohola, PA: Reprinted from the *News Eagle*, Hawley, PA, 1976.

_____. *Pike County: Highlights of History in Northeastern Pennsylvania*. Shohola, PA: George J. Fluhr, 1975.

Foster, David R., ed. *Hemlock: A Forest Giant on the Edge*. New Haven: Yale University Press, 2014.

Fox, Stephen. *The American Conservation Movement: John Muir and His Legacy*. Madison: University of Wisconsin Press, 1985.

Fox, William F. *History of the Lumber Industry in the State of New York*. Harrison, NY: Harbor Hill Books, 1976.

Franklin, Wayne. *James Fenimore Cooper: The Early Years*. New Haven: Yale University Press, 2007.

French, J.H. *Gazetteer of the State of New York*. Syracuse: Pearsall Smith, 1860.

Funk, Robert E. *Archaeological Investigations in the Upper Susquehanna Valley, New York State*. Buffalo, NY: Partners Press, 1993.

_____. *An Ice Age Quarry-Workshop: The West Athens Hill Site Revisited*. Albany: The University of New, New York State Museum Bulletin 504, 2004.

Golley, Frank Benjamin. *A History of the Ecosystem Concept in Ecology*. New Haven: Yale University Press, 1993.

Goulden, C.E., ed. *The Changing Scenes in the Natural Sciences, 1776–1976*. Philadelphia: Academy of the Natural Sciences, 1977.

Graham, Frank Jr. *The Adirondack Park: A Political History*. Syracuse: Syracuse University Press, 1984.

Graves, Henry S. *The Use of Wood for Fuel*. Washington, D.C.: United States Department of Agriculture, Bulletin No. 753, March 10, 1919.

Harding, Walter. *The Days of Henry Thoreau: A Biography*. New York: Dover Publications, 1965.

Harlow, Alvin F. *The Road of the Century: The Story of the New York Central*. New York: Century Age Press, 1947.

Harper and Brothers. *New York and Erie Rail-Road Guide Book*. New York: Harper and Brothers, 1851.

Harwood, Herbert H., Jr. *Impossible Challenge: B&O*. Baltimore: Barnard, Roberts and Company, 1979.

Hedrick, Ulysses Prentiss. *A History of Agriculture in the State of New York*. New York: Hill and Wang, 1933.

Heinrich, Bernd. *The Mind of the Raven: Investigations and Adventures with Wolf-Birds*. New York: HarperCollins, 1999.

Helferich, Gerard. *Humboldt's Cosmos: Alexander von Humboldt and the Latin American Journey That Changed the Way We See the World*. New York: Gotham Books, 2004.

Hilfiker, Earl L. *Beavers: Water, Wildlife and History*. Interlaken, NY: Windswept Press, 1990.

Hindle, Brooke, ed. *America's Wooden Age: Aspects of Its Early Technology*. Tarrytown, NY: Sleepy Hollow Press, 1975.

_____. *Material Culture of the Wooden Age*. Tarrytown, NY: Sleepy Hollow Press, 1981.

Hitakonanu'laxk. *The Grandfathers Speak: Native American Folk Tales of the Lenapé People*. New York: Interlink Books, 2012.

Hoff, J. Wallace. *Two Hundred Miles on the Delaware River*. Trenton, NJ: The Brandt Press, 1893.

Hofstadter, Richard. *Social Darwinism in American Thought*, reprint ed. Boston: Beacon Press, 1992.

Holman, J. Alan. *Ancient Life of the Great Lakes Basin: Precambrian to Pleistocene*. Ann Arbor: University of Michigan Press, 1995.

Homberger, Eric. *The Historical Atlas of New York City: A Visual Celebration of Nearly 400 Years of New York City's History*. New York: Henry Holt and Company, 1994.

Hornocker, Maurice, and Sharon Negri, eds. *Cougar: Ecology and Conservation*. Chicago: University of Chicago Press, 2010.

Hubbard, Elbert. *Old John Burroughs*. East Aurora, NY: The Roycroft Shop, 1901.

Hungerford, Edward. *Men of Erie: A Story of Human Effort*. New York: Random House, 1946.

Hunter, Douglas. *Half Moon: Henry Hudson and the Voyage that Redrew the Map of the New World*. New York: Bloomsbury Press, 2009.

Hunter, Louis C. *Water-Power in the Age of the Steam Engine*. Charlottesville: University of Virginia Press, 1979.

Irving, Washington. *A History of New York*. New York: Penguin Books, 2008.

_____. *The Legend of Sleepy Hollow and Other Stories; or, The Sketch Book of Geoffrey Crayon, Gent*. New York: Penguin Books, 2001.

Isachsen, Y.W., E. Landing, J.M. Lauber, L.V. Rickard and W.B. Rogers, eds. *Geology of New York: A Simplified Account*, 2nd ed. Albany: New York State Museum Educational Leaflet 28, 2000.

Jacox, Diane L. *Delaware and Hudson, Past and Present*. Philadelphia: National Parks Service, Division of History, 1979.

Kanze, Edward. *The World of John Burroughs: The Life and Work of One of America's Greatest Naturalists*. San Francisco: Sierra Club Books, 1996.

Kauffman, Henry J. *The American Farmhouse*. New York: Bonanza Books, 1975.

Kingsland, Sharon E. *The Evolution of American Ecology, 1890–2000*. Baltimore: Johns Hopkins University Press, 2005.

Klein, Milton, ed. *The Empire State: A History of New York*. Ithaca: Cornell University Press, 2001.

Knight, Edward H. *Knight's American Mechanical Dictionary*. 3 vols. Boston: Houghton, Mifflin and Company, 1876.

Kuchler, A.W. *Potential Natural Vegetation of the Conterminous United States*. New York: American Geographical Society, Special Publication No. 36, 1964.

Kudish, Michael. *The Catskill Forest: A History*. Fleischmanns, NY: Purple Mountain Press, 2000.

Lange, Ian M. *Ice Age Mammals of North America*. Missoula, MT: Mountain Press Publishing, 2002.

Leopold, Aldo. *For the Health of the Land: Previously Unpublished Essays and Other Writings*. ed. J. Baird Callicott. Washington, D.C.: Island Press, 2001.

Leslie, Vernon. *Faces in Clay: The Archaeology and Early History of the Red Man in the Upper Delaware Valley*. Middletown, NY: T. Emmett Henderson, 1973.

Lister, Adrian, and Paul Bahn. *Mammoths: Giants of the Ice Age*. Revised ed. Berkeley: University of California Press, 2007.

Lotterer, Elizabeth Stephens. *Stockport on the Delaware*. Hancock, NY: Hancock Herald, 1964.

Lovejoy, David. *The Glorious Revolution in America*. Middletown, CT: Wesleyan University Press, 1987.

Lutts, Ralph H. *The Nature Fakers: Wildlife, Science, and Sentiment*. Golden, CO: Fulcrum Publishing, 1990.

Major, Judith K. *To Live in the New World: A.J. Downing and American Landscape Gardening*. Cambridge: The MIT Press, 1997.

Mancall, Peter C. *Hakluyt's Promise: An Elizabethan's Obsession for an English America*. New Haven, CT: Yale University Press, 2007.

Marchand, Peter J. *Autumn: A Season of Change*. Hanover, CT: University Press of New England, 2000.

_____. *Life in the Cold: An Introduction to Winter Ecology*, 2nd ed. Hanover, CT: University Press of New England, 1991.

_____. *North Woods: An Inside Look at the Nature of Forests in the Northeast*. Boston: Appalachian Mountain Club, 1987.

Marsh, George Perkins. *Man and Nature: or, Physical Geography as Modified by Human Action*. New York: Scribner's, 1864.

Martin, Calvin. *Keepers of the Game: Indian-Animal Relationships and the Fur Trade*. Oakland: University of California Press, 1982.

Martin, Justin. *Genius of Place: The Life of Frederick Law Olmsted, Abolitionist, Conservationist, and Designer of Central Park.* Cambridge, MA: DaCapo Press, 2011.

Martin, Paul S., and R.G. Klein. *Quaternary Extinctions: A Prehistoric Revolution.* Tucson: University of Arizona Press, 1984.

Mathews, Alfred, ed. *History of Wayne, Pike, and Monroe Counties, Pennsylvania.* Philadelphia: R.T. Peck, 1886.

Matteson, John. *The Lives of Margaret Fuller: A Biography.* New York: W.W. Norton, 2012.

Matthiessen, Peter. *Wildlife in America*, rev. ed. New York: Viking, 1987.

McCracken, Harold. *George Catlin and the Old Frontier.* New York: The Dial Press, 1959.

McGregor, Robert C. "Radical Environmental Change: Deforestation in the Upper Delaware River Valley, 1800–1875," Ph.D. Dissertation, State University of New York at Binghamton, 1984.

McGregor, Robert Kuhn. *A Wider View of the Universe: Henry Thoreau's Study of Nature.* Champaign: University of Illinois Press, 1997.

McManis, Douglas R. *Colonial New England: A Historical Geography.* Oxford: Oxford University Press, 1976.

McNett, Charles W. Jr., ed. *Shawnee Minisink: A Stratified Paleoindian-Archaic Site in the Upper Delaware Valley of Pennsylvania.* Orlando: Academic Press, 1985.

Meltzer, David J. *The Great Paleolithic War: How Science Forged an Understanding of America's Ice Age Past.* Chicago: University of Chicago Press, 2015.275

Melville, Herman. *Pierre, or The Ambiguities.* New York: Penguin Books, 1996.

Merchant, Carolyn. *Reinventing Eden: The Fate of Nature in Western Culture.* New York: Routledge, 2004.

Meyers, Arthur N. *Douglass: The Delaware Valley City, 1867-78.* Narrowsburg, NY: Delaware Valley Press, 1969.

Miller, Char. *Gifford Pinchot and the Making of Modern Environmentalism.* Washington, D.C.: Island Press, 2001.

Millhouse, Barbara Babcock. *American Wilderness: The Story of the Hudson River School of Painting.* Hensonville, NY: Black Dome Press, 2007.

Minnis, Paul E., and Wayne J. Elisens. *Biodiversity & Native America.* Norman: University of Oklahoma Press, 2000.

Moretta, John. *William Penn and the Quaker Legacy.* New York: Pearson, 2006.

Morgan, Edmund S., and Helen M. Morgan *The Stamp Act Crisis.* New York: Collier Books, 1962.

Morgan, Lewis Henry. *The American Beaver: A Classic of Natural History and Ecology.* New York: Dover Publications, 1986.

Muller, Gilbert H. *William Cullen Bryant: Author of America.* Albany: State University of New York Press, 2008.

Muller-Schwarze, Dietland, and Lixing Sun. *The Beaver: Natural History of a Wetlands Engineer.* Ithaca: Cornell University Press, 2003.

Mumford, Lewis. *Technics and Civilization.* New York: Harcourt, Brace and Company, 1934.

Munsell, W.W., ed. *The History of Delaware County.* New York: W.W. Munsell and Company, 1880.

Murray, David, ed. *Centennial History of Delaware County, New York: 1797-1897.* Delhi, NY: William Clark, Publisher, 1897.

Nash, Roderick Frazier. *Wilderness and the American Mind*, 5th ed. New Haven, CT: Yale University Press, 2014.

Novak, Barbara. *Nature and Culture: American Landscape and Painting, 1825-1875.* Oxford: Oxford University Press, 2007.

Numbers, Ronald L. *Darwinism Comes to America.* Cambridge, MA: Harvard University Press, 1998.

O'Toole, Judith Hansen. *Different Views in Hudson River School Painting.* New York: Columbia University Press, 2005.

Outwater, Alice. *Water: A Natural History.* New York: Basic Books, 1996.

Panetta, Roger, ed. *Dutch New York: The Roots of Hudson Valley Culture.* New York: Fordham University Press, 2009.

Perles, Stephanie J., Gregory S. Podniesinski, Mary Ann Furedi, Bradley A. Eichelberger, Aissa Feldman, Greg Edinger, Elizabeth Eastman, and Lesley A. Sneddon. *Vegetation Classifica-*

tion and Mapping at Upper Delaware Scenic and Recreational River. Philadelphia: National Park Service Technical Report NPS/NER/ERMN/NRTR, 2008/133.

Petulla, Joseph M. *American Environmental History*. San Francisco: Boyd and Fraser Publishing Company, 1977.

Pickett, S.T.A., and P.S. White. *The Ecology of Natural Disturbance and Patch Dynamics*. Orlando: Academic Press, 1985.

Pielou, E.C. *After the Ice: The Return of Life to Glaciated North America*. Chicago: University of Chicago Press, 1991.

_____. *The World of Northern Evergreens*, 2nd ed. Ithaca: Comstock Publishing Associates, 2011.

Pike Outdoors: A Public Land Guide for Sportsmen and Outdoor Enthusiasts. Pittsburgh: Pennsylvania Environmental Council, 2012.

Pinchot, Gifford. *A Primer of Forestry*, 2 vols. Washington, D.C.: U.S. Department of Agriculture, Division of Forestry, Government Printing Office, 1900.

Powell, Earl A. *Thomas Cole*. New York: Harry N. Abrams, 1990.

Primack, Richard B. *Walden Warming: Climate Change Comes to Thoreau's Woods*. Chicago: University of Chicago Press, 2014.

Quinlan, James E. *History of Sullivan County*. Liberty, NY: G.M. Beebe and W.T. Morgans, 1873.

Ra, Croker. *Stephen Forbes and the Rise of American Ecology*. Washington, D.C.: Smithsonian, 2001.

Redman, Charles L. *Human Impact on Ancient Environments*. Tucson: University of Arizona Press, 1999.

Reynolds, David S. *Walt Whitman's America: A Cultural Biography*. New York: Alfred A. Knopf, 1995.

Reynolds, R.V., and Albert H. Pierson. *Fuel Wood Used in the United States, 1630–1930*. Washington, D.C.: United States Department of Agriculture, Circular No. 641, February, 1942.

Rink, Oliver A. *Holland on the Hudson: An Economic and Social History of Dutch New York*. Ithaca: Cornell University Press, 1986.

Ritchie, William A. *The Archaeology of New York State*. Revised ed. Harrison, NY: Harbor Hill Books, 1980.

Ruttenber, E.M., and L.H. Clark. *History of Orange County, New York*. Philadelphia: Everts and Peck, 1881.

Schaefer, Paul, ed. *Adirondack Explorations: Nature Writings of Verplanck Colvin*. Syracuse: Syracuse University Press, 1997.

Schutt, Amy C. *Peoples of the River Valleys: The Odyssey of the Delaware Indians*. Philadelphia: University of Pennsylvania Press, 2007.

Schwarz, Philip J. *The Jarring Interests: New York's Boundary Makers*. Albany: State University of New York Press, 1979.

Shaughnessy, Jim. *Delaware and Hudson*. Berkeley, CA: Howell-North Books, 1967.

Sheriff, Carol. *The Artificial River: The Erie Canal and the Paradox of Progress, 1817–1862*. New York: Hill and Wang, 1996.

Silverman, Stephen M., and Raphael D. Silver. *The Catskills: Its History and How It Changed America*. New York: Alfred A. Knopf, 2015.

Sivertsen, Barbara F., and Barbara L. Covey, eds. *The Legend of Cushetunk: The Nathan Skinner Manuscript and the Early History of Cochecton*. Westminster, MD: Heritage Books, 2011.

Sloane, Eric. *An Age of Barns*. New York: Funk and Wagnall's, 1963.

Smith, Bruce D. *The Emergence of Agriculture*. New York: Scientific American Library, 1988.

Smith, Richard. *A Tour of Four Great Rivers: The Hudson, Mohawk, Susquehanna and Delaware in 1769*, ed. Francis Whiting Halsey. New York: Charles Scribner's Sons, 1906.

Soll, David. *Empire of Water: An Environmental and Political History of the New York City Water Supply*. Ithaca: Cornell University Press, 2013.

Starr, Timothy. *Railroad Wars of New York State*. Charleston, SC: The History Press, 2012.

Stell, Mark. *Protestantism, Capitalism, and Nature in America*. Albuquerque: University of New Mexico Press, 1997.

Stradling, David. *Making Mountains: New York City and the Catskills*. Seattle: University of Washington Press, 2007.

_____. *The Nature of New York: An Environmental History of the Empire State*. Ithaca: Cornell University Press, 2010.

Strong, Paul. *Beavers: Where Waters Run*. Minocqua, WI: Northword Press, Inc., 1997.

Tawney, R. H. *Religion and the Rise of Capitalism*. London: Penguin Books, 1977.

Taylor, Alan. *William Cooper's Town: Power and Persuasion on the Frontier of the Early American Republic*. New York: Random House: 1995.

Thoreau, Henry David. *The Natural History Essays*. Salt Lake City: Peregrine Smith, 1980.

_____. *Walden*. Princeton: Princeton University Press, 1989.

Thurston, Robert H. *The Growth of the Steam Engine*. New York: D. Appleton and Company, 1878.

Titus, Robert. *The Catskills in the Ice Age*, revised ed. Fleischmanns, NY: Purple Mountain Press, 2003.

Trebilcock, Evelyn D., and Valerie A. Balint. *Glories of the Hudson: Frederic Edwin Church's Views from Olana*. Ithaca: Cornell University Press, 2009.

Turner, Frederick. *Beyond Geography: The Western Spirit Against the Wilderness*, 2nd ed. New Brunswick, NJ: Rutgers University Press, 1992.

Turner, Frederick Jackson. *The Significance of the Frontier in American History*. Madison: State Historical Society of Wisconsin, 1894.

Van Kirk, Sylvia. *Many Tender Ties: Women in Fur-Trade Society, 1670–1870*. Norman: University of Oklahoma Press, 1983.

Van Tassel, Alfred J. *Mechanization in the Lumber Industry*. Philadelphia: Works Progress Administration National Research Project Report #M-5, 1940.

Van Valkenburgh, Norman J., and Christopher W. Olney. *The Catskill Park: Inside the Blue Line* Hensonville, NY: Blackdome Press, 2004.

Van Wagenen, Jared Jr. *The Golden Age of Homespun*. Ithaca: Cornell University Press, 1953.

Venema, Janny. *Beverwijck: A Dutch Village on the American Frontier, 1652–1664*. Albany: State University of New York Press, 2003.

Vogel, Robert M. *Roebling's Delaware & Hudson Canal Aqueducts*. Washington, D.C.: Smithsonian Institution Press, Smithsonian Studies in History and Technology, No. 10, 1971.

Wakefield, Manville B. *Coal Boats to Tidewater*. Steingart Associates, 1965.

Wallace, Anthony F.C. *King of the Delawares: Teedyscung, 1700–1763*. Syracuse, NY: Syracuse University Press, 1949.

Weiss, Harry B., and Grace M. Weiss. *Rafting on the Delaware*. Trenton: New Jersey Agricultural Society, 1967.

West, Darrell C., Herman H. Shugart, and Daniel B. Botkins, eds. *Forest Succession: Concepts and Application*. New York: Springer-Verlag, 1981.

Whitford, Noble E. *History of the Canal System of the State of New York*. Albany: Brandon Printing Company, 1905.

Whitman, Walt. *Leaves of Grass: First and "Death-Bed" Editions*. New York: Barnes and Noble Classics, 2004.

Wiebe, Robert H. *The Search for Order: 1977–1920*. New York: Hill and Wang, 1966.

Williams, Michael. *Americans & Their Forests: A Historical Geography*. Cambridge: Cambridge University Press, 1992.

Williams, Robert C. *Horace Greeley: Champion of American Freedom*. New York: New York University Press, 2006.

Wood, Leslie. *Rafting on the Delaware River*. Livingston Manor, NY: Livingston Manor Times, 1934.

Woodruff, Robert E. *Erie Railroad—Its Beginnings!* New York: Newcomen Society of England, 1851.

Wormuth, Guy. *My Memories of Acid Factories*. Hancock, NY: N.p., 1977.

Worster, Donald. *Nature's Economy: A History of Ecological Ideas*. Cambridge: Cambridge University Press, 1994.

Unpublished Documents

Citizen's Advisory Council, Upper Delaware Scenic and Recreational River, 1978 (unpublished transcript)

"Documents Collection." Hanford Mills Museum, East Meredith, New York.

Lord, John. "Personal Notebooks, 1838–46," Unpublished manuscript. On file at the Minnisink Valley Historical Society, Port Jervis, New York.

"Uriah Gregory Papers." Broome County Historical Society, Roberson Center, Binghamton, New York.
Works Progress Administration. "Rafting," 3 vols., unpublished, on file, Minnisink Valley Historical Society, Port Jervis, NY.

Online Sources

CCClegacy. *CCC Camps*. Edinburg, VA: www.ccclegacy.org/CCC_Camps_New_York.html, 2015.
Section of Archaeology at the State Museum of Pennsylvania, "This Week in Pennsylvania Archaeology," www.twipa.blogspot. *com*., 2015.
State of New York. *Catskill Park State Land Master Plan*. Albany: www.dec.ny.gov/docs/lands_forests_pdf/cplsmp.pdf, August, 2008.
"Stourbridge Lion Historical Marker," www.Explorepahistory.com, 2011.
www.nysparks.com/parks
www.dec.ny.gov/lands
www.dec.ny.gov/animals
www.denr.state.pa.us/stateparks
www.dcnr.state.pa.us/forestry
www.eaglecreekre.com/facilities/northeast-region/mongaup-river-ny
www.esf.edu/chestnut
www.nj.gov/drbc/about/accomplishments
www.nps.gov/upperdelawarescenicandrecreationalriver/purposeandmanagementgoals
www.upperdelawarecouncil.org/history
www.waterdata.usgs.gov/pa/nwis

Index

www.ingramcontent.com/pod-product-compliance
Lightning Source LLC
Chambersburg PA
CBHW031129270326
41929CB00011B/1559